Organizational Change and Development

Organizational Change and Development

Kumkum Mukherjee

Professor

Head of the Department of Masters of Human Resource Management

Indian Institute of Social Welfare and Business Management

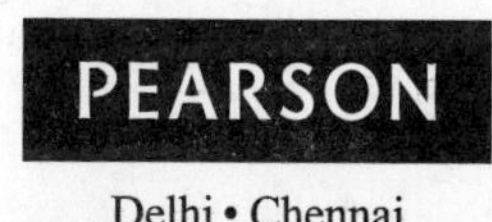

Delhi • Chennai

Associate Editor–Acquisitions: Varun Goenka
Editor–Production: G. Sharmilee

The aim of this publication is to supply information taken from sources believed to be valid and reliable. This is not an attempt to render any type of professional advice or analysis, nor is it to be treated as such. While much care has been taken to ensure the veracity and currency of the information presented within, neither the publisher nor its authors bear any responsibility for any damage arising from inadvertent omissions, negligence or inaccuracies (typographical or factual) that may have found their way into this book.

Copyright © 2016 Pearson India Education Services Pvt. Ltd.

This book is sold subject to the condition that it shall not, by way of trade or otherwise, be lent, resold, hired out, or otherwise circulated without the publisher's prior written consent in any form of binding or cover other than that in which it is published and without a similar condition including this condition being imposed on the subsequent purchaser and without limiting the rights under copyright reserved above, no part of this publication may be reproduced, stored in or introduced into a retrieval system, or transmitted in any form or by any means (electronic, mechanical, photocopying, recording or otherwise), without the prior written permission of both the copyright owner and the publisher of this book.

ISBN 978-81-317-7342-0

First Impression

Published by Pearson India Education Services Pvt. Ltd, CIN: U72200TN2005PTC057128, formerly known as TutorVista Global Pvt. Ltd, licensee of Pearson Education in South Asia.

Head Office: A-8(A), 7th Floor, Knowledge Boulevard, Sector 62, Noida 201 309, Uttar Pradesh, India.
Registered Office: Module G4, Ground Floor, Elnet Software City, TS-140, Blocks 2 & 9, Rajiv Gandhi Salai, Taramani, Chennai 600 113, Tamil Nadu, India.
Fax: 080-30461003, Phone: 080-30461060.
www.pearson.co.in, Email: companysecretary.india@pearson.com

Compositor: PageTech Publishing Services Pvt. Ltd.
Printed in India - Sai Printo Pack (P) Ltd

Dedication

To those, near and far, who supported me unconditionally when I needed it most

Contents

Preface

The present book on *Organizational Change and Development* aims to present the primary forces for Change in the organizational context in depth in the first ten chapters. Thus an effort has been made to scrutinize each of the possible factors in and around an organization behind any change as exhaustively as possible within the limited space. It thus touches the issues of organizational culture and climate, leadership, development of groups and the group dynamics, the power game within the organization, to name a few, and tries to identify the impact of all these on resultant organizational change. In the second part of the book, focus is specifically on Organization Development (OD) where a brief history of organization change is traced, the specific steps of OD, along with some detailed description of OD intervention strategies have been presented. An attempt has been made to incorporate the latest researches in this field as well as the current reality scenario in the business today. In addition, each chapter starts with an opening case and includes cases at the end of the chapter to apply the knowledge presented in the chapter.

WHY STUDY CHANGE AND ORGANIZATION DEVELOPMENT?

As they say, it is only change that is constant today all around us at this time of constant flux. Things are always changing. Sometimes small, yes, but at times even dramatic and quite often too fast for our full comprehension. In order to survive, and of course to thrive, in the world of constant change, it is mandatory for the managers and the people in charge of the organizations to observe and understand the nature and forces of change so that they can benefit from change itself.

Objectives of the Book

The primary objective of the current title is to present the knowledge and practical understanding in the area of Organizational Change and Development in a lucid and reader friendly way, both for the students in management as well as managers and practitioners in the field. It also tries to incorporate the current issues and happenings in the corporate world so that the readers may relate better. There are case studies that have been incorporated in each chapter so that a reader's entire effort would be a practice in more active learning than a passive one.

The Structure of the book

The first part (Part One) of the book deals with change in the organizational context, the nature and forces for change while the second part (Part Two) deals with organization development in details.

Key Features

- Each chapter starts with an Opening Case that initiates the reader in to the particular area of study.
- At the beginning of each chapter the Learning Objectives are given clearly to enable the reader to comprehend what follows.
- Features like 'Managers Essence' offer a real life glimpse for the readers to understand and relate more specifically.
- The *Concept Check* and *Interactive Exercises* help the reader to be engaged in active learning in contrast to the passive learning.
- The definitions and important concepts presented prominently also would help in clear understanding.
- The Glossary at the end of the chapter would present a quick recapitulation of the concepts in the chapter. It also helps to clarify any specific concept discussed in the chapter.
- The Review questions at the end of the chapter offers a self check of the understanding.

Acknowledgement

I owe a deep sense of gratitude to my family in the first place for bearing with me in spite of me being continuously preoccupied with my project. Undoubtedly they were the greatest source of support in my endeavor of writing the book. I am also immensely indebted to my beloved students who always made my teaching a challenging task by questioning my every idea and offering scores of their own. I do like to thank them for keeping me always alert and on my toes. I of course must thank my colleagues for their fiercest and scathing criticisms, valuable suggestions and a relentless drive to complete the book, in addition to the unconditional support that they always showed towards me. And, lastly, and certainly not the least, my Institute, IISWBM! Without all the support I got from my Institute, I could never write the book.

Acknowledgements

[illegible]

About the Author

Kumkum Mukherjee, a renowned professor and Head of the Department of Masters of Human Resource Management at the prestigious IISWBM, is a holder of Ph.D. in Organizational Behavior, Organizational Development and Change Management from the Calcutta University. With nearly three decades of extensive teaching experience in the field of Management Studies, she was also welcomed in the Budapest University of Technology, Budapest, Hungary to teach Economics and several other short term courses. She also took part as the State Co-Investigator of West Bengal in the worldwide recognized GLOBE (Global Leadership Organizational Behavioral Effectiveness) study that involved 62 nations across the world. She has presented several papers in various conferences and seminars and also published some of them for national and international journals.

PART 1

Organizational Change

Chapter 1

Understanding Organizations

Opening Case: What a Day!

It was already 7.30 a.m.! Vinod cursed himself as he was getting late for office. He had to reach office on time as a urgent meeting with the sales team was scheduled to take place in the morning! While rushing into the bathroom, he called his wife at the top of his voice for breakfast. Among all the chaos, Vinod thought that it had never been easy for Rupa. She had to prepare their two-and-half-year-old daughter Neha for her school, get ready for her office, instruct the maid, pack lunch for herself, Vinod and for Neha and then she would have to drive to her office before dropping Neha to her school. A busy schedule to say the least! But still she is able to manage everything with a smile in her face. Almost nonchalantly, she went to the kitchen to instruct the maid to make breakfast.

Miraculously Vinod finally managed to catch his carpool in time. Rupa and Neha could afford to start a little late as Neha's play school and Rupa's NGO start later than Vinod's. Not only her office hours are flexible, but the office is nearby to her home also. Rupa would pick Neha around 1.30 p.m., drop her back home under the care of Shova and go back to her office. Vinod was thanking his luck and was hoping to reach the office almost in time with a clear 15 minutes time to organize his thoughts and points for the meeting. But while he was immersed in his thoughts, he did not notice the traffic jam because of some rowdy protesters with the traffic constable helplessly looking at the other side!

The opening case not only depicts a glimpse of an everyday familiar scene, but an idea that at almost every moment of our existence, we have to depend on so many people, both known and unknown.The range varies from the domestic help to the ones who have made the toothpaste or the cereals. And we also keep on playing different roles all the time—from a father and a husband to a corporate executive, belonging to various set-ups of people that could be roughly called organizations—as in the case of Vinod here.

In this chapter, we will try to understand the term 'organization' and how modern lifestyle is intricately related to organizations in some form or the other.

LEARNING OBJECTIVES

- Basic components of an organization
- Types of organizations

- View of organization as an open system
- Strategy and organizational design
- Recent challenges

NATURE OF ORGANIZATIONS

Definition of Organization

The concept of organization is rather vague and abstract in nature. We might visualize some parts of the term, for example through, a building or some of the employees, but organization as a coherent concept is often difficult to perceive, as there are many layers in it.

Organizations are all around us. In fact, it is practically impossible to name a moment in our life when we are not within or part of some organization or the other. Most of us are born in hospitals, we grow in a family, get education in schools and colleges, worship in temple, church or mosque, work in offices or factories, avail of public transport and live in a country run by the government. All these are examples of organizations. According to Daft, organizations are social entities that are

1. goal directed,
2. designed as deliberately structured and coordinated activity systems and
3. linked to the external environment.

In a nutshell, an organization is the rational coordination of activities of a number of people for the achievement of some common goal, through division of labour and function, and through a hierarchy of authority and responsibility.

An organization is the rational coordination of activities of a number of people for the achievement of some common goal, through division of labour and function, and through a hierarchy of authority and responsibility.

Concept Check

What is an organization? Identify the typical characteristics of an organization.

Importance of Organizations Today

Organizations are relatively new entities and were not in existence even in the late 19th century. The Industrial Revolution and the subsequent development of large organizations have changed the fabric of our entire society today. As mentioned previously, right from the moment of one's birth to one's last journey, any individual in today's society is dependent on one organization or the other. Organizations are all around us and shape our lives in many ways.

It is, however, should be noted that an organization is not just a building or a set of policies or strategies. Organizations are made up of people and their relationships with each other. Recent trends in managerial approach have recognized the importance of human resources in organizational context. Organizations are not a illogical assortment of individuals either. People in charge of organizations deliberately coordinate organizational resources to achieve the organization's objectives and purpose.

The specific contributions made by organizations have been summed up by Daft (2004) as follows:

- **Organizations Bring together resources to achieve desired goals and outcomes:** Though in the distant past, people used to consume home-grown products like food, clothing and other necessities in life. For everything else, the barter system used to be practiced. The consumption system used to be very simple before as the sources for procuring food were uncomplicated. But gone are those simplistic days of cottage and small-scale manufacturing units. After the Industrial Revolution, machines were put into use to speed up the process of production phenomenally and many factories were created with sufficient labour force. So, a number of people with their individual capabilities and inputs were brought in together to achieve the desirable outcomes.
- **Organizations Produce goods and services efficiently:** Organizations can always produce—be it products or services—much more efficiently than individuals. When a particular job is broken down into specific activities and each part is assigned to different employees, things will naturally be achieved faster and better than an individual.
- **Organizations Facilitate innovation:** The possibility for innovation and creativity is much higher in an organization primarily because of the strength of the people as well as other available resources that could be brought in an organization in contrast to the individual efforts.
- **Organizations Use latest available technology:** Organizations can seek and procure latest technology, which may not be possible for individuals.
- **Organizations Are primarily collective social units or socio-technical entities:** Organizations are deliberately created with some specific purpose. Still, the functioning of organizations is not necessarily restricted to the pursuance of only that goal(s). People in an organization may indulge in activities like gossiping about trivial issues or arguing with each other which are quite unrelated to the pronounced purpose of the organization. Look at yourself. You are pursuing a management course in a reputed college or university and your aim is ostensibly to study hard to get the degree. Fine? But don't tell me you are *only* studying! You do definitely had fun when you organized that fest or debate or meet, which all have almost nothing to do with your earning the degree at the end of your course. You would pick up friends here with whom you would plan so many things that has hardly anything to do with your degree.
- **Organizations Adapt to and influence a changing environment:** In order to survive, organizations, at one hand, have to undergo various changes so that they can adapt themselves to the demand of the ever-changing external environment. On the other hand, in turn, may bring in changes in their external environment as well and facilitate their own sustenance. A body of organizations may put pressure and change even the governmental policies.
- **Organizations Create value for owners, customers and employees:** The very purpose of creating any organization is to satisfy the stakeholders, including *any one* who might have any interest in the functioning of the organization. Thus, the investors and founder members of the organization would eagerly wait for the handsome return of their money put into the organizations, through generation of profit and sustainability of the business. Customers would prefer the products or services of a particular organization as long as they would find them better than those offered by other organizations. Employees, who are the ultimate asset of any organization, would stay in the organization only when they find their current organization better than others.
- **Organizations Accommodate ongoing challenges of diversity, ethics, motivation and coordination of employees:** Organizations are like living entities that can always change themselves in order to face the challenges that they are continuously exposed to. The demography of the available

workforce has undergone major changes over the recent years. Different types of people from all over the world, irrespective of their racial, cultural, geographical and religious backgrounds, are found to work together. People join the organizations primarily to achieve their own individual goals, but when within an organization, they learn to align these individualistic pluralistic goals to the organizational objectives.

Organizations shape our lives and well-informed managers can shape organizations to become better equipped in attaining their objectives in an effective way.

Interactive Exercise

Refer to the opening case 'What a Day!' at the beginning of this chapter. What are the different types of organizations mentioned there? Categorize them.

Organizations as Systems

The functioning of organizations can be best understood if we consider organizations as systems. A system is *a set of interacting elements that acquires inputs from the environment, transforms them, and discharges outputs to the external environment.* The need for inputs and outputs reflects the dependency of the organization on the external environment. Interacting elements mean that people and departments depend on one another and must work together. It also implies that whatever happens to one part or subsystem of the organization will not be restricted there only but will affect the entire system. It is very similar to the internal organs inside our body. If you suffer from an infection in the digestive system, your entire body functions and faculties would be disturbed. You would not only stop taking food but will also feel low and have difficulties in following your class lectures though there is nothing wrong in your brain or other body parts.

Closed Systems vs Open Systems View of Organizations

Closed-system view perceives organization as an entity independent of its environment; it views organization as autonomous, enclosed and sealed off from the outside world. Although a true closed system can never exist in reality, early organizational studies focused mainly on the internal systems of an organization. This view took the environment for granted and assumed that organizations could be made more effective through internal design only.

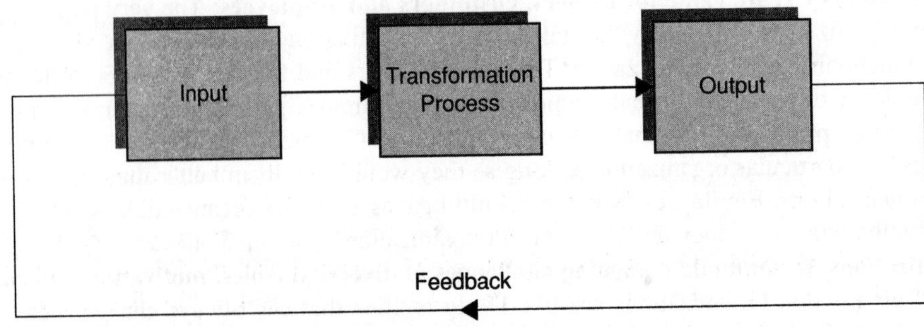

Figure 1.1 An Open System Model of Organization

An *open system,* in contrast, views the organization as one which constantly interacts with the environment in order to survive. It cannot seal itself off from the environment, as it is dependent on the external environment for its inputs and outputs. Therefore, it must continuously change itself to adapt to the environment. Open systems can be enormously complex where the internal efficiency is just one of the many important issues and a minor one for that.

Organizational Configuration

According to Henry Mintzberg, the various parts of the organization that are designed to perform the key subsystem functions are—technical core, top management, middle management, technical support and administrative support. These five parts of the organization may vary in size and importance, depending on the organization's environment, technology and other factors. The following is a brief description of each of these parts:

- **Technical core:** The technical core includes people who do the basic work of the organization. It is concerned with the actual production process and the service outputs of the organization. This is where the primary transformation from input to output takes place.
- **Technical support:** The technical support function helps the organization adapt to the environment. The technical support employees include engineers and researchers who are responsible for creating innovations in the technical core and helping the organization to change and adapt.
- **Administrative support:** The administrative support function is responsible for the smooth operation and upkeep of the organization, including its physical and human elements. This includes human resource activities such as recruitment and selection. Also establishing employee compensation and benefit policies and training and development as well as other maintenance activities such as cleaning and repairing and upkeeping of machines and equipment, etc are also included.
- **Management:** The management is a distinct subsystem, responsible for directing and coordinating the different parts of the organization . It has usually three distinct levels, identified as the top, middle and the first-line or supervisory category of managers. We will discuss these in the subsequent chapters of this book.

Interactive Exercise

Refer to any organization you are associated with—be it your management institute or the company your working currently. Now try to identify the different parts described and how you had interacted with those.

Dimensions of an Organization

The dimensions of an organization describe the organization and help us to understand organizations in a better way. Organizational dimensions are of two broad types—structural and contextual. Structural dimensions provide labels to describe the internal characteristics of the organization, whereas the contextual dimensions characterize the whole organization including its size, technology, environment and goals.

Structural Dimensions:

The following six components comprise the structural dimensions of an organization:

1. **Formalization** refers to the amount of written documentation in the organization including job descriptions, procedures, rules and regulations and policies, etc. Organizations vary in terms of the degree of formalization. This can be very high in large bureaucratic organizations such as the University of Calcutta or the Income Tax Department of the Government of India, which tends to make them rather rigid and inflexible. The same can be relatively low in newly formed organizations, particularly during its initial days.
2. **Specialization** is the degree to which the organizational tasks are subdivided into separate jobs. If the level of specialization is high, this means that the employees perform a particular type of activity only, whereas in organizations with a lower level of specialization, employees perform a wide range of tasks in their jobs.
3. **Hierarchy of authority** describes who reports to whom and the *span of control* for each manager, which refers to the number of employees managed efficiently by a manager. When the span of control is narrow, it gives rise to a taller hierarchy or organizational structure, whereas a wider span will result in flatter organizations.
4. **Centralization** refers to the hierarchical level that has the authority to make a decision. When the decision-making is restricted at the top level, it is called a centralized organization and when the decision-making authority is distributed among the various levels of an organization, it is known as a decentralized organization.
5. **Professionalism** is the level of formal education and training of the employees in the organization. It is considered high when employees require a long period of training and education to hold a job in the organization, like doctors or university teachers.
6. **Personnel ratios** refer to the deployment of people to various functions and departments.

Contextual Dimensions:

The following five components comprise the contextual dimension of an organization.

1. **Size** is the organization's magnitude as reflected in the number of people in the organization. Size is typically measured by the number of employees though other measures of size are also used such as the volume of production or amount of profit, etc.
2. **Organizational technology** refers to the equipment, techniques and actions used to transform the input into output.
3. The **environment** includes all elements outside the boundary of the organization. The key elements of environment include the industry, government, customers, suppliers and the financial community, for instance.
4. The **organization's goals and strategies** define the purpose and competitive techniques that set the organization apart from other organizations. Goals and strategies determine the scope of operations of the organization and relationship with employees, customers and competitors.
5. An **organization's culture** is the set of values, beliefs, understandings and norms shared by the majority of the people in the organization.

The eleven contextual and structural dimensions discussed previously help us to define and understand a particular organization in its required perspectives. It is, however, to be noted that these are often highly interdependent on each other.

Concept Check

1. What are the two broad dimensions to describe an organization?
2. Describe the different components of these dimensions.

TYPES OF ORGANIZATION

Organizational Typology

Organizations can be of big scale or small scale doing various types of businesses like service or manufacturing. The legal status of an organization is also to be considered—whether it is of sole proprietorship or partnership, joint-stock companies, profit or non-profit ones, voluntary or philanthropic in nature or cooperative societies. Organizations also differ in terms of what they produce or what service they intend to offer, and so we have organizations producing automobiles or computers or in the services sector such as banking, insurance, hotels, legal firms or medical services.

Organizations have been categorized in different ways by different researchers. Etzioni (1975) classified organizations into the following categories on the basis of the particular activities it is engaged in should precede the Exhibit 1.1: Etzioni's Typology of Organizations.

Exhibit 1.1 Etzioni's Typology of Organizations

Type	Sectors in the Society where these are Found
Coercive (use of force)	Applied in prisons
Utilitarian (use of rewards)	Applied in shops or retail outlets
Normative (reliance on commitment)	Applied in voluntary organizations, NGOs

Blau and Scott (1966) use a different way to classify organizations on the basis of the primary beneficiary, that is, the group who benefits from the organization.

Exhibit 1.2 Blau and Scott's Types of Organizations and the Prime Beneficiary

Type of Organization	Mutual Benefit Organization
Mutual benefit association (professional body)	Members
Business concerns (privatized utility)	Owners or shareholders
Commonwealth organizations (civil services)	Public at large

Organizational Goals

An organization is created and designed to achieve some goals or end objectives. The steps to achieve this goal are normally decided by the top management team. The final shape of a organization depends primarily on these. Thus, the most important task of the top management is to determine

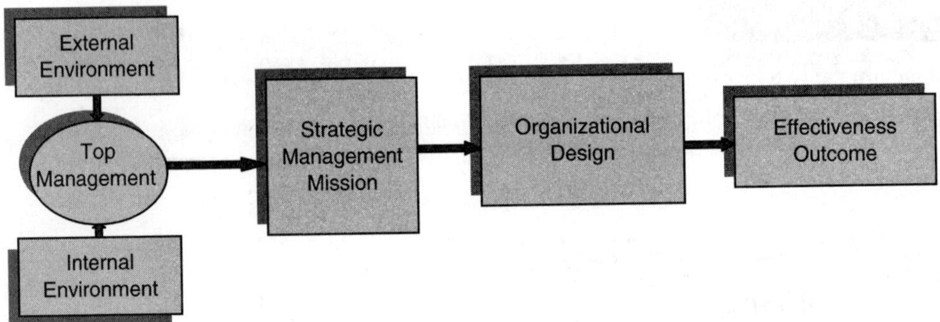

Figure 1.2 Top Management's Role

an organization's goals, strategy and design in order to make the organization adaptive to face the demands of the external environment. Figure 1.2 depicts the top management's role in an organization's direction, design and effectiveness.

The process of setting the direction for an organization typically begins with an assessment of the opportunities and threats in the external environment. Organizations exist in a complex and changing environment. For this reason, managers are required to understand the environment carefully and position and reposition the organization as necessary to sustain it. The top management also assesses the internal strengths and weaknesses to define the organization's distinctive competence compared with others in the market. This usually includes an evaluation of each department along with the effect of leadership and the influences of the top management. The next step is to clarify the overall mission and official goals which is defined in terms of an appropriate fit between external opportunities and internal strengths. Specific operational goals or strategies can then be formulated to define how the organization is to accomplish its overall mission. Finally, managers have to evaluate the effectiveness of organizational efforts or the extent to which the organization realizes its goals.

It is to be noted that the choices of top managers regarding the selection of goals, strategies and organizational design have a tremendous impact on the organizational effectiveness. It is also to be remembered here that goals and strategies are not fixed or taken for granted. The setting up of goals should rather be viewed as a continuous process that needs constant monitoring.

There are many types of goals which exist in an organization. Some have been described below:

Mission: This refers to the overall goal of an organization that provides the very reason for its existence. The mission describes the organization's vision, its shared values and beliefs and its reason for being. The mission is also called the official goals which are the formally stated objectives of the organization, its values, the customers and the probable market it would look for. Understandably, these have a powerful impact on an organization.

Operative Goals: After having the mission statement for an organization, the next requirement is to decide the specific steps to be taken on a short-term basis to attain those broader objectives. Operative versus official goals represent the actual versus stated goals.

Operative goals can be of various types such as:

- **Overall performance:** Profitability reflects the overall performance, which can be measured in terms of net income, earning per share, or return of investment. For non-profit organizations, profitability is not the measure of overall performance but they have other goals that determine the quality of services rendered within a specified budget.

- **Resources:** Resource goals are concerned with the acquisition of needed material and financial resources from the environment. Examples of resource goals could be obtaining finance for a particular project or locating less expensive sources for raw materials.
- **Market:** Market goals relate to the market share desired by the organization. These are the responsibility of the marketing, sales and advertising departments of an organization.
- **Employee development:** Employee development pertains to the training, promotion, safety and growth of employees.
- **Innovation and change:** These refer to internal flexibility and the readiness to adapt to unexpected changes in the environment. These are defined in terms of development of new services, products or the production process.
- **Productivity:** Productivity goals are concerned about the amount of output achieved from the available resources.

Importance of Organizational Goals

Organizational goals, variously referred to as purpose, missions, objectives or targets, are, therefore, something that the organization seeks to achieve. Setting organizational goals serves the following purposes for the organization.

- **Legitimacy of existence**—as setting up the organization's missions or objectives provides the very reason for its creation.
- **Employee motivation**—as the process of goal setting itself serves as a powerful motivating purpose.
- **Decision guidelines**—can only be obtained when there are clearly set goals or targets to achieve.
- **Reducing uncertainty**—as having clear goals automatically helps to reduce the uncertainty in the mind of its members.
- **Provides a sense of direction**—as without goals it is difficult for individuals as well as organizations to achieve what they really wish to achieve.
- **Goals focus our efforts**—as every organization has to work with limited resources, goals will help to allocate these resources wisely.
- **Goals help us evaluate our progress**—as clearly stated goals provide a standard for performance.

Organizational Strategies and Design

An organization's structure is a means to help the management achieve its objectives. Since objectives are derived from the organization's overall strategy, it is obvious that organizational strategies will have a definite impact on the structure of the organization. A strategy is a plan to attain the organizational objectives in a competitive environment. Goals define where the organization wishes to go, whereas strategies define how to get there. Deciding on a strategy will essentially involve choosing whether the organization will perform different activities than its competitors or whether it will execute similar activities more efficiently than its competitors. Two models for formulating strategies are the Porter's model of competitive strategies and the Miles and Snow's strategy typology.

Michael E. Porter studied a number of businesses and introduced a framework describing three competitive strategies: low-cost leadership, differentiation and focus. The *low-cost leadership strategy* tries to increase the market share by emphasizing on low cost of the product/service compared to that offered by the competitors. In the *differentiation strategy*, organizations attempt to distinguish their products

Table 1.1 The Strategy–structure Relation

Strategy	Structural Options
Innovation	Organic structure
Cost minimization	Mechanistic
Imitation	Mechanistic and organic structure

and services from others in an industry. An organization using this strategy will advertise the distinctive product features, exceptional service or new technology used to achieve the product perceived as unique. The *focus strategy* of Porter encourages the organization to concentrate on a specific regional market or buyer group.

According to Miles and Snow, organizational strategies can be broadly divided under the following categories:

- The **prospector strategy** is to innovate, take the risks, seek out new opportunities and grow. This strategy is suitable for a dynamic and growing environment.
- The **defender strategy** is almost opposite to the prospector strategy where instead of taking risks and seeking new opportunities, the defender strategy is concerned with stability and holding onto the current market or customer.
- The **analyzer strategy** tries to maintain a stable business while innovating on the periphery. It seems to be in the midway between the prospector and defender strategies.
- The **reactor strategy** is in fact not a strategy at all. Reactors respond to the environmental threats and opportunities in an ad hoc fashion.

Different strategies will give rise to different types of organizational structure and design. Table 1.1 presents the strategy–structure relationship.

Emerging Organizational Designs

In today's world, we encounter organizations which are so different from their traditional counterparts that ruled the world only a decade ago. In contrast to the yesteryears' organizations, which were typically large and complex with distinct boundaries between functional departments and other organizations, and mostly run by autocratic leaders, in which communication was typically formal and predominantly top-down in nature, organizations today seem to thrive on 'chaos'! There is hardly any order or predictability around us, and the world seems to be full of surprises, rapid changes and confusions. The present century is experiencing organizations going through a whopping change, which is more flexible and decentralized with a strong emphasis on horizontal collaboration and widespread information sharing and a high degree of adaptability. A new generation of organization has come into prominence, known as the Learning Organization (LO).

An LO promotes communication and collaboration so that everyone is engaged in identifying and solving problems, enabling the organization to continuously experiment, improve and increase its capability (Daft, 2004). The typical characteristics of LOs are as follows:

- **From vertical to horizontal structure:** In contrast to the traditional vertical organizations, in learning organizations, emphasis is given on creating the structure around horizontal workflows or processes rather than vertical hierarchy.

- **From routine tasks to empowered roles:** While a task is a narrowly defined set of work activities, a role, in contrast, is a part to be played by an individual within the dynamic context of the social environment. A task is relatively rigid in terms of individual or group input, but a role is more about the responsibility and allows the person to use his/her discretion in order to achieve the objective.
- **From formal control systems to shared information:** Traditionally, information system has acted as a major tool for controlling the behaviour of the members of the organization. But, in learning organizations, the widespread sharing and accessing of information by organizational members facilitates the organization to function at the optimum level.
- **From competitive to collaborative strategy:** In traditional organizations, extreme emphasis has always been placed on competition and the efficient use of organizational resources. The organizational strategies are typically set by the people at the top echelon of the hierarchy, with employees from the lower rung having hardly any say in that sacred piece of document. But, in the learning organizations, each and every one is encouraged to think and contribute to the overall strategy of the firm. In addition, in these modern organizations, strategy may evolve from the partnerships with suppliers, customers and even from competitors.
- **From rigid to adaptive culture:** In learning organization, in a sharp difference with the traditional organizations, a conscious effort is taken to create a culture that is characterized by openness, mutual respect, strive for continuous improvement and acceptance and adaptation of change.

In the subsequent chapters, we will learn more about different organizational structures. It is, however, to be remembered that the function and effectiveness of any organization is dependent on its environment. More specifically, an organization's environment typically refers to the forces that are outside the organization and can potentially affect the performance of the organization. These include suppliers, customers, competitors, governmental regulatory agencies, activists and the like.

GLOSSARY

- **Organization:** The rational coordination of activities of a number of people for the achievement of some common goal, through division of labour and function, and through a hierarchy of authority and responsibility.
- **Technical core:** The technical core includes people who do the basic work of the organization.
- **Technical support:** The technical support function helps the organization adapt to the environment. The technical support employees include engineers and researchers who are responsible for creating innovations in the technical core and helping the organization to change and adapt.
- **Administrative support:** The administrative support function is responsible for the smooth operation and upkeep of the organization, including its physical and human elements.
- **Management:** The management is a distinct subsystem, responsible for directing and coordinating the different parts of the organization.
- **Mission:** This refers to the overall goal of an organization that provides the very reason for its existence. The mission describes the organization's vision, its shared values and beliefs and its reason for being.
- **Learning organization:** A learning organization promotes communication and collaboration so that everyone is engaged in identifying and solving problems, enabling the organization to continuously experiment, improve and increase its capability.

QUESTIONS

1. What is an organization? Compare and contrast among the following organizations—an IT firm, a multi-facility medical care and hospital and a management institute.
2. What do you understand by the term 'learning organization'? What are the typical characteristics of a learning organization?
3. Why do you think organizations have mission statement? What purposes are served by an organization's mission statement?
4. Briefly describes the two dimensions of organizations and the various parameters.
5. If you want to start a readymade garment business, what considerations will you keep in mind and how would you plan the entire thing?

REFERENCES

1. A. Etzioni, *A Comparative Analysis of Complex Organizations* (New York: Free Press, 1975).
2. P.M. Blau and W.R. Scott, *Formal Organizations* (London: Routledge & Kegan Paul, 1966).
3. R.L. Daft, *Organization Theory* and *Design* (South-Western, 2004).
4. B. Srivastava, *Organizational Design and Development* (Biztantra, 2007).

Case Study: Blooming on the Offshore

Organizations can be best understood as a organic entity. Its location also matters a lot as it affects the functioning of an organization rather significantly. Digital Softech started its operation in 1981 in California, USA. The company claims that it has changed the standard of creating, storing and consuming the digital information around the world. LSI, which pioneered system-on-a-chip integration, is the only company that can provide a complete offering of silicon-to-system solutions for the storage and consumer markets. The organization is focused on providing systems and software solutions for the storage and consumer markets. Digital Softech is powering some of the most popular consumer electronics products today, including GPS navigation systems, electronic toys, educative and entertainment applications, personal media players and handheld products. Digital Softech also provides entry-level market solutions such as single-drive DVRs (digital video recorder) as well as complex, integrated consumer solutions, such as hybrid analog and digital personal DVR, set-top boxes (STBs) and hard disk drive/DVD recorder combination products that involve high levels of software complexity. Till date, more than 350 million consumer electronic devices with Digital Softech silicon have been shipped to market.

Digital Softech leverages its in-depth system-level expertise, innovative technologies, understanding of customer requirements and a philosophy of providing best-of-breed silicon, systems and software to meet the specific needs of their partners and customers. With a long history in developing and driving industry standards for silicon, systems and software solutions, LSI is creating the technologies that drive the evolution of industry ecosystems.

Sound Corporate Policy

In addition to its recognized status as the market leader in its area of operation, Logitech is also known for its fair policy and sound corporate governance. It has developed stringent guidelines to be followed strictly in the company, which reflect the board's commitment to monitor the effectiveness of policy and decision-making at both the board and management levels, with a view to enhancing long-term stockholder value. These are also subject to modification from time to time by the board.

Digital Softech has empowered the board to function in an extremely fair manner. Anything regarding the business of the company is managed by the board. It chooses the chairman of the board in any way that it deems best for the company at any given point in time. A director is expected to spend the time and effort necessary to properly discharge such director's responsibilities. Accordingly, the director is expected to regularly attend meetings of the board and committees where the director reviews various agendas. A director who is unable to attend a meeting is expected to notify the chairman of the board or the chairman of the appropriate committee in advance of such meeting.

Employee Benefit Programmes

Digital Softech looks after the employees very well. In a world perennially short of talented employees, retaining quality human capital is always a challenge for most organizations today. To retain its competitive advantage and unique position in the market, Logitech employees are offered a competitive and comprehensive benefits package designed to meet diverse needs to attract and retain talented, dedicated and innovative employees. The company strongly believes that it is the talent and determination of the employees that have made Logitech the market leader. The company offers the following advantages:

Time-off Benefits:

Holidays and Vacation: Digital Softech full-time employees receive 10 paid holidays a year and are eligible to accrue vacation hours commensurate with the years of service. Thus, employees with less than 6 years of service will be eligible to accrue 120 hours, while those with six or more years will get 160 hours of vacation.

Education and Training:

Sabbatical Leave: A unique policy in Logitech is that after ten years of continuous service, employees are eligible for a four-week sabbatical leave.

Opportunity for Further Study: Many Digital Softech employees have achieved bachelor and advanced degrees from accredited universities with the aid of Logitech's education assistance programme. The organization encourages learning that benefits the employee and the company. Many at Digital Softech continue education, technical training, seminars, online learning and other activities with the approval of their manager.

Author's Award: Another special feature of Digital Softech is its Author's Award Programme, which disburses approximately $100,000 annually as monetary awards to deserving authors.

Recognition Award and Patent Award Programmes

When an employee displays exceptional effort in his/her department in achieving corporate goals, or produces an invention accepted for a patent by the US Patent and Trademark Office, that individual receives a cash award. This surely motivates the employees to put into use their innovative talents at work.

Overseas Operations

Digital Softech, with its strong presence in the industry, was naturally eager to open operations across the globe and India obviously featured in the list. Rupert Dillon, Senior Software Engineer Manager, RAID Application Software Development, RAID Storage Adapter Division, was the logical choice to handle offshore, especially Indian, operations, not only because of his superb technical knowledge and expertise but also because of his previous exposure to this part of the globe.

Digital Softech's Success Story in India

The company's Indian operation started around a year back with the initiative of only two young Indians who were then posted in the US. They took the challenge of setting up the operations here in Kolkata, India. They came back in India, started operating from a small rented place with only two laptops, and started hunting for local talents from universities and institutes. Within less than a year, the India operation became a force to reckon with, shifting to a huge state-of-the-art office located in the heart of the city's IT district with a highly sophisticated computer laboratory and a team of young and talented engineers. Instead of only implementing the software already developed in the US, the newly established India operation started *designing and developing various unique software programmes* here after successfully attracting the best talents in the area. Not only just that, they developed a unique software package, which generated a huge demand from the customers all over the world and continues to be in great demand till now. This helped to earn huge revenue for the company and became a showpiece to impress the customers all over the world. But all the fairy tale did not happen by sheer magic. It took a lot of determination and hard work on the part of the new team in India. The main credit most probably goes to a person named Rupert Dillon, who joined the firm around the time the Kolkata operation started taking place. The success of the Kolkata operation certainly did happen because of the talents in India, but it was also because of the policies of the firm that changed a great deal after Bob joined. He could correctly understand the psyche and culture of Kolkata and tapped the brilliance and talent of the people here by empowering them and treating them with genuine respect. He also understood the importance of communication, particularly when the operations of the firm involve several continents and widely different time zones.

Questions

1. What kind of organization is Digital Softech?
2. What reasons would you ascribe for the success of Digital Softech in Kolkata?

Chapter 2

Organizational Effectiveness and Change

Opening Case: The Changing Time

Rajeev was truly amazed. At the age of 25, he left India after obtaining a prestigious scholarship from the USA for his postdoc and eventually joined a university to teach physics. He married an American and settled there happily with two children. He was never overly sentimental about his country and came to India only once after the death of his mother. Though Rajeev was the only son, his mother preferred staying at their ancestral house near Bhawanipur, Kolkata. She had a couple of loyal old servants and was well looked after. Rajeev's real problems started after her death. To clear the financial tangles regarding fixed deposits, lockers and such formalities with the banks was an uphill task. He had to go to the banks so many times and was always facing so many difficulties that he lost count! He had to take three weeks' leave to settle down all of these. That was 25 years back. This time he came with his wife for holidaying. His wife had never been to India. At the time of his mother's death, she could not accompany him, as the kids were too young to travel.

They had checked in at a five star hotel near the south of the city, not too far from his ancestral house. As he was now getting old and with the children grown up and all settled for themselves, perhaps nostalgia was slowly gripping him! The house at Bhawanipur was still robust and fine, though it was in need of some repairing. Rajeev decided to speak to the person who looked after the house and start the repairing soon. It was perhaps not altogether a bad idea to have a spot of his own in Kolkata! However, for all these he would require to open a bank account and transfer some money into it. But the very thought of going to a bank was scaring him to death. He had not yet overcome the memories of banks in the past. However, with much prodding from his wife, he finally made a trip to the branch where his mother had her account. And he was truly amazed! The manager was cordial and helpful! He even met him at his hotel to sign the papers and promised to activate the account before they return.

The Opening Case illustrates the strong focus on the urge for improving organizational effectiveness that is now found everywhere. No one can possibly ignore it anymore now, particularly in the present era of globalization and the intense competition that closely follows.

After reading this chapter, you will be able to understand different aspects of organizational effectiveness. You will also have an understanding about the nature and forces of change faced by an organization at any given point of time.

The topics which we will touch in this chapter are as follows:

LEARNING OBJECTIVES

- What is effectiveness?
- Different approaches to measure effectiveness
- Need for change
- Types of change
- Resistance to change
- Implementing change successfully

ORGANIZATIONAL EFFECTIVENESS

What do we understand by the term 'organizational effectiveness' and why this term has become so important today? Whatever an organization does, it has to be done efficiently in order to keep pace with today's intense competitive environment. Any organization, therefore, has now to perform not only at par with their competitors, but would also need to outperform them in order to stay in business. As mentioned in the opening case, the functioning of the nationalized banks had to undergo a lot of changes due to stiff competition from private players which were aggressively capturing the market. The notion of effectiveness will help an organization identify its present state vis-à-vis the ideal state of existence. This in turn will help the organization to identify ways the ideal state can be achieved and sustained.

Efficiency and effectiveness are two similar yet different concepts. The term 'organizational effectiveness' is never easy to define, since it is essentially multidimensional in nature. According to Barnard (1938), organizational effectiveness refers to the degree to which operative and operational goals of the organization have been achieved. In contrast, efficiency primarily refers to the ratio of input and output: the greater the value, the less the wastage and better the output. Thus, just being efficient alone will not ensure the long-term survival and well-being of the organization. Sometimes these two may even create conflict among each other. The American car-making industry in the early 19th century may be considered as a classic example. The American car-making industry was extremely efficient and rolled out a record number of car of a particular model every 5 minutes. But around this time, the market for big cars guzzling on oil was depleting fast, and no matter how efficient the production process was, the decision of making big cars itself was not the right choice. That was the time when the American car market was almost taken over by the Japanese auto makers and America is perhaps yet to recover from the jolt. Peter Drucker, the famous management Guru, distinguished between the often confusing terms efficiency and effectiveness as *doing things right* (efficiency) and *doing the right thing* (effectiveness).

Organizational effectiveness refers to the degree to which operative and operational goals of the organization have been achieved. Organizational efficiency primarily refers to the ratio of input and output.

Concept Check

1. What is organizational effectiveness?
2. Distinguish between efficiency and effectiveness.

Today all kinds of organizations are almost compelled to establish their effectiveness to justify their existence. It is, however, not easy to define organizational effectiveness in a clear and unambiguous way. The concept of effectiveness has undergone a noted shift over the years, with the progress and development of management and organizational theories. The criteria of effectiveness actually depend on how the organization is viewed and conceptualized. This typically involves organizational forms and structure on one hand and organizational activities and functions on the other, and they have significant implications for how organizational processes and people are managed. If, for example, organizations are viewed simply as means of producing products and thus help in increasing the profit margin only, the whole emphasis will be on austerity to increase productivity and minimizing waste. If, on the other hand, organizations are seen as going through flux and transformations, then 'the fundamental role of managers is to shape and create "contexts" in which appropriate forms of self-organization can occur' (Morgan 1997). Burns and Stalker (1961) first coined the term 'organic organizations' in contrast to the mechanistic ones. According to this categorization, mechanistic organizations are characterized by large-scale, low-complexity work activities and are best suited to stable environments that do not require adaptive change and innovation. Organic organizations are characterized by small-scale, high-complexity work and are better suited to changing environments that do require adaptation and innovation.

The mechanistic views of an organization were prevalent during the 19th and early 20th centuries, with the entire focus on efficient production and utilizing manpower. This trend of thought, known as scientific management, was initiated by scholars like Taylor, Fayol and Weber. Slowly, over the years, management theories started acknowledging the complexities of human nature as one of the determining factors along with its interplay with other organizational factors. The importance of external contextual factors was also highlighted by modern theorists like Mayo, McGregor, Likert and others, who subscribed to what was called the human relations school. The concept of organic organizational structures were now more favoured, with provision for change and flexibility built in the system.

Researchers in the field of organizations eventually offered various models in an effort to understand organizations more clearly where they recognized the organizational and systems complexity, organizational diversity and the interplay of the external environment (March and Simon 1958; Blau and Scott 1962; Mintzberg 1979).

The earlier models of organizations were largely closed system models, where organizations were typically viewed as closed, rational systems (Scott 1987) and were characterized by a focus on internal interaction with an emphasis on organizational order and control. Later on, increasing recognition of the limits of the rational system perspective led to the emergence of the *natural system* perspective. The natural system perspective views organizations as first and foremost social entities where the primary interest is the survival of the system. A natural system perspective stresses on the need to emphasize the importance of informal social relations over formal structures (Likert 1961).

Thus, organizational effectiveness does not necessarily mean only productivity or profitability of an organization. Keep in mind that organizational effectiveness is essentially a multidimensional concept which can hardly be measured by a single criterion. The concept of organizational effectiveness is an abstract concept and has to resort mostly to indirect measures rather than direct ones. The indirect or what is known as 'proxy measures' of organizational effectiveness may include factors like number of people served, types and sizes of population segments served, and the demand within those segments for the services the organization supplies. In this context, we will also have to consider the different ways to view an organization.

The concept of effectiveness varies from one organization to another, depending upon its mission, environmental context, nature of work, the product or services it produces and customer demands. Thus, it is imperative to make an effort to understand the organization in its totality and detail—its functions, structures and values—before defining the measure(s) of its effectiveness. The perspectives of looking at organizational effectiveness have, however, undergone a lot of change. As pointed out earlier, during the early days of management science, the sole preoccupation of the owners/managers was an enhanced rate of productivity from the employees. This was the legacy of the school of scientific management, started primarily by F.W. Taylor, H. Fayol and some others. The entire effort was directed towards increasing the productivity of the employee and concepts of employee well-being were in place only to increase productivity and thus the profitability of the organization. Over the years, however, this outlook was slowly replaced by a genuine concern for employee welfare and development, which became one of primary objectives of the organizations. This was the offshoot of the human relations movement, originated from the famous Hawthorn studies conducted over a decade by Sir Elton Mayo and his group of researchers from Harvard Business School. They acknowledged the presence of higher order needs, not just basic ones, operative across employees at all levels. In fact, the human relations movement actually established the belief that employees are the most valuable resources in any organization that has to be carefully nurtured to reap the richest dividend.

With these shifts in management thoughts over the years, the concept of organizational outcomes and the desirability of these outcomes have also undergone noted change. Increasingly, more emphasis has been given to balancing the technical or structural aspects of the organization, while considering the needs and interests of the organizational members. Accordingly, a number of approaches to the measurement of organizational effectiveness have evolved over the years. We will have a brief discussion on each of the four major models of organizational effectiveness, and finally an integration of all four to arrive at a comprehensive one. We shall now discuss the four models in detail.

Rational Goals Model

The goals approach is the most traditional one in measuring organizational effectiveness, which tries to identify what the purported goals of the organization are and how well these have been achieved. The emphasis is given largely on operative goals, which are easier to measure, rather than broad generalized ones. But the fact of the matter is that it is not always *really* easy to measure the operative goals of an organization either. In this approach, organizations as well as their members are largely viewed as having a purely rational orientation, which may not always come true. The disadvantages of this approach are that goals are not always tangible, neither are they easily measurable; in addition, organizations are often found to pursue multiple goals rather than a single one, which may be conflicting in nature. The justification in pursuing the stated goals of an organization may also not always be there. In addition, as noted by Srivastava (2007), the goals approach focuses on the end result, that is the result of effectiveness.

Open Systems Model

The systems approach acknowledges the constant interaction between the external and internal environments of an organization. Thus, to understand organizational effectiveness, one must understand the nature of the continuous interplay between these two. Instead of finding out *what* the objectives of an organization are, the systems approach focuses on *how* the same will be achieved. Thus, the systems approach attempts to discern the organizational processes that are involved in the functioning of an organization and typically include communication, cooperation, tolerance and the amount of nurturing of the human capital or investment in them. According to this view, an organization's effectiveness depends on its ability to maintain a productive relationship with both its external and internal environments. This includes all the stakeholders, namely, shareholders, employees, customers, suppliers, government and other regulatory bodies and the like. The criteria for effectiveness in the systems approach are the flexibility and adaptability of the organization to meet the demands of the external environment and the adequate management of the organizational processes.

Internal Process Model

According to the internal process model, the effectiveness of any organization depends on the effective internal transformation processes of the organization. More specifically the internal transformational processes would include the 7 Ss of the McKinsey framework. Strategy, structure and systems of the organization are considered to be the 'hard Ss' whereas skills, shared values, staff and style are considered to be the softer and more intangible aspects of the organization. All in fact are intricately interrelated with each other and essential in determining the effectiveness of any organization. Other researchers in this area have tried to identify various indicators of internal effectiveness as predictors of organizational effectiveness. These include flexibility, maintaining a simple organizational structure, employee autonomy and empowerment, focusing on people's development, action bias instead of long-term planning (Peters and Waterman, 1982) or maintenance and production cost, contribution of new members, youthfulness of members, workforce growth, employee loyalty and the like (Steers, 1977).

Human Relations Model

This view focuses on the development of the organizational members as the key to organizational effectiveness and success. It emphasizes various organizational processes as the predictors of organizational effectiveness. These are corporate culture and positive work ethics, decentralized decision making, trust and open communication, organizational loyalty and commitment, and rewarding managers for the development of their subordinates, to name a few.

Competing Value Model

According to Quinn and Rohrbaugh (1983), the competing value model of organizational effectiveness requires that an organization scrutinize the balance among the above four effectiveness models, namely, rational goal model, open system model, internal process model and human relations model.

Thus, in the competing value model, there are three sets of competing values:

1. **Internal vs external focus:** The tension between the two has to be balanced as a mark of effectiveness.
2. **Flexibility vs control:** Flexibility allows quick response to changing conditions and values innovation, whereas control values just the opposite.
3. **People vs task orientation:** Concern with the feelings, needs and development of the people making up the organization vs the organization and its requirement to accomplish its tasks.

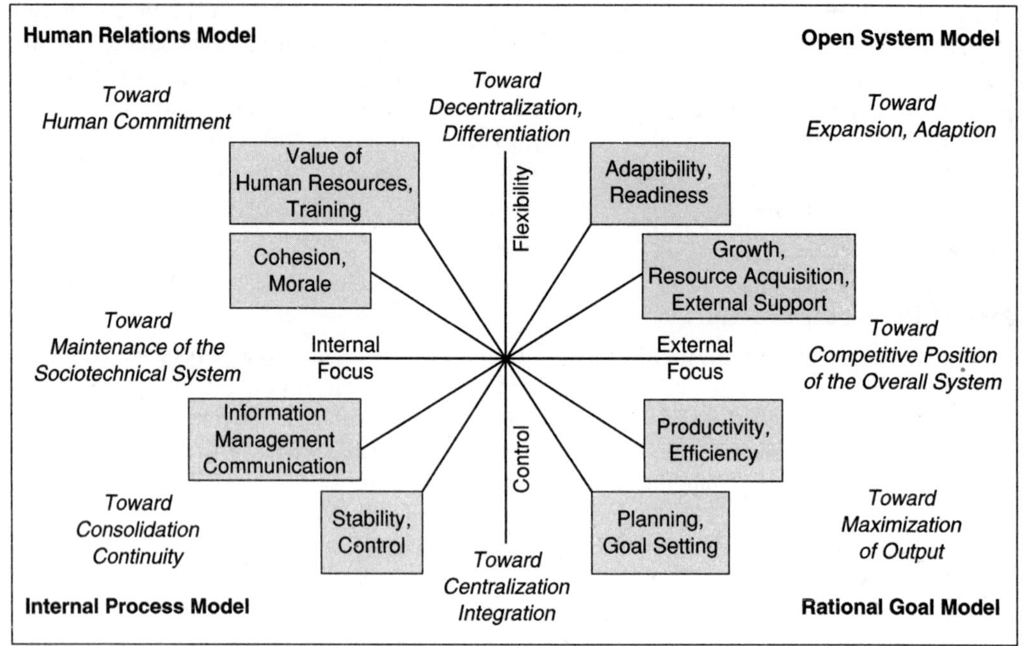

Figure 2.1 Competing Values Framework: Effectiveness

Source: Quinn and Rohrbaugh (1983).

According to the Quinn and Rohrbaugh (1983) model of the competing values of organizational effectiveness, organizations have a need for some level of stability as well as a need to be flexible and adaptable; it has a need for control and discipline as well as a need to allow some degree of freedom and autonomy; a need for rational formal structures and non-rational informal relations. Thus, as noted by Quinn and Rohrbaugh, organizational effectiveness depends upon the ability of an organization, and its managers, to strike the right balance among these critical attributes, as required by the organization's objectives and situation.

Concept Check

1. Why is it difficult to measure organizational effectiveness?
2. What are different approaches to measure organizational effectiveness?

Interactive Exercise

Have a fresh look at the organization you are a part of. How could you determine its effectiveness? Analyze and determine the effectiveness of this particular organization following the competing value model as described earlier.

NEED FOR CHANGE

These days change is the only constant and it is pervasive all around us. Organizations need to change and redefine themselves continuously if they desire to stay in the business. Organizations may want and actively seek change or are forced to change because of the environmental forces. Even organizations at the prime of their business need to change if they want to retain their positions in the market. Staying at the top and in good condition is never easy as one can easily slip and fall down anytime. Thus, to keep on retaining the same position requires a conscious and continuous effort from the organizations. From the viewpoint of organizational development, organizations must always strive to change the way they function in order to be more effective in the ever changing environmental demands. Hence, before implementing any change in programme in an organization, we must carefully try to understand the nature of the forces acting upon it at that point in time.

But before we proceed, we must first try to define change. Simply put, any change is *a relatively enduring alteration of the present state*. Organizational changes, more specifically, refer to *transformations in the organization's design and structure, technology and/or people, which may be either a planned effort or an unplanned one.* Change may occur as a natural process in an organization, or it may be initiated deliberately within the organization.

Any change is a relatively enduring alteration of the present state.
Organizational changes refer to transformations in the organization's design and structure.

Nature of Organizational Change

Whether the organization is deliberately introducing change or is compelled to change as a result of external or internal forces, we have to remember that any change in effort will have a pervasive influence over the entire organization. In other words, it hardly happens that change would remain where it has been initially introduced, as it will always have its presence felt at almost every corner of the organization. This would happen both in the case of planned as well as unplanned change. Also in this context, change may occur either at the behest of the managers or it may slowly evolve from within the organization. Apart from this, change could also take place because of the external pressures operating on the organization.

Forces for Change

There are various factors that may be responsible for driving change in any organization. These may arise from many sources. Some of these are external, arising from outside the company, whereas others are internal, arising from sources within the organization. We will now have a look at each of these separately.

EXTERNAL FORCES FOR CHANGE

Some of the major external forces for change are globalization resulting in fierce competitions, workforce diversity, technological change, government regulations, changing economic conditions and world politics that compel organizations to change.

- **Globalization:** In today's open market economy, power players are multinationals or transnationals having their presence felt in every country across the globe. This has undeniably increased the level of competition for every concerned party. To survive and remain afloat, an organization will have to compete not only with others in its own country but also with the best ones around the world. In order to keep pace with the changing demands across the world, organizations have to undergo changes themselves.

- **Workforce diversity:** This is one of the powerful forces behind organizational changes in recent times. It is quite apparent that the composition of today's workforce has changed significantly over the past few years. Today, we find more women reporting to work as well as in other arenas of life than before. In general, the level of education is higher. The average age of the working people today is found to vary a great deal with more and more people joining the workforce after retirement, with a number of students doing either summer or part-time jobs. To accommodate all these different types of people under the same roof requires a lot of understanding, patience and tolerance as well as embracing changed policies and practices.
- **Technological change:** Advances in technology compel organizations to change. The introduction of computers has probably revolutionized the workplace as nothing before. Uses of internet and intranet have changed the basic functioning of many organizations. New advancements in the manufacturing process also force organizations to change, which are not only restricted to the application of technology but also involve the people applying them.
- **Government regulations:** Organizations have to cope with governmental rules and regulations, which are hardly known beforehand.
- **Changing economic conditions:** The constantly changing economy, not only in the country of operation but also all over the world, is posing considerable challenges for organizations in recent years. The worldwide recession in recent times has forced changes like freezing recruitment and cost cutting in many organizations. Organizations have to struggle real hard to adjust to these changing times and have to undergo changes themselves.
- **World politics:** Whatever happens even at the remotest corners of the world inevitably starts creating ripples within an organization. Events such as the 9/11 attack, the Afghan war, the USA war against Kuwait, changes in the Indo–Pak relationships, the recent upsurge of terrorist movement across the world and the Maoist rebellion have critical impacts in the way business can be conducted.
- **Managing ethical behaviour:** Recent scandals like Satyam, 3G scam and numerous others have brought ethical behaviour in organizations as well as the country to the forefront of public consciousness. All these have forced organizations to maintain a minimum level of transparency and change the way they function.

INTERNAL FORCES FOR CHANGE

Pressures for change that originate inside the organization are generally recognizable in the form of signals indicating that something needs to be altered. The following may be considered as pointers for change within organizations:

- **Declining effectiveness** is often a pressure to change. A company that experiences its third quarterly loss within a fiscal year is undoubtedly motivated to do something about it. Some companies react by instituting layoffs and massive cost-cutting programmes, whereas others look at the bigger picture, view the loss as symptomatic of an underlying problem, and seek the cause of the problem.
- **A crisis** may also stimulate change in an organization. Strikes or an alarming rate of employee turnover may lead the management to change the wage structure. The resignation of a key decision-maker

is one crisis that causes the company to rethink the composition of its management team and its role in the organization. Sometimes, a much-publicized crisis in the organization might lead to change as in the case of the Union Carbide Corporation in India after the Bhopal gas-leak tragedy.

- **Changes in employee expectations** can also trigger change in organizations. A company that hires a group of young newcomers may be met with a set of expectations very different from those expressed by older workers. The workforce is more educated than ever before. Although this has its advantages, workers with more education demand more from their employers. The workforce belonging to the new generation is not only career minded but also more concerned with family balance issues, thus often favouring flexitime or opportunities to work at their own pace. The many sources of workforce diversity hold potential for a host of differing expectations among employees.
- **Changes in work climate** at an organization can also stimulate change. A workforce that seems lethargic, unmotivated and dissatisfied must be addressed. This symptom is common in organizations that have experienced layoffs. Workers who have escaped a layoff may grieve for those who have lost their jobs and may find it hard to continue to be productive. They may fear that they will be laid off as well, and many feel insecure in their jobs.

Types of Change

Change may thus be of two types—*planned* or *unplanned.* Planned change results from a *deliberate decision to alter the organization*. Companies that wish to move from a traditional hierarchical structure with its age-old approach to one that encourages more customer orientations must use a proactive, carefully orchestrated approach; however not all changes are planned. Unplanned change is imposed on the organization and is often unforeseen. Changes in government regulations and changes in the economy, for example, are beyond the control of an organization and thus are often unplanned, particularly, the response to those changes imposed upon. Responsiveness to unplanned change requires tremendous flexibilityand adaptability on the part of the organizations. Managers must be prepared to handle both planned and unplanned forms of change.

In order to further understand the nature of change, we may distinguish between the first-order and second-order change as given in the following:

__First-order change__ refers to the change that is continuous in nature and involves no major shifts in the way an organization operates.
__Second-order change__ refers to more radical change involving major shifts at different levels and different aspects of the organization.

- **First-order change:** This refers to the change that is continuous in nature and involves no major shifts in the way an organization operates. We can notice this type of change taking place in the functioning of, for example, a major steel mill, where they continuously try to improve the efficiency of its production process. Similarly, a restaurant may be seen as making first-order changes as it gradually adds new items to its menu after an initial success.
- **Second-order change:** This refers to more radical change involving major shifts at different levels and different aspects of the organization. When organizations face the second-order change, the basic purpose of the organizations' existence seems to be questionable. An organization going through a second-order change has to revisit its mission, vision and strategy and must make an effort to redefine these in order to position itself better in the market. This is a process of self-renewal when the organization tries to develop an insight into its functioning.

Change can also be either ***fundamental*** or ***incremental*** in nature. Fundamental changes refer to those changes that question the very basic existence of the organization and start exploring better ways of functioning, whereas incremental changes are small changes in the line of the organization's business. Understandably, incremental changes are less disturbing for the organizational members, but in the case of fundamental changes, organizational members are often taken in for a rude shock.

> ***Fundamental changes*** *refer to those changes that question the very basic existence of the organization and start exploring better ways of functioning.*
> ***Incremental changes*** *are small changes in the line of the organization's business.*

Similarly, when adjustments and related strategies are decided in apprehension of possible changes, these are called ***proactive*** changes. But when the organization accommodates itself when facing already imposed changes, these are called ***reactive*** changes. In fact, reactive changes as a change strategy are actually no strategy, as the organization has to adjust at a considerable cost and waste useful resources; proactive changes, however, are wise and offer an effective change strategy that an organization could adopt. Note that it is not always feasible to adopt a proactive change strategy, as it requires meticulous supervision who can successfully scan the environment and discern the possible nature of change well in advance to formulate the change strategy.

> ***Proactive*** *changes occur when adjustments and related strategies are decided in apprehension of possible changes.*
> ***Reactive*** *changes take place when the organization accommodates itself when facing already imposed changes.*

Another way of looking at change is to distinguish between ***individual*** vs ***collective*** changes. It depends on the focus of change. If an individual employee becomes the target (How to improve the performance level of employee X?) of the organizational change effort, their activities will certainly be different from when they aim to initiate change at a collective level (How to improve the daily attendance of a particular department?).

THEORIES OF PLANNED CHANGE

Warren Bennis, one of the pioneers in the field of organization development (OD), claimed OD to be a particular type of change process designed to bring about a particular desirable end result. This 'change' as referred to in the context of organization development, no doubt means planned change. These are the the changes that deliberately induced in the organization, with or without the help of an OD practitioner, with the intention of leading the organization to greater heights. The theoretical models of planned changes provide us with the basis of strategic planning and ways to implement the change processes in the organization.

Lewin's Force Field Analysis

Borrowing the concepts from physical science, Kurt Lewin tried to understand any state as a state of balance or equilibrium of two sets of forces, which he called driving and restraining forces. As long as the balance is maintained, the status quo will remain the same. If an organization wants to be successful consistently, firstly it has to identify the forces acting upon the organization at a point of time. The next step is to strive to actively disrupt the equilibrium.

The force field analysis is a brilliantly simple and logical approach in understanding the organization's current status and planning strategies for further improvement. The steps are also pretty clear and down to earth, which are as follows:

- **Identification of driving and restraining forces:** These may be external and/or internal to the organization. The process of identifying the forces is done in a collaborative way, involving the employees of the organization. This not only encourages the flow of thoughts and new insights, but also helps a greater bonding among organizational members. After identifying the forces, their perceived relative strengths are also ascertained by the members.

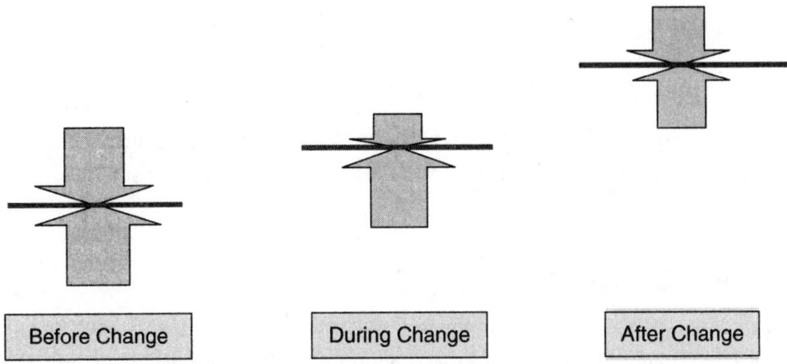

Figure 2.2 Lewin's Force Field Analysis

Source: Lewin, K. (1943). "Defining the field at a given time". *Psychological Review*, 50.

- **Deciding on strategies:** The action plan for achieving the change is rather simple and straight which is to increase the driving forces and decrease the restraining forces and for maximizing the effect, doing both simultaneously. Relative importance to be given to each of these forces is also decided.

Planning a strategy is never enough for initiating change. To make the change effective, it must be accepted by the organizational members through whom the change will have to be implemented. But if people think that they are quite fine the way they and their organization function, they will surely not trouble themselves for undergoing any change. We will note in the next section why people reject and resist change and ways to overcome that. But Lewin's three-step model of change gives valuable insight into the process of change and the means to implement it.

LEWIN'S THREE-STEP MODEL OF CHANGE

Kurt Lewin, one of the pioneers in the field of organization development, proposed his now famous three-step model of change. According to him, to make any effective change, one must be led through the following three typical stages:

1. **Unfreezing:** This involves encouraging individuals to discard their present behaviour by deliberately disrupting the equilibrium state that maintains the status quo and 'shaking' them up from their complacency and comfort zones. This becomes particularly difficult when things are seemingly going fine.
2. **Moving:** After the unfreezing state, when people are aroused from their 'slumber' and start realizing the need for change, they feel almost devastated and rather vulnerable. They have realized that what they were doing in the past were not the right thing. But the perplexing question for them at the moment is what the right thing is for them to do now. This is the stage when new attitudes, values and behaviours are to be provided as substitutes for old ones.
3. **Refreezing:** Enabling change alone is not enough. The success of any effort depends on how well these are maintained afterwards. This is the stage that involves the establishment of new attitudes, values and behaviours as the new status quo.

Figure 2.3 Lewin's Three-step Model of Change
Source: Lewin, K. (1951) Field Theory in Social Science. Harper and Row.

RESISTANCE TO CHANGE

People often resist change even when they are not satisfied with the way the organization functions. They tend to be apprehensive about any proposed change for various reasons. Many of these occur as people usually develop a negative reaction whenever they have to face something different and feel that their personal freedom is at threat.

To understand the nature of resistance to change, we can divide this broadly into two categories: resistance at the ***individual level*** and at the resistance at the ***organizational level***.

INDIVIDUAL RESISTANCE

The major reasons for resisting change by the individual concerned are due to the basic nature of human beings that can be summarised as follows:

- **Fear of the unknown:** Change often brings with it substantial uncertainty. Employees facing a technological change, such as the introduction of a new computer system, may resist change simply because it introduces ambiguity into what was once a comfortable situation for them. This is especially a problem when there has been a lack of communication about the change.
- **Fear of loss:** When a change is impending, some employees may fear losing their jobs, particularly when an advanced technology like computer controls is introduced. Employees may also fear losing their status because of a change. The professional chartered accountants, for example, may feel threatened when they feel their expertise is eroded by the installation of new computer software.
- **Fear of failure:** Some employees fear change because they doubt their own ability. Introducing computers into the workplace often arouses self-doubts about the ability to master the required computer skills. Often, resistance can arise from a fear that the change itself will not be as effective as it is being projected.
- **Force of habit:** Jobs that are well learned and become part of habit are easy to perform. The prospect of change might imply developing new job skills that might be threatening to employees.
- **Economic factors:** Usually, any change in job has the potential to threaten one's livelihood either in the form of loss of job or reduced pay. Thus, resistance to such change is but natural.
- **Disruption of interpersonal relationships:** Employees may resist change that threatens to limit meaningful interpersonal relationships on the job. The prospect of too much automation can be seen as losing the opportunity to interact with their colleagues.
- **Personality conflicts:** When the personality of the person in charge of change (the change agent) engenders negative reactions, employees may resist the change. A change agent who appears insensitive to employee concerns and feelings may meet considerable resistance, because employees perceive that their needs are not being taken into account.

- **Politics:** Organizational change may also shift the existing balance of power in the organization. Individuals or groups who hold power under the current arrangement may be threatened with losing these political advantages in the advent of change. Unless employees are fully convinced about the need for change, they will not support the change.
- **Breach of psychological contract:** People usually develop a psychological involvement with the organization they come to work for. Apart from the clear, tangible contracts between the employer and employee, this gives rise to what is called the *psychological contract.* Any threat of change, particularly the harsh ones, might disrupt this. For example, in the time of ruthless downsizing, people become sad with the prospect of losing their jobs even when it is clearly mentioned in their appointment letter that the nature of the job is purely contractual. They tend to feel betrayed as they feel that the organization has not kept their promise and lacked the reciprocity of feeling.
- **Cultural assumptions and values:** Sometimes cultural assumptions and values can be impediments to change, particularly if the assumptions underlying the change are alien to employees. This form of resistance can be very difficult to overcome, because some cultural assumptions are deep rooted and largely unconscious.

Organizational Resistance

Like individuals, organizations also do resist change in various ways. These can be summarised as follows:

- **Structural inertia:** Organizations are created to ensure stability, and jobs in an organization are designed in a standardized way. Thus, it often becomes difficult to change all these because of the inherent inertia.
- **Work group inertia:** Inertia to continue performing jobs in a specified way comes not only from the job incumbents themselves but also from the social work group.
- **Limited focus of change:** Organizations are made up of a number of interdependent subsystems. Change at one subsystem can only be effective when the other subsystems also change accordingly. But often this is difficult to attain.
- **Threat to expertise:** Changes in organizational patterns and functioning may threat the expertise of specialized groups and that is why it may be strongly resisted by the concerned members.
- **Threat to existing power equation:** Any redistribution of decision-making authority and allowing others into the process can threaten long-established power relationships within the organization and is hence resisted by those enjoying the power.
- **Threat to establish resource allocation:** The groups in the organization who had access to more resources often see change as a threat.
- **Commitments or contracts already made:** Sometimes organizations resist any prospect of change because of commitments already made. For example, in the case when the organization has signed a contract of supplying a certain quantity of a product, it is not possible for them to reduce the workforce immediately.
- **Previously unsuccessful change efforts:** Any organization that has faced a disaster in the past will naturally be resistant to initiate any new change.

MANAGING RESISTANCE TO CHANGE

Resistance to change makes it difficult for the organizations to implement the proposed changes required for the development of the organization. As discussed earlier, resistance to change is an innate psychological response of human beings to anything new, and it is wise to acknowledge it. Instead of trying to overcome it, this can be treated as valuable feedback from the people subject to the change scenario and can be used to effectively manage the change process in the organization.

There are various approaches for managing resistance to change that can be summarized as follows:

- **Identify and convince key individuals:** For changes to be effective and accepted, it is often essential to win the support of the most powerful individuals in the organization. This surely facilitates the change process.
- **Identify and neutralize those who resist change:** During times of impending change, some people become too nervous and tend to openly verbalize their apprehension. The whole thing might be quite infectious and more and more people start panicking. The authority should be prompt in responding to such situations and clarify the doubts of the concerned people as candidly as possible.
- **Education and communication:** Resistance to change can be reduced significantly if employees are helped to appreciate the need for change. This can be achieved through clear and extensive communications. Open communication, participation, and emotional support can go a long way towards managing resistance to change. Managers must realize that some resistance is inevitable; however, they should plan ways to deal with resistance early in a change process.
- **Involve employees in the decisions for change:** In order to win the support of employees, it is always wise to involve them in the decision-making process. This way, they feel the decision is their own and hence commit to it.
- **Facilitation and support:** During times of change, offering support in the form of counselling or arranging training programmes for mastering new skills required in the changed situation help reducing resistance considerably.
- **Reward constructive behaviour:** A time-tested tactics for accepting change is to reward those who have learned to adopt the changes successfully.

BEHAVIOURAL REACTIONS TO CHANGE

In spite of attempts to minimize the resistance to change in an organization, some reactions to change are inevitable. People may show four types of basic, identifiable reactions to change: disengagement, disidentification, disenchantment and disorientation.

Disengagement is psychological withdrawal from change. The employee may appear to lose initiative and interest in the job. They lack drive and commitment, and they simply comply without real psychological investment in their work. The basic managerial strategy for dealing with disengaged individuals is to confront them with their reaction and draw them out so that they can identify the concerns that need to be addressed.

Another reaction to change is ***disidentification***. Individuals reacting in this way feel that their identity has been threatened by the change, and they feel vulnerable. Often, they cling to a past procedure because they had a sense of mastery over it. When employees are allowed to participate, they are more committed to the change. Another strategy for managing resistance is providing empathy and support to employees who have trouble dealing with change.

Disenchantment is also a common reaction to change. It is usually expressed as negativity or anger. Disenchanted employees lives in their past obsessively. They may try to enlist the support of other employees by forming coalitions, resulting in destructive behaviours like sabotage and backstabbing. It is often difficult to reason with disenchanted employees. Thus, the first step in managing this reaction is to bring these employees from their highly negative, emotionally charged state to a more neutral state. They can then be dealt in such a way to acknowledge that their anger is normal. This can reduce the negativity in their feeling.

The final reaction to change is ***disorientation***. Disoriented employees are lost, confused and often unsure about their feelings. They waste time and energy trying to figure out what to do instead of exploring the correct way to do things. They ask lots of questions and become detail oriented. It may appear that they need proper guidance and may leave their work undone unless all of their questions have been answered.

A final note of caution on organizational change: The success of any change in fact depends on the person handling the change. His capability of handling any change sensitively and winning the trust and confidence of those facing the change will determine the effectiveness of any change.

GLOSSARY

- **Organizational effectiveness:** A multidimensional concept involving more than one criteria of measurement.
- **Rational goals model:** Identifying what the purported goals of the organization are and how well these have been achieved by the organization.
- **Open systems model:** An organization's effectiveness depends on its ability to maintain a productive relationship with all aspects of both its external and internal environments including all stakeholders.
- **Internal process model:** The effectiveness of any organization depends on the effective internal transformation processes of the organization.
- **Human relations model:** The development of the organizational members as the key to organizational effectiveness and success.
- **Competing value model:** Organizational effectiveness requires a balance among four effectiveness models, namely, rational goal model, open system model, internal process model and human relations model.
- **Organizational change:** A relatively enduring alteration of the present state.
- **Planned change:** Change resulting from a deliberate decision to alter the organization.
- **First-order change:** Change that is continuous in nature and involves no major shifts in the way an organization operates.
- **Second-order change:** More radical change involving major shifts at different levels and different aspects of the organization.
- **Lewin's three-step model of change:** For any effective change, three typical stages, unfreezing, moving and refreezing, are involved.

QUESTIONS

1. What do you understand by the term 'organizational effectiveness'? Why is the concept of effectiveness important? Discuss different perspectives of organizational effectiveness.
2. Define change. Why is the understanding of organizational change important for today's managers?
3. Distinguish between planned and unplanned changes. Which type of change is better from the view point of an organization? Why are unplanned changes sometimes inevitable in an organization?
4. What are the major sources of resistance to change? What are some of the ways to overcome these resistances?

REFERENCES

1. P.M. Blau and W.R. Scott, *Formal Organizations: A Comparative Approach* (San Francisco: Chandler Publishing Company, 1962).
2. Bernard, C. I. (1938). *The Function of Executive.* Harvard University Press
3. T. Burns and G.M. Stalker, *The Management of Innovation* (London: Tavistock, 1961).
4. Cummings, T. G. and Worley, C. G. (2005). *Organization Development and Change.* 8th Edition. Thomson/South Western.
5. R. Likert, *New Patterns of Management* (San Francisco: Jossey-Bass, 1961).
6. J.G. March and H.A. Simon, *Organizations* (New York: John Wiley & Sons, 1958).
7. E. Mayo, *The Social Problems of an Industrial Civilization* (Boston: Graduate School of Business Administration, Harvard University, 1945 (copyright 1933)).
8. D. McGregor, *The Human Side of Enterprise* (New York: McGraw-Hill, 1960).
9. H. Mintzberg, *The Structuring of Organizations* (Englewood Cliffs, NJ: Prentice-Hall, Inc, 1979).
10. G. Morgan, *Images of Organization*, 2nd ed. (Thousand Oaks, CA: Sage, 1997).
11. K. Mukherjee, *Principles of Management and Organizational Behaviour* (Tata McGraw-Hill, 2008).
12. Peters, T., and Waterman, R. H. Jr. (1982). *In Search of Excellence: Lessons from America's Best Run Companies* (New York, Harper & Row).
13. R.E. Quinn and J. Rohrbaugh, 'A Spatial Model of Effectiveness Criteria: Towards a Competing Values Approach to Organizational Analysis', *Management Science*, 1983, 29:363–377.
14. R.W. Scott, *Organizations: Rational, Natural, and Open Systems* (Englewood Cliffs, NJ: Prentice Hall, 1987).
15. Srivastava, B. (2007). *Organization Design and Development: Concepts and Applications*. Biztantra.
16. Steers, R. M. (1977). Antecedent and outcomes of organizational commitment. *Administrative Science Quarterly*, Volume 22(1).
17. F.W. Taylor, *The Principles of Scientific Management* (New York: Harper, 1911).

18. E. Trist, 'The Evolution of Sociotechnical Systems', in A. Van de Ven and W. Joyce (eds.), *Perspectives on Organizational Design and Behavior* (New York: Wiley-Interscience, 1981).

19. Steers, R. M. (1977). *Antecedent and Outcomes of Organizational Commitment*, Administrative Science Quarterly, Volume 22(1).

20. Quinn, R. E., and Rohrbaugh, J. (1983). "A Spatial Model of Effectiveness Criteria: Towards a Competing Values Approach to Organizational Analysis", *Management Science*, 29.

Case Study: Logicom Corporation

Logicom Corporation is the leading supplier of communication chips for broadband, data networking and wireless and set-top box applications. Logicom started operating its business in 1981 in California and has developed products that they claim have changed the way people around the globe create, store and consume digital information. With over $1 billion in storage market revenue annually, Logicom is uniquely positioned to deliver technologies, products and software to its global markets.

Overseas Operations

Logicom started its operation in India in 2005. Robert Carey, Senior Software Engineer Manager, was given the charge of the project because of his in-depth knowledge and technical expertise as well as his previous exposure to this part of the globe. Since Robert, or Bob as he is usually known by people around him, was global head of entire software development team, therefore he could not shift base to Kolkata permanently. The management was therefore on the lookout for people who can stay in Kolkata and take charge of the operations of the the Kolkata office. At that time, two young Bengali software professionals originally from Kolkata, who were then working with Logicom in the USA, got selected for the positions.

They returned to Kolkata and started operating from a small rented place with only two laptops, while hunting for local talents from universities and institutes. In less than a year, the India office became a force to reckon with, shifting to a huge state-of-the art office located in the heart of the city's IT district with a highly sophisticated computer laboratory and a team of young and talented engineers.

Instead of running the India operations on the basis of only implementing the software designs already developed in the USA, the newly established India operation started designing and developing various unique software programmes after successfully attracting the best talents in the area. They also developed a unique software package that generated huge demand from global customers. This helped the company to earn revenues and become a hot favourite with many customers worldwide.

Of course, the turnaround was a result of the hard work put in by the team. The credit goes to Bob, who was in charge of the Kolkata operation. The success of this operation was, in fact, the resultant effect of the policies of the firm that changed the fortunes of the company. He correctly understood the psyche and culture of Kolkata and tapped the brilliance and talent of the people by empowering them and treating them with respect. He also understood the importance of communication, particularly when the operations of the firm involve several continents and widely different time zones.

There was certainly nothing 'bossy' about this boss. In spite of his dazzling academic and technical brilliance, Bob did not think too much of his own technological prowess. However, he struggles to manage people effectively and mentor future leaders out of the highly competent group of technological experts and computer engineers. A strikingly handsome and mild-natured person, Bob hardly showed the mental toughness he possesses. He was an uncompromising perfectionist and had the ability to instill the same sense of commitment in his juniors. He never believed in shooting orders, as he believed that if values and ethos are not internalized by people, it is never possible to elicit the best out of them. He had respect for the people working under him and he was a staunch believer of delegation of power and authority.

Question

How did Bob develop his style of interaction to facilitate the growth of Logicom in Kolkata?

Chapter **3**

Organizational Culture and Climate

Opening Case: Identical Across the World

Swami Vivekananda was one of the most renowned disciples of Shri Ramakrishna Paramhansa Dev. A vastly read person with a strong spiritual base, he introduced the concepts of Indian philosophy, Vedanta and yoga to the Western world. His captivating speech at the Parliament of World's Religion at Chicago in 1915 touched the heart of millions and he became a legend overnight.

Born to a rich and aristocratic Bengali family in late 19th century, Narendranath (his original name before he became a monk) had an urge to know God from an early age. He eventually came in touch with Shri Ramakrishna at Dakshineswar and became his disciple. After the death of his Guru, Vivekananda became a *Paribrajak* or wandering monk and travelled throughout India to know the people and their conditions in the subcontinent. He attained the highest level of spirituality in his personal life. Vivekananda could very well devote his life in the pursuit of God as a hermit, away from people and civilization. But following the instructions of his Guru, he devoted his life to the well-being of his fellow countrymen and set up a chain of ashramas in the name of his Guru, Shri Ramakrishna, as 'Ramakrishna Math' or Ramakrishna Missions. The first *math* was set up in a dilapidated building in Baranagar, chiefly because of the low rent of the building and its proximity to the burning ghat near the Ganges, where Shri Ramakrishna was cremated. Initially, there was a strong financial constraint with the cost of the establishment being borne by the householder disciples only. Eventually the financial constraint got over and the Baranagar *math* eventually shifted to Belur, a small township located in the Howrah district. Over the years, the institution became recognized worldwide.

If you go to a *math*, you will be struck by way it has been maintained over the years. You would never find a speck of dust anywhere, every individual member is found to be wearing clean robes according to the order he belongs to. You will find a similar pattern of behaviour in all of them, which may be described as polite, firm and perfectly orderly. All the activities are precisely time bound. From keeping the shoes of the visitors in neatly arranged piles with token numbers to help in identification, to organizing pujas and festivals, to distributing *bhog* or *prasadas* to huge number of devotees and visitors, to organizing relief activities for victims of natural calamities such as floods or tsunamis, there will always be an exact order and meticulous execution of every simple task with unfailing clockwork precision. If the evening prayer is to start at 6.00 pm, by 5.45 pm all the sanyasis conducting the prayer and puja will take their seats.

Among the major focuses of Swamiji were cleanliness and orderliness. These values, among other things, are found to be strongly present in each of the mathas across the globe even today.

After going through this chapter, you would be able to understand what culture is and what could possibly affect the effective functioning of an organization. In addition, you would also be able to appreciate the interplay of national culture with the specific organizational culture. In this chapter, you will learn about the following:

LEARNING OBJECTIVES

- What is organization culture?
- Levels of organizational culture
- Types of culture
- Sustaining organizational culture
- Stages of organizational culture
- Culture and climate
- Changing organizational culture
- Organizational culture vs national culture

WHAT IS ORGANIZATIONAL CULTURE?

Imagine being in any of the nationalized banks of India before you visit a modern age bank, both situated in the same city. Even if you are unaware about the names of the banks, you will notice stark difference between these two banks. From the ambiance to the way people greet or interact with each other, their dress to the general ambience, everything would seem distinctly different. To understand this, just take an example of the person sitting next you in the classroom. You two are pursuing the same course, have paid the same course fee, but it is least likely that you two are similar personalities. In the same way, we may assign the difference between two organizations as organizational culture that distinguishes it from other organizations.

Like individuals, organizations are also different from each other. This is what may be roughly referred to as the *culture* prevailing in any organization.

The most commonly used definition of organizational culture is that it is 'a system of shared meaning held by majority of members that distinguishes the organization from others'. Schein (1985) also describes organizational culture as a 'cognitive framework consisting of attitudes, values, behavioural norms, and expectations shared by organizational members'. In other words, this refers to *a set of basic assumptions that are embraced and shared by organizational members without any question*. You will find an analogy of this in your family which has a distinctive culture and plays an important role in your day to day activities. Say, for example, when all your friends are planning to go to an evening movie show, you had to excuse yourself as you know that it would never be allowed. It will be useless even

Organizational culture is a system of shared meaning held by the majority of members that distinguishes the organization from others.

to try to argue as what you would hear from them would invariably be 'Oh, this is never done in our family, and you know that!' This is the culture prevailing in your family and you have learned to simply accept that. The set of values and beliefs such as these are what have made your family stand distinctly different from other families.

As noted earlier, organizational culture is similar to what the personality is in the individual context. However, Martin (1996) has identified six core organizational values that can distinguish one organizational culture from others. These are as follows:

- **Sensitivity to the needs of customers and employees:** As an organization matures over time, it tends to lose its flexibility and focus on customers and employees. This sets the tone of the organization, which denotes a sense of aloofness and unconcern. In contrast, some organizations are warm, caring and pay good attention to their both internal and external customers. It is, however, not quite uncommon to note that an established organization, like a nationalized bank, is forced to shake its inertia and try to pay more attention to their customers and employees when faced with steep competition in the market, and reset the priorities.
- **Interest in employees generating new ideas:** Some organizations prefer uniform and standardized behaviour from their employees and take adequate care to 'train' them to ensure the uniformity of behaviour, while some organizations encourage diverse inputs from their employees, which can create a rich and innovative atmosphere in the organization.
- **Willingness to take risks:** Some organizations are traditionally risk avoiders, whereas in some organizations taking risks is encouraged. Examples include traditional financial institutions vs modern players in the same sector, which are more daring and aggressive in their approach.
- **Value placed on people:** Some organizations truly believe the employees to be their asset while some consider them valuable only as long as they can contribute to enhance the profit margin by increasing their productivity. The latter is called a toxic organizational culture, which tends to lose the valuable workforce and thus suffer in the long term. In contrast, the former is known as the healthy culture as organizations having the healthy culture are found to have low turnover and generally prosper. Examples of healthy culture could be found in the Tata group of companies where employees are usually treated well and with respect. Eight characteristics of healthy organizational culture are summarized in Table 3.1.

__Toxic culture:__ Where people feel they are not valued
__Healthy organizational culture:__ Where people feel they are valued

- **Open communication:** In some organizations, members are free to communicate with each other, irrespective of the hierarchical level, whereas in some, usually large organizations, in public and private sectors alike, channels of communication are found to be too formal and rather restricted.
- **Friendliness and congeniality among employees:** In some organizations, people get along well with each other and tend to develop long-term relationships, often beyond the work place. But, in some organizations, a strong feeling of competitiveness is found to prevail.

There are a few unmistakable signs of a healthy organizational culture that seem to clearly distinguish them from toxic cultures, which may be summarized as in Table 3.1.

Table 3.1 Some Typical Indicators of Healthy Organizational Culture

Openness and humility	Openness and humility are shown by the members, and haughtiness or high-handedness is absent. This clearly enhances good interpersonal relationships among the members and facilitates learning from each other. This is typically found in most software firms where people are hardly stuck in hierarchical positions and are warm and friendly towards their juniors.
Accountability and responsibility	Members own up their personal *responsibility* and are *accountable* for their actions, thus minimizing blame games or excuses. This leads to better compatibility and cooperation.
Risk taking	People are found to *take risks* to a reasonable extent, thus encouraging the flow of new ideas. However, in large bureaucratic organizations, both public sector and private sectors alike, risk taking is hardly encouraged and more reliance is given on precedence and rule book instead.
Personal commitment	A high level of *commitment* to the job as well as the organization is shown by the majority.
Tolerating mistakes	Mistakes, up to a limit, are tolerated as these are viewed as learning effort.
Personal integrity	Members' level of personal integrity is very high and dishonesty is seldom.
Collaborative and friendly environment	People are found to work together in an open and friendly environment and collaborate beyond the individual or departmental boundaries.
Persistence of efforts	Members are encouraged to persist in their efforts, even in the face of failure which is accepted in a challenging work.

LEVELS OF ORGANIZATIONAL CULTURE

Schein (1965) identifi ed three distinct levels of culture that are found in any organization. These are as follows:

- **Level I—Artefacts:** This refers to the tangible part of organizational culture that hits our senses. It gives you the first glimpse of the typicality or distinctiveness of the culture of any organization. Examples of artefacts include physical space, layout, technical output, spoken language, dress code and so on, which are readily reckoned by anyone stepping even for the first time inside the organization.
- **Level II—Values:** This refers to values shared by the majority of the people in the organization. These values develop over time in a particular organization out of past experiences of successfully tackling any important problems or issues in the life of the organization. Typical examples include customer focus in a bank as it has proved to generate customer loyalty and thus better business prospect, and so has been accepted by the majority of the employees in the bank.

__Level I—Artefacts:__ This refers to the tangible part of the organizational culture that hits our senses.

__Level II—Values:__ This refers to values shared by the majority of the people in the organization.

Elements of Organizational Culture

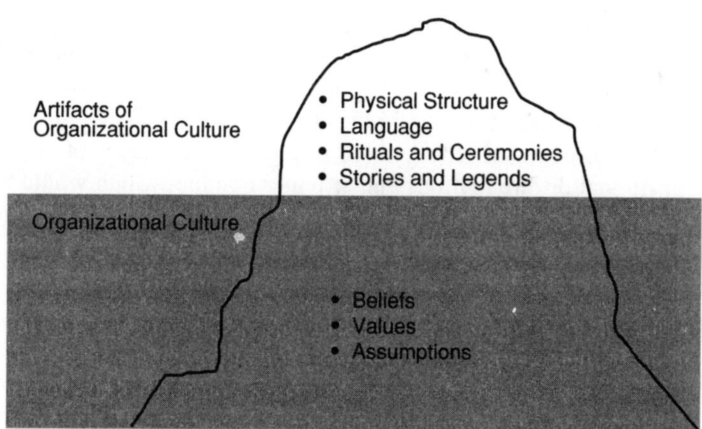

Figure 3.1 Levels of Organizational Culture

Source: Adapted from Stanley N. Herman, "TRW Systems Group".

- **Level III—Basic underlying assumptions:** This refers to the 'distilled' value sets or things that are taken for granted and accepted without question. Take the example of the bank which has come to value its customers because of its positive outcome. Therefore, the 'customer focus' or willingness to treat customers as 'kings' will eventually be accepted across the entire organization without question.

> ***Level III—Basic underlying assumptions:*** *This refers to things that are taken for granted and accepted without question.*

ORGANIZATIONAL CULTURE: UNIFORM OR POCKETS OF DIFFERENT CULTURES

Organizational culture is the generalized subjective perception of the organizational members regarding the prevalent culture in an organization. It may or may not necessarily tally with the measures or practices that are adopted in the organization. *Core* organizational values are the basic or fundamental values accepted by the majority of the organizational members. Interestingly, organizational culture is hardly a uniform entity in any organization. In spite of the existence of an overall culture in an organization, we can often spot pockets of *subcultures* across the organization, particularly in large organizations. In addition to subscribing to core cultures, organizational subcultures are distinguished from the

> ***Core values:*** *The basic or fundamental values held by the majority of the members.*
> ***Dominant culture:*** *Core values shared by the majority of the organizational members.*
> ***Subculture:*** *Pockets of culture that typically develop across the organization, usually due to belongingness to different departments or geographical locations.*

overall organizational culture in terms of the functional typicality or locational characteristics, such as physical space or geographical characteristics.

Subcultures might not always be completely aligned with the dominant culture of any organization. Some typical characteristics may be more pronounced and this could at times result in a conflicting perception among members. Nevertheless, subcultures should not necessarily be seen as a threat to the dominant culture of the organization. Rather, the presence of subcultures often helps the organization to check and question its prevailing dominant cultures and can thus provide opportunities of self-evaluation and reality checking. Values that are mostly shared at the corporate head offices may not be the same at plants at remote areas of a power development company. People at plants may have less positional differentiations and stronger bonding which would not be found in city offices. This might set the thinking process of the utility of holding the hierarchical differences too tightly.

WEAK vs STRONG ORGANIZATIONAL CULTURE

Organizational culture also does vary in terms of its perceived strength and thus can give rise to strong or weak cultures. A *strong* organizational culture is the one which is *passionately* embraced and accepted by the majority of the people in an organization. If customer focus is strongly accepted by most of the employees in a bank, it would be a strong culture in that organization. But, if the same is rather weakly accepted by the members, this will give rise to a *weak* culture. Thus, if an organization has only limited and/or passive acceptance of the organizational values, it would give rise to a weak organizational culture.

> ***Strong culture:*** *Organization's core values are both passionately held and widely accepted across the organizational members.*
> ***Weak culture:*** *There is only limited agreement with respect to core organizational culture among the organizational members.*

Thus, in organizations with a strong culture, core values are held intensely and shared widely (Greenberg and Baron 2009). A strong organizational culture typically denotes an organization where most of the members accept the core values and have a higher degree of commitment towards these values. Stronger organizational cultures are usually found in newer organizations with a relatively smaller number of employees than in larger and older organizations. Apparently, in older organizations, the effect of culture seems to be diffused and the influence of founder members gets diminished over time.

ROLE OF ORGANIZATIONAL CULTURE

Organizational culture serves several important roles within an organization. These may be described as follows:

- **Sense of identity:** With the presence of a strong and dominant culture in an organization, bonding and cohesion among organizational members increase noticeably. This helps in developing a strong corporate identity. For example, in the Tata group of companies, a strong commitment towards corporate social responsibility differentiates them from other companies and in turn creates a sense of pride and belongingness towards the company.
- **Commitment towards the organization and its purpose:** In organizations, where there is a well-established culture, members tend to submit their individual interests for the sake of attaining overall organizational objectives with which they identify themselves. Thus, in not-for-profit

organizations trying to provide social support to people, even when employees accept a monthly salary, they keep in mind the spirit of rendering services to the poor and deserving.

- **Ensures uniformity of behaviour:** The presence and acceptance of an organizational culture helps organizational members to have a better and clearer idea regarding what is expected from them. This ensures uniformity of behaviour on the part of the organizational members who tend to conform to the expectations.
- **Provides control:** Organizational culture, once established, helps to control members' behaviour, as they naturally pick up the desired forms of behaviour from other members around them. Any deviations from the desired behaviour are automatically controlled, not by rules or punitive measure, but by the sheer presence of a culture that is embraced by the majority of the members. It is thus like winning a hard battle nonchalantly.

TYPES OF ORGANIZATIONAL CULTURE

Various types of organizational cultures may typically be categorized in terms of two defining dimensions—flexibility vs control and internal vs external focus. This gives rise to four distinct types of organizational culture which are as follows:

1. **Hierarchy culture:** Hierarchy culture is denoted by a strong concern for internal focus and a high level of control. The major emphasis is given on maintaining uniformity of behaviour which is followed and enforced according to the rule books and/or manuals. This type of culture is typically noticed in large bureaucratic organizations—in both public and private sectors alike. Thus, in organizations such as the Indian Railways or Tata Group of Companies, very little discretion is allowed and a high level of emphasis is given to conformity and uniformity of behaviour.

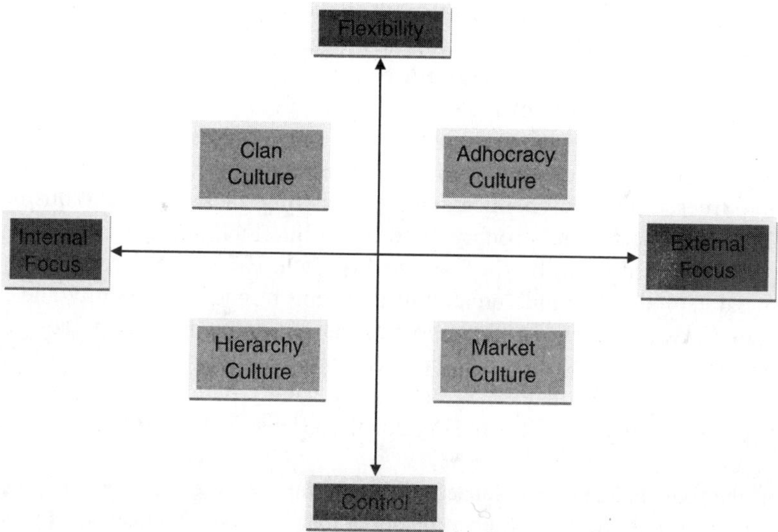

Figure 3.2 Types of Organizational Culture

2. **Market culture:** Similar to hierarchical culture, market culture also places strong emphasis on control, but at the same time it is more outward in comparison to the hierarchical culture. Thus, in these types of organizations, more emphasis is given on the competition and prevalent market scenario. The focus is result-oriented, on better productivity, in order to survive the competition. Modern players in the telecommunication sector, namely, Vodafone, Airtel or Aircel are good examples of market culture who fiercely compete with each other by frequently and drastically lowering the tariff rates or rental plans.
3. **Clan culture:** Organizations with a clan culture are denoted by a strong internal focus along with a high degree of flexibility in their operations. Organizational goals are strongly held by members and this leads to a better cohesiveness among them. Understandably, clan cultures, where employee well-being is given maximum emphasis, will make the organization an enjoyable place to work. However, stressing only on employee well-being at the cost of losing important business goals will surely be detrimental to the organizational survival and prosperity.
4. **Adhocracy culture:** Organizations having a high concern for flexibility along with a strong emphasis on the external environment give rise to the adhocracy culture. These organizations are found to have a strong emphasis on innovativeness and a constant environmental analysis to capture future opportunities. Typically, software firms, filmmaking and entertainment businesses and research laboratories reflect the adhocracy culture.

HOW DOES ORGANIZATIONAL CULTURE START?

The culture of any organization typically starts with the founder members. They start the company and bring their personal values and passions into the organization. They select people for the organization and their values guide them considerably in the selection process. This becomes particularly true during the initial stages of the organization when the influence of the founder members is found to be still alive, though this can very well continue for a pretty longer period. Take the case of the Tata group of companies founded by Jamsetji Nusserwanji Tata around one and a half centuries back. It has 90 companies as part of the conglomerate, fondly referred to as 'family'. They are a $70.8 billion commercial enterprise with about 350,000 employees in 80 countries and are engaged in diverse types of business including steel manufacturing, mining, consumer goods, hotels, telecommunication, trucks and cars, chemicals and engineering, IT services and business process outsourcing. All of these sectors are strongly bond by an interlocking governance structure and a set of corporate values passed down by the founder J.N. Tata. He used to strongly believe a company thrives on 'social capital', the value created in investing in good community and human relationships, in the same way as the hard and tangible assets of a company may possess. Along with this, there is a strong commitment towards social responsibility which is fervently followed across all the companies under the group. To date, these beliefs and values are found to be strongly shared by the large majority of the employees across the organization. This can be described as a multi-step process as given in Figure 3.3.

Apart from the founder members, subsequently, the top management becomes responsible in creating and sustaining a culture. With human resource management practices such as selection of new employees, performance appraisals, promotional policies, training activities and so on that are followed in an organization ensure that the employees fit into the organizational culture.

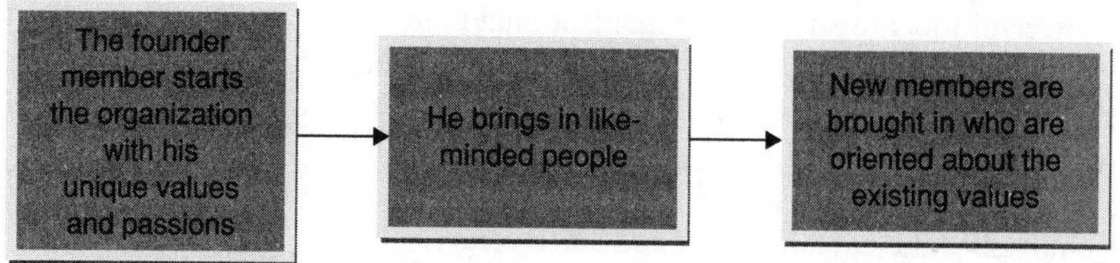

Figure 3.3 The Steps of Organizational Culture

THE STAGES OF ORGANIZATIONAL CULTURE

When a new employee enters an organization, he does not embrace the culture immediately. It takes some time for the new entrée to get accustomed with the existing culture that prevails in the organization. Before finally embracing the culture, the employee passes through several distinct phases which are given in Figure 3.3.

Socialization process is the process through which employees adopt the organizational culture.

Rebellion, when the employee rejects all the values and norms of the existing culture.
Conformity, where the employee fully accepts all the values and norms of the existing culture.
Creative individualism, where the employee accepts only the pivotal values of culture and rejects the rest.

Pivotal norms: Norms essential to accomplishing the organization's objectives.
Peripheral norms: Norms that support the pivotal norms but are not essential for attaining the organization's objectives.

The adjustment of a new employee to the cultural norms of the organization may however take three possible routes:

1. **Rebellion,** when the employee rejects *all* the values and norms of the existing culture.
2. **Conformity**, where the employee fully accepts all the values and norms of the existing culture.
3. **Creative individualism**, where the employee accepts only the pivotal values of culture and rejects the rest.

The pivotal norms are those that are essential to accomplishing the organization's objectives, whereas peripheral norms refer to those that support the pivotal norms but are still not essential for attaining the organization's objectives. Thus, the pivotal norms for a teaching institute are acquiring and maintaining excellent standards of teaching for the faculty members, whereas the peripheral norms may, say, be the dress code and presentability of the faculty members.

HOW DOES ORGANIZATIONAL CULTURE GET TRANSMITTED?

How does the organizational culture sustain? How do the employees come to know the culture in the first place? There are several ways through which the culture gets transmitted in an organization, which include stories, slogans, language, and rituals.

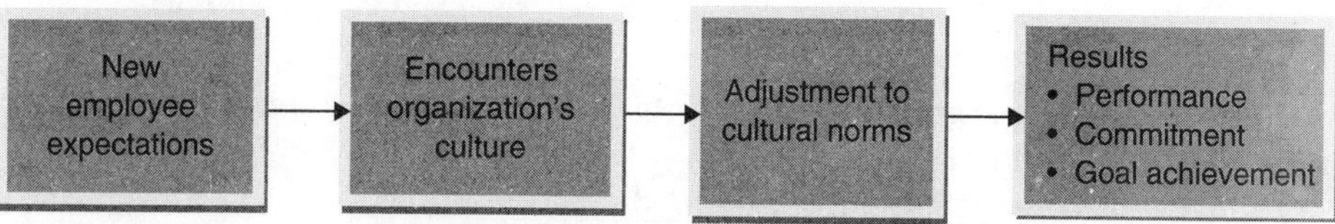

Figure 3.4 The Socialization Process

- **Stories** are powerful tools to sustain an organizational culture. These usually highlight the basic philosophy behind the organization. And these are circulated throughout the company so that people learn them fast. For example, the founder of a multi-crore paper machinery manufacturing company who started his life collecting wastes from the rag pickers to be supplied to paper mills as the ingredient of paper pulp eventually became a millionaire, and used to boast about his early struggles to emphasize the need for thrift and hard work.
- **Slogans** that an organization chooses are never just advertisement gimmicks but actually reflect a lot about the inner values and deeper philosophies held by the company. In fact, slogans showcase the important part of the organizational culture to both the internal employees and the external world at large. A short overview of some of the noted Indian organizations clearly conveys the culture of the organizations, as shown in Table 3.2.
- **Material symbol:** When you enter an organization, the first things that hit your senses, such as the layout or the décor, the office arrangement—open cubicles or close cabins—the sizes of the cabins, the furniture, the colour scheme, the interior, and so on and so forth, are tangible in nature and have been noted in the earlier section as 'artefacts'. These speak quite loudly about the culture of the organization. For example, beautiful flower arrangements in government offices are never expected, whereas a spick and span office is usually found in modern private-sector organizations. The allowances and privileges given were also found to vary at different levels, such as while the top managements are allowed to fly in the business class, the middle-level managers are entitled to the economy class only. And this certainly reflects the culture of the organization.
- **Language:** Organizations are often found to develop some typicality in the language the members use. For example, software professionals are found to dwell on using acronyms (some examples are ABAP, advanced business application programming; JSP, Java server pages; FYI, for your information; PFA, please find attachment), the meanings of which are understood by members of the particular community only. Over time, the new entrants start picking up the typical language usage and feel as one belonging to the organization.
- **Rituals:** Rituals are the activities repeated over and over in the organization and highlight the key thrust areas of the organization. For example, before starting the day all the employees of the showroom of a renowned watch maker would assemble for the morning meeting and decide and agree upon the day's target or any typical strategy. It is not so much about deciding on the day's target and strategy but about being together before starting the day; this reflects the emphasis on people

Table 3.2 Some Interesting Slogans of Present Organizations

Company	Slogan	Underlying Culture
Tata Steel	■ *We also make steel* ■ *Values stronger than steel*	■ Though we happen to make steel, our main thrust is nurturing human capital and taking care of the society at large. ■ Strongly ethical corporate culture.
Big Bazaar	*Isse sasta kahin nahi milegi (You won't get it cheaper anywhere)*	You can rely on us for offering the lowest possible price.
LIC	*Jeevan ke sath bhi, jeevan ke bad bhi (We are with you through your life, we are with you even after your life)*	We are caring and always will be by your side. You can rely on us.
Vodafone	*Happy to help*	A strong supporting spirit.

force within the organization. In the same way, organizations are found to adhere to some activities no matter what and even when the activities as such may not be essentially work related, such as a monthly 'dinner meet' or the first day programme of the beginning of a course.

- **Stories:** Organizations have their share of stories in the round, just like the families have. You keep on hearing, perhaps the thousandth time, how your great grandfather amassed the fortune by working so hard and being so thrifty in his personal habit. Take the case of Bajaj group of industries, which was established by Jamnalal Bajaj in the pre-independence era. Jamnalal was a staunch follower of Gandhiji and was considered as his confidante. He devoted himself to the cause of freedom and lent considerable financial support to the movement. These values and sentiments were deeply shared by the successive generations of people who took charge of the business empire and are still strongly reflected across the group of industries. The company is abounding with stories of the selfless sacrifice and commitment of the founder member. The sentiment is still reflected in various corporate social responsibility efforts taken up by the company. Thus, the stories in fact do depict the success attained by the organization (or in the case of families as well) on a typical situation or describe a mistake and the fallouts, and all these in fact offer a great learning experience for the members. The new entrants get to know what is cherished in the organization (or in the family) and what is to be avoided at all cost.

SUSTAINING ORGANIZATIONAL CULTURE

Once a culture develops within an organization and particularly when it gives 'good dividend', maintaining it becomes the next challenge. It is worth noting that the culture does not simply be retained by default. It takes some serious thought on the part of the people in charge of the organization and some detailed and careful planning strategies are to be implemented. The various strategies could be as follows.

- **Choosing the new entrants carefully:** Though the ostensible purpose of any selection process is to choose the people who possess the required skill set and expertise, checking only these will never ensure 'the right person' for any particular organization. The entire process should also focus on identifying the people who will be compatible with the prevailing organizational culture, just like any matrimonial alliance initiated by the parents where the selection of the bride/bridegroom takes serious consideration of, among other things, the cultural compatibility of the two families. In the organizational context, this is one of the reasons behind multiple phases of interview processes found in various organizations where the candidate is asked to meet people at different levels on more than one occasion. This also helps the candidate to take a decision regarding the possibility of 'gelling' with the organization in question.
- **The people at the helm:** Just as creating the culture, the top management has a major role in sustaining the culture within the organization. This is achieved predominantly by the behaviour and the practices adopted by them rather than 'preaching' anything grand and lofty, as actions invariably speak louder. For example, Narayan Murthy, the Director of Infosys, one of the major IT companies in the country, believes in simple living, and he never travels in business class. Thus, the emphasis on simple living is loud and clear across the organization.
- **Orientation process:** The initial period after joining an organization is very crucial for the new entrants as this is their encounter stage when they learn to pick up 'the ropes' around the organization. If sustaining the organizational culture is among the list of priorities for the organization, the orientation programme should be carefully planned and the important dimensions of the prevailing culture of the organization are duly highlighted. In addition, the expectations from the new joinees could also be made crystal clear

through various planned processes of interaction. Typically, the dress code, patterns of accepted behaviour, usage of language, and so on can be established rather easily during a well-designed orientation programme along with carefully prepared guidelines and manuals that are handed out to them.

WHEN ORGANIZATIONAL CULTURE BECOMES A LIABILITY?

However, organizational culture is not always a boon. With the presence of a strong organizational culture, people tend to follow this with least deviation. Organizational culture not only regulates the behavioural pattern of the members, but also tends to control the pattern of thinking, ways of problem solving, and significantly affects their attitude. And the stronger the organizational culture, the deeper is the acceptance and conformity among the members. It will be extremely difficult to bring in any change in the organization because of the strong adherence of the members and the inevitable pull towards the prevailing culture. More specifically, the presence of a strong (and not necessarily conducive) organizational culture affects the organizational culture in the following ways:

- **Difficulty in bringing in change:** As mentioned earlier, the strong adherence to an existing culture would prohibit implementation of change, as people would resist that. And the implication of this could prove to be seriously detrimental for the well-being and survival of any organization, as the success any organization, particularly at the time of flux, lies with its ability to change as per the need of the situation. Take, for example, the case of nationalized banks vis-à-vis the new age, fiercely competitive private banks, which aggressively seek to widen the customer base. Now, even when the large nationalized banks appreciate the need for being more proactive and customer oriented, they face a huge difficulty in changing the mindset of their employees. Nothing would happen overnight, and it took a considerable amount of time for this sector to bring in the desired change.
- **Difficulty in promoting diversity:** Since the presence of a strong culture ensures conformity and uniformity of behaviour among the members, it becomes difficult to accept people who are different from the rest in terms of say, gender, race, caste and creed, nationality, ability/disability, etc. On the one hand, organizations seek for diversity for various reasons, such as complying with the employment laws as well as to bring in different types of abilities and approaches in the organization as these will help in better creativity. However, this becomes very difficult in reality, primarily for the pressure for conformity arising out of the presence of a strong culture.
- **Difficulty cropping up after merger and acquisition:** Whenever an organization takes over another organization, or when two organizations merge, often various problems crop up which are not necessarily financial in nature. These are found even when the financial issues and/or product lines are thoroughly discussed and agreed upon. These problems mainly arise because of a seemingly cultural incompatibility of the two and may even result in the failure of the merger or acquisition. This becomes particularly true when one or both organizations have strong organizational cultures shared by the majority of the members. In such cases, it becomes difficult to merge these two cultures, and employees of the two previous organizations tend to retain their own culture even when they become one organization.

CHANGING ORGANIZATIONAL CULTURE

Even when an organizational culture seems to be set and well established, it does not guarantee that it would remain the same forever. The very concept of organizational culture is dynamic in nature and never static. So it is often found that a well-accepted culture changes with time. The reasons could be of various types, such as changes in the workforce, the environment, the organization arising out of merger and acquisition, or sometime due to a deliberate attempt to change the existing culture altogether. We would be discussing each of these in brief.

Changing Workforce

With the changes in the demography of the workforce, there will be changes in the overall organizational culture. The people who now come to work are different from yesteryear's workforce in terms of educational qualification, gender, age, and family structure, to name a few. The demographical characteristics of the workforce today are much different from the yesteryears. They are more educated, have a wider variations in age with a good mix of freshers and retired people. Apart from these, there are more number of women who now come for work now compared to the past. With this, the culture of the organization is bound to undergo change. What used to happen and accepted earlier cannot be expected to happen or accepted today.

- **Environmental Changes:** The changes in the external environment often force an organization to change its culture in order to adapt to those changes. Even an orthodox and rather rigid organizational culture may change over time and become flexible and more accepting.
- **Merger and Acquisition:** When an organization takes over or merges with another organization, a considerable amount of change takes place in the resultant organizational culture. In fact, there could be various possibilities that would determine the emerging culture after any organizational merger and/or acquisition. These may be
  - *Assimilation,* when the acquired company suspends its own values and beliefs and embraces the acquiring firm's values completely.
  - *Deculturation,* is the second possibility when the acquiring firm forcefully imposes its own culture on the acquired firm, even when these are not willingly accepted.
  - *Integration,* is the best possible outcome of merger and acquisition when the two organizations evolve an acceptable common culture which is neither of the organizations' previously existing culture.
  - *Separation,* is a state when both the merged companies retain their own culture and remain separated from each other.
- **Deliberate attempt to change:** At times organizations need to look inside and may decide to change its culture in an attempt to improve the organizational effectiveness.

ORGANIZATIONAL CLIMATE

Organizational climate can be understood as the general perception of the organizational members regarding the nature of environment or the general ambience of their place of work. Put in a slightly different way, organizational climate refers to a set of attributes as perceived by the organizational members regarding the particular organization and/or its subsystems. This primarily depends on how the organization and/or its subsystems deal/s with its members as well as the environment where they exist. Thus, organizational climate may be defined as the *perceived attributes of an organization and its subsystems as reflected in the way it deals with its members, groups, and issues.*

Organizational climate is the perceived attributes of an organization and its subsystems as reflected in the way it deals with its members, groups, and issues.

More specifically, organizational climate depends largely on the organizational *processes*, which are reflected through the following aspects of an organization, namely, nature of leadership, ways of

Table 3.3 Six Dominant Motives and the Typical Organizations

Motives or the Driving Forces	Typical Organizations Where These are Found
Achievement motive: Concern for excellence, competition with self and others, setting challenging goals for oneself.	Industrial and business organizations where the profit making is important.
Affiliation motive: Concern for maintaining close and personal relationships, emphasis on friendship, and a tendency to express one's emotions.	Clubs, where the main purpose is to enjoy the company of others.
Expert power: Concern for making an impact on others, a desire to make others do what one thinks right, an urge to change situations and develop people.	University departments, scientific research labs, R&D units of an organizations.
Control: Concern for orderliness and a desire to stay informed; an urge to monitor events and take corrective actions when required.	Bureaucratic organizations where strong emphasis is given on following the rules and no deviation is tolerated.
Extension: Concern for others, interest in superordinate goals, and an urge to be relevant and useful to larger groups of people including society.	Mostly not-for-profit organizations offering community services.
Dependency: Characterized by a desire for the assistance from others to develop oneself.	Traditional teaching-learning organizations as well as in organizations involving typical command groups.

communication, how goals are set and decisions are made in the organization, the control mechanism, and the usual ways of motivating people within the organization, to name a few.

Usually, six distinct sets of motives (Pareek 2006) are found to exist underlying any organizational culture and give rise to six distinctly different climates in the organization as perceived by the members. The Table 3.3 depicts the six dominant motives along with the types of organizations where they are most commonly found.

Though the terms culture and climate often seem to be synonymous, there are indeed some definite differences between these two. While organizational culture could be understood as the precipitating cause, climate may be described as the manifestations of the underlying culture in an organization in terms of the members' perception of the organizational culture. Put in a simple way, organizational culture tends to identify the nature of expectations within a given organization, and organizational climate is more concerned about what is really found to happen there in reality.

ORGANIZATIONAL CULTURE vs NATIONAL CULTURE

It is not surprising that organizational culture would be significantly influenced by the national culture of the country where it is situated, because of the strong interplay between external and the internal environmental characteristics of any organization. This explains why we find a great deal of difference between various organizations situated at different parts of the globe even when these are within the same sector.

It was Geert Hofstede (1980) who first systematically analysed the wide variations across cultures. When he was working at IBM, he conducted an extensive survey on 116,000 IBM employees at different locations around the world, regarding their work-related values and found astonishing differences among them. He identified five distinct dimensions of national culture which are as follows:

***Power distance:** This refers to the degree to which people in a culture accept that there is an inequality of power among individuals.*

1. **Power distance:** This refers to the degree to which people in a culture accept that there is an inequality of power among individuals. This could vary from being relatively equal (low power distance) to extremely unequal (wider power distance). South Asian countries, for example, are found to have a wider power distance compared to those in the US.

***Individualism vs collectivism:** A loosely knit social framework in which people emphasize only on themselves and their immediate family vs a tight social framework in which people expect others in their groups to look after and protect them.*

2. **Individualism vs collectivism:** Individualism refers to a loosely knit social framework in which people emphasize only on themselves and their immediate family. In contrast, collectivism refers to a tight social framework in which people expect others in their groups to look after and protect them. Most oriental cultures value collectivism over individualism.

***Masculinity vs feminity:** The extent to which assertiveness and materialism are accepted as desired social values, emphasis on relationship, and concern for others.*

3. **Masculinity vs feminity:** This dimension is also known as 'quantity of life vs quality of life'. *Masculinity* or *quantity of life* refers to the extent to which assertiveness and materialism are accepted as desired social values, whereas *feminity* or *quality of life* is the extreme opposite where major emphasis is placed on relationships and concern for others. While the US culture is found to be strongly masculine in nature, countries like Sweden value quality of life over material prosperity.

***Uncertainty avoidance:** This refers to the extent to which a society feels threatened by uncertain and ambiguous situations and tries to avoid them.*

4. **Uncertainty avoidance:** This refers to the extent to which a society feels threatened by uncertain and ambiguous situations and tries to avoid them. In some cultures, people prefer clear guidelines and instructions whereas in some others, France being one of them, people feel rather claustrophobic with too many instructions.

***Long-term vs short-term orientation:** Long-term orientation refers to the emphasis on the future, thrift, and persistence, while the short-term orientation emphasizes on the respect for the present and fulfilling social obligation.*

5. **Long-term vs short-term orientation:** Long-term orientation refers to the emphasis on the future, thrift, and persistence, while the short-term orientation emphasizes on the respect for the present and fulfilling social obligation. India is a country with a predominately long-term focus (the future for the Hindu could well be the next life even), while people in the US typically focus on the present.

All the characteristics would be reflected in the values and attitudes of people who would bring these into their work life as well.

A recent extension of the Hofstede study was taken up by the GLOBE (Globe Leadership and Organizational Behavior Effectiveness) foundation research which investigated the effect of cross-cultural variations in 62 nations and found significant variations.

There are, however, some typical characteristics of Indian culture as identified by Pareek (2004) which help us to understand the typical Indian ethos and provide an insight as to why they behave in certain ways. According to Pareek, the dimensions of Indian values are as follows:

- *Karta* or the head of the family which is typically patriarchal in nature. These 'father figures' are found to be nurturing, caring, dependable, sacrificing yet demanding, and authoritative and are found both in families and organizations alike.
- *Relationships* which are usually warm and close not only between spouses and parents and the offspring but also among the members of the extended family. Thus, an average Indian enjoys an extended childhood as he/she remains a son/daughter, son-in-law/daughter-in-law, grandson/granddaughter, or nephew/niece till the ripe old age and gets both pampered and disciplined by the members of the extended family.
- *Proximity to power* that reflects a strong desire to be near powerful people and almost worshipping them, which is generated perhaps due to the strong feeling of helplessness during the childhood and adolescence.
- *Security* is generated by the wide network of extended family ties. People learn to respect senior family members and share more responsibility. More emphasis is put on peace and comfort rather than being competitive and adventurous.
- *Simple living and high thinking* is a value that is typically reflected in the general reverence to saints who lead a simple life rich in inner values. Mahatma Gandhi was perhaps an epitome of Indian cultural values who led a life of a hermit renouncing material comfort.
- *Survival*, where Indians have a strong faith in luck and destiny (bhabitabya) and believe that the karma of one's past life governs one's present life.

All these lend typical characteristics to an average Indian and these would also have a significant impact on the organizational culture.

QUESTIONS

1. What is organizational culture? Distinguish between a strong and a weak culture. Identify the characteristics of a healthy organizational culture.
2. What do you understand by the term 'socialization processes' in an organization? Describe the steps a new member goes through before being accepted by the organizational culture. Distinguish between pivotal and peripheral norms of an organizational culture.
3. How does the culture of an organization start? Describe ways to sustain the organizational culture. When does the culture become a liability?
4. Differentiate organizational climate from organizational culture. Describe how national culture might affect organizational culture.
5. Compare and contrast the cultures of two of the organizations you have been a member of.

REFERENCES

1. K.S. Cameron and R.E. Quinn, 'Diagnosing and Changing Organizational Culture: Based on the Competing Values Framework', *Journal of Extension*, 1999, 41(2).
2. Greenberg, J. and Baron, R. A. (2008). *Behaviors in Organizations*. 9th Ed. PHI Learning Private Limited.

3. G. Hofstede, *Culture's Consequences: International Differences in Work Related Values* (Beverly Hills, CA: Sage, 1980).
4. J. Martin, *Culture in Organizations* (New York, Oxford University Press, 1996).
5. U. Pareek, *Understanding Organizational Behaviour* (New Delhi: Oxford University Press, 2011).
6. Pareek, U. (2006). *Organisational Culture and Climate*. The ICFAI University Press, Hyderabad.
7. E.H. Schein, *Organizational Culture and Leadership* (San Francisco: Jossey-Bass, 1985).
8. Schein, E. H. (1965). Organizational Psychology. Prentice-Hall, (Englewood Cliffs, NJ).
9. Cameron, K. S., and Quinn, R. E. (1999). *Diagnosing and Changing Organizational Culture: Based on Competing Values Framework*. Reading, MA: Addison-Wesley.
10. Stanley N. Herman, "TRW Systems Group", in Wendell L. French and Cecil H. Bell, Jr., *Organization Development: Behavioral Science Interventions for Organization Improvement*, 3rd ed. 1984, Prentice Hall, Englewood Cliffs, N.J.

Case Study: On Your Face

Ashoke looked incredulously at professor Srivastava. Professor Srivastava pointed towards Professor Saha and in his normal calm voice said, 'Do you expect him to do anything good? He is so terribly weak and all the time yielding to whatever demands the students are coming with. Is that the way to run a department?' Professor Saha was the head of the Executive MBA Programme, which was attended by working executives. Since these students attend the classes after office hours, punctuality and regularity were both nagging administrative problems for the department. As professor Srivastava was conversing with Ashoke, professor Saha was well within the proximity to hear everything as three of them were invigilating in an examination hall. Ashoke felt acutely uneasy. He had joined rather recently as an assistant professor in this old and prestigious management institute after a stint of working as a marketing executive in an MNC. He had always been a very good student. After graduating in chemical engineering from a premier engineering college in the country, Ashoke had opted to join the campus job in a pharma giant. Being the only son and having lost his father when he was still in the college, Ashoke did not have much of a choice. He would have to look after his mother and ailing grandfather. Though his first calling was academics, he knew he could not have any suitable teaching job without either a PhD or good work experience, as a prerequisites of a teaching career. So he had accepted the job offer, worked hard to climb up the corporate ladder rather fast, and was certainly in the good books of his higher management. But he still yearned for the teaching position. Hence, when he saw an advertisement for a position of a marketing faculty in this good old institute, he decided to try his luck. He was selected for the post as he had enough work experience.

Ashoke felt very happy, even though he did not get a very good package. He was tired of being a part of the corporate rat race and perennially fulfilling daily 'targets'; this change was refreshing. Ashoke still remembers his first day at the Institute which he found very different. The Head of the Department introduced him to colleagues among whom Ashoke had a warm conversation with Prof Srivastava and Prof Mrs Patra. The whole vibe was different from what he had experienced so far. He soon found that this institute was remarkably different from his previous organization, where he had learned the nuances of corporate existence. The 'addas', or chit chats were not just idling without doing any work. It was certainly an ennobling experience apart from being highly educative as well. Those 'conducting' the addas were remarkable. Of course they all were learned men and ladies, holding the highest university degrees after their names and having specialized knowledge in their subject areas, but they were also experts in so many other areas! He found at least three to five professors who could so easily and so expertly talk on anything under the sun, from ancient dance forms and the evolution of Indian and other classical dances to recent experiments in English literature to the latest movies around the world. These addas were punctuated by rounds of teas and sometimes even a few snacks. And the 'addas' would go on! If somebody has to take a class at that point in time, others feel genuinely disturbed and accused him of spoiling the entire atmosphere: 'Couldn't you take it sometime later? This discussion is so important, and how could you leave like that?'

Ashoke had often mulled over the differences between these two organizations. In his previous organization everybody always seemed to be in a hurry. Ashoke could hardly remember people enjoying leisure time; but it was completely different here. Other areas of striking differences include openness in interaction! Nobody seemed to think twice about what they say! They prefer being straightforward, often irrespective of even the hierarchical positions. It is not that people in Ashoke's previous office were all devoid of any blemishes; however, they would never criticize upfront. You would be very selective and careful regarding whom you can say these things to! But here things were almost diametrically opposite. Ashoke could never imagine speaking about others the way Professor Srivastava was talking about Professor Saha.

Questions

1. Identify the culture of the organization.
2. Why do you think Ashoke feels so perplexed?

Chapter 4

Conflict and Negotiation in Organization

Opening Case: Life is Like That

Vijay Mallya, the Chairman of United Breweries Group and Kingfisher Airlines, is clearly facing some trouble for the past few months or so. He was born in Kolkata and graduated from the city's much celebrated St. Xavier's College. He took over as the chairman of the United Breweries at a young age of 28 after the sudden demise of his father. He infused some freshness into the company and captured more than 50 per cent of the market's share of India's beer market. Kingfisher beer is now available in 52 countries outside India. In fact, he is the one who first put India in the international beer market and transformed UB into the largest beer producing company in the world it is today. He eventually brought in all the companies under the umbrella of UB Group.

From the very beginning, Vijay Mallya was an extrovert and flamboyant person. He was a keen sports lover and an avid motor race enthusiast. He has taken part in various track racing events in India and abroad and also owns one of the first ever Formula 1 team in India. Apart from that, he also owns a cricket team named Royal Challenger Bangalore which plays in Indian Premiere League.

His love for speed perhaps prompted him to start the Kingfisher Airline. He started the airline with such a grandeur that was unprecedented—from engaging fleets of beautiful girls as hostesses and offering top quality service to the customers. But, within 7 years since its inception, Kingfisher Airline ran into deep trouble and is almost on the verge of bankruptcy now. It is unable to pay the salaries of the staff for the past few months, and as the deadline of paying the dues went unfulfilled, the staff and pilots are prepared to start a fresh agitation and even threatened to take the matter to the labour court. The airline has also been officially asked to vacate its rented premise in Mumbai due to non-payment of rents. The market is still watching them closely and waiting to see what takes shape now.

So, as one of the most extravagant and upbeat chairman of a business group, Vijay is now facing more problems and ill reputes than he could perhaps handle. Even if the financial deficiency is somehow overcome, what is more damaging is the loss of trust and support of his staff along with earning a bad reputation in the market that might stay on.

We all have had our fair shares of conflicts and agonies, even if not always of this magnitude as faced by Vijay Mallya. After reading this chapter, you would know what a conflict is and why it arises, and how these could be controlled. More specifically, you will learn the following:

LEARNING OBJECTIVES

- What is a conflict?
- Difference between task and relationship conflicts
- Conflict process
- Causes of conflict
- Strategies for conflict resolution
- Competitive and collaborative strategies
- 5-step negotiation process
- Cultural impact on negotiation process

WHAT IS A CONFLICT?

Put in a rather simple term—when two parties oppose against each other, conflict ensues. In essence, this refers to an interpersonal process that arises from disagreements over the goals to attain or methods to attain those goals. Thus, in the present case study, we find that Vijay Mallya and his staff are not exactly seeing 'eye to eye', in simple terms. What Vijay is striving to achieve is not what his men are looking for. Even when both the parties may agree to enhance organizational profitability, they might widely differ as to the ways to attain it.

Conflict is an interpersonal process that arises from disagreements over the goals to attain or methods to attain those goals.

However, by no means, it always requires at least two individuals to have a conflict. Conflict may well happen when there is nobody else but you, that is to say, it can start within an individual. Thus, we may say that conflict occurs at individual, interpersonal, inter group or inter-organizational levels.

Conflict may occur at individual, interpersonal, intergroup or interpersonal levels.

INTRA-INDIVIDUAL CONFLICT

Individuals may experience conflict even when there is no one else. There are various types of intra-individual conflict.

Conflict due to frustration takes place when one is denied of what he is looking for. This happens when an individual's motivated drive is blocked and he fails to attain a desired goal. It is interesting to note that the 'barrier' may be overt which is outward and tangible, such as a locked door for an individual who yearns to go out. But quite often the barrier may be covert and socio-psychological in nature rather than physical. Thus, a student might feel frustrated whenever she faces problems involving numbers as she *believes* that she is not good in numbers. Therefore, the block in her case is mental rather than physical.

Individuals may show a wide array of interesting behaviour in an unconscious effort to cope with frustration, particularly when he cannot remove the barrier—be it physical or socio-psychological. These are known as defence behaviour. Thus, when an individual is not getting what he desires, say a promotion which goes to someone else, he may now declare that he never wanted a promotion, and it is rather a good thing for him that he did not get it, as promotion would certainly involve relocation which is impossible for him. If you see the proverbial 'grapes are sour' syndrome here, it is not surprising as this certainly is quite an effective coping behaviour and is known as 'rationalization'. This is called 'defense mechanism', which is adopted unconsciously by an individual to protect his mind from undue

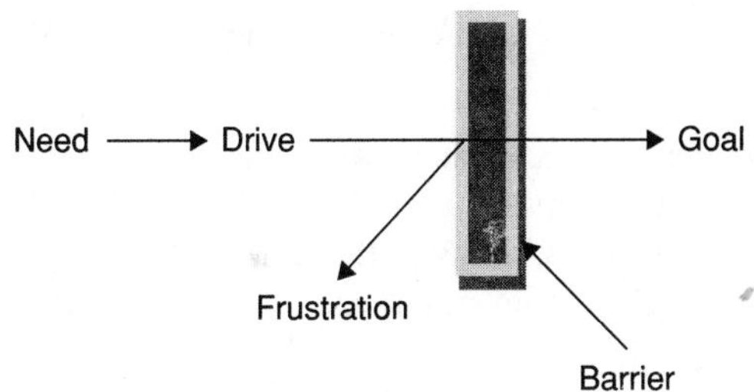

Figure 4.1 Frustration Due to Barrier

worries and anxieties. There are a host of other interesting behavioural manifestations of defence mechanism, such as 'displacement' when you bang the door after getting a good redressing from your boss. The poor door has to bear the brunt of your grudge against your boss which you could not show him for obvious reasons.

Apart from conflict due to frustration, there are two more types of intra-individual conflicts, which are goal conflict and role conflict.

Goal conflict occurs whenever an individual is facing a goal that has both positive and negative features or when he faces two or more competing goals—equally good or equally bad. This results in three types of goal conflicts:

1. *Approach-approach conflict*, when the individual is faced with two positive goals. This type of conflict is usually quickly resolved by the individual as he counts the positives and negatives and chooses the option that has more positives. He also decides on the basis of lessening the dissonance or discord in mind towards attaining mental comfort.

***Approach-approach conflict**, when the individual is faced with two positive goals.*

2. *Approach-avoidance conflict* occurs more often in the organizational context. It takes place when a particular goal typically has both positive and negative aspects for the individual. This makes him vacillate anxiously, particularly when the positive aspects equal the negative aspects. One interesting point to note in this context is that the positive aspects become more prominent over a period of time, but the negatives become more pronounced when the individual comes closer to it. When the date of joining for your dream job comes near you may now even dread the possible workload and the loss of freedom it might entail.

***Approach-avoidance conflict** takes place when a particular goal typically has both positive and negative aspects for the individual.*

3. *Avoidance-avoidance conflict* takes place when an individual faces options both of which are unacceptable to him. Like the approach-approach conflict; the avoidance-avoidance conflict is also usually resolved rather fast. If both the options are equally unacceptable for the individual, he would leave the place. If leaving, however, is not possible for the individual, he would become very frustrated.

***Avoidance-avoidance conflict** occurs when both the options are equally unacceptable for the individual.*

Role Conflict

A *role* is a position that has expectations arising out of established norms. An individual assumes succession of roles throughout his life. Apart from that, he is also expected to play multiple roles at a given point in time, which could be conflicting or incompatible at times. *Role conflict* can also be of three types:

1. *Person-and-the-role conflict* takes place when the person's basic nature or personality is in conflict with his role. A soft-natured person might have difficulties in assuming the position of a strict administer, for example.

***Person-and-the-role conflict** takes place when the person's basic nature or personality is in conflict with his role expectations.*

2. *Intra-role conflict* occurs when there are contradictory expectations regarding how a given role should be played. Whether a supervisor would be supportive or exacting may create a dilemma in the mind of the role incumbent.

***Intra-role conflict** occurs when there are contradictory expectations regarding how a given role should be played.*

3. *Inter-role conflicts* take place because of role overlap or differing requirements of two or more roles to be played simultaneously by the individual. A lady, who is a mother of two and is a senior manager, might face difficulty as to which role she should play or give priority—mother or manager?

***Inter-role conflicts** take place because of role overlap or differing requirements of two or more roles to be played simultaneously by the individual.*

Concept Check

1. What is a conflict?
2. What are the different levels of conflict?

INTERPERSONAL CONFLICT

However, whenever we discuss conflict, we usually mean the conflict that takes place between individuals. This is known as interpersonal conflict, that includes the conflict between two parties as well. Interpersonal or inter-group conflict, thus, may be best described as a process in which one party perceives that its interests are being opposed or negatively affected by another party. In other words, when one party feels that he might be harmed by what the other party would do, a conflict will ensue between the two. It is to be noted that interpersonal conflict may arise out of two types of disagreements:

Interpersonal conflict takes place when one party feels that he might be harmed by what the other party would do.

1. Disagreements regarding the goals to achieve
2. Methods to be adopted to attain these goals

As we have noted earlier, even when the parties may agree as to the goal (as in the opening case study of this chapter, organizational well-being is an objective which both the Chairman of Kingfisher and his staff would heartily agree to attain, but they would differ in the means to attain them).

FUNCTIONAL AND DYSFUNCTIONAL CONFLICT

Conflict is everywhere, be it within ourselves or when we are with other people. It may be seen as an inevitable entity of life. However, not all conflicts are bad! Though initially it may sound like an oxymoron, certain conflicts can indeed be beneficiary for the organization. For example, instead of being just 'yes men', if organizational members choose to disagree, this will help generate ideas and bring in fresh air into the organization. Thus, in an organization, the goal of the management should not be to eliminate all types of conflicts! The effect of conflict should always be judged in terms of the impact it creates on the organization's well-being, and identify functional or positive conflicts from dysfunctional or harmful conflicts. Needless to say, the former types of conflicts should rather be nurtured, while the latter should be eliminated as soon as possible. We may, thus, distinguish these two types of conflicts as follows:

1. **Functional conflict:** It is the interaction between individuals or groups that leads to positive results from the organizational perspective and is a prerequisite for change and creativity. From the disagreements of the members over a certain issue, new and better ideas will flow. A passionate disagreement is always better than a weak agreement. When you present an idea to your peers and everybody seems to tear your idea to shreds, believe it to be a very good sign! You can be sure that a productive idea would surely develop from these heated arguments. The organization should take adequate care to create and maintain an atmosphere where healthy and positive conflicts may take place, which helps to build up what may be called a 'creative tension' in the organization.

__Functional conflict__ is the interaction between individuals or groups that leads to positive results from the organizational perspective.

2. **Dysfunctional conflict:** In contrast to the functional conflict, dysfunctional conflict refers to the interaction between individuals and groups that impedes the attainment of organizational objectives. This would result in disruptive outcomes which would be harmful for the organization. Dysfunctional conflicts are quite often found to affect the individual and group performance negatively as the members' attention strays away from the task and directed more towards 'fixing others'. This kind of conflict must be stopped from occurring in an organization at any cost.

__Dysfunctional conflict__ refers to the interaction between individuals and groups that impedes the attainment of organizational objectives.

Concept Check

Differentiate functional conflict from dysfunctional conflict.

Another way of analysing conflict is from the perspective of *task vs. socio-emotional conflict.* The task-related conflict takes place when the focus of the conflict is on the issues and not the parties. Thus, in the *task-related conflict*, both the parties are concerned only about the task in hand and are committed to find a solution to the problem; it never matters who said what or whose suggestions are finally accepted as long as the solution is achieved. Evidently, this type of conflict is potentially healthy and valuable for the organization as it helps to recognize problems, understand issues related to the problem

In __task-conflict__, both the parties focus on the tasks or issues.
In __socio-emotional conflict__, individuals get identified with their views more, and any contradiction is seen as a personal attack.

Table 4.1 Possible Effects of Intergroup Conflict

Level of Intergroup Conflict	Probable Impact on Organization	Typical Characteristics	Level of Organizational Performance
Low or none	Dysfunctional	▪ Stagnation ▪ Few changes ▪ Little stimulation of ideas	Low
Optimal	Functional	▪ Innovation and change ▪ Enhanced goal achievement ▪ Adaptation	High
High	Dysfunctional	▪ Disruption and chaos ▪ Difficulty in coordination	Low

Source: Gibson, J. L., Ivancevich, J. M., Donnelly Jr., and Konopaske, (2006).

better and identify the best possible solution. Thus, task conflict refers to functional conflict. *Socio-emotional* conflict, on the other hand, is a conflict situation where the individuals get identified with their views and any contradiction is seen more as a personal attack on their self. Most commonly this gives rise to the sentiment 'how YOU could tell this to ME!' Thus 'you' and 'me' become more important than the issue or the problem and emotions take the driver's seat, and issues and problems often become secondary. This evidently will result in dysfunctional conflict.

Effect of conflict between two parties on organizational performance is mixed, and there seems to be an optimum level of conflict that varies from organization to organization. A too low level of conflict fails to arouse individuals to put in their best, and thus can result in poor performance. Nevertheless, a very high level of conflict will indeed lower the performance as well and would certainly be detrimental to the organizational performance and effectiveness.

There is, however, always a possibility of even the functional conflict to slip into the zone of dysfunctional conflict. It depends both on the nature of the task and the group members' psycho-social characteristics including tolerance of stress and pressure of disagreement, that is, how the functional conflict changes to the dysfunctional conflict.

INTERPERSONAL CONFLICT PROCESS

No conflict comes out of the blue. Nobody just starts screaming at another person without any reason. There has to be always an antecedent of any conflict, though at times these may be obscure or unclear or too complex to identify easily. Figure 4.2 depicts the conflict process, as described by McShane et al. (2006). The first block denotes the source from which it starts. It has to start from something—an event, thwarting of one's desire or an opposition from someone. In the organizational context, it could be the negative opinion of your superior towards you. Nevertheless, to get this fully blown into a conflict, in the first place you need to perceive it. If you do not perceive the opposition, there would hardly be any conflict between you and the other person.

Even when you perceive the opposition, but if it is over some minor issues, the conflict may not occur at all. But the moment it touches your emotion, it will lead to a conflict. For example, if your supervisor declares that he does not like the colour of your shirt, it would be a minor issue and you wouldn't be too bothered. But if he comments negatively about your capability or intelligence, say, you might be roused

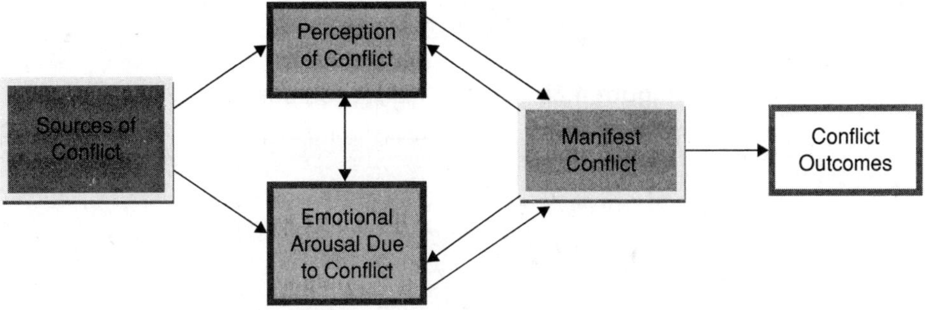

Figure 4.2 Conflict Process

Source: Adapted from the model given by McShane, S. L., Glinow, and Sharma, (2006)

badly and a full-fledged conflict may ensue between you two. Now, more you react, the more will the previous two components, viz., perception of the conflict and emotional arousal due to conflict, be stoked further, pitching the feeling of conflict to an even higher level. This is what is called 'escalation of conflict cycle' (Witteman, 1992). And then it would result in various untoward outcomes—from lack of cooperation among individuals, lowering of productivity, acute dissatisfaction of the organizational members and so on. All of these would undoubtedly have a negative impact on the overall organization.

CAUSES OF CONFLICT

Causes of conflict within an organization may be put into the following broader categories:

Organizational Factors

- **Task interdependence:** Conflict increases with task interdependence. The more the interdependence between tasks, more acute the conflict. There could be three possible types of task interdependences: pooled interdependence, sequential interdependence and reciprocal interdependence.
  - *Pooled interdependence* occurs in an organization when organizational resources are shared among different groups, but that does not necessarily require any amount of interaction or interdependence among various groups or individuals. Like the library in an institute which is shared by all the students, with a minimum level of interdependence among them. Pooled interdependence also refers to the situation when different units or branches of an organization perform without any dependence or interaction, but all these will eventually contribute to determine the overall organizational effectiveness, like the performance across all the branches of Tata Consulting Services will determine the total output of the company. Possibility of conflict in pooled interdependence is relatively low.
  - In a *sequential interdependence*, one group cannot start or complete its task before the other group finishes its task. This happens most typically in a manufacturing plant, say in a jute mill.

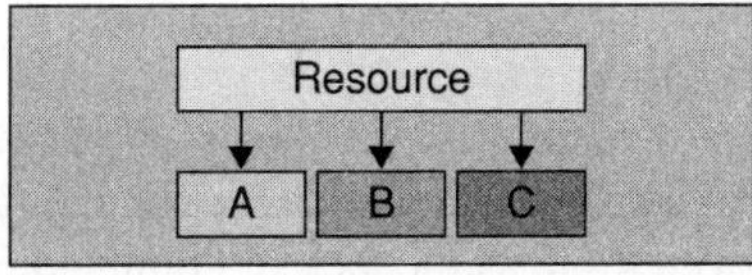

Figure 4.3a Pooled Interdependence

Figure 4.3b Sequential Resources

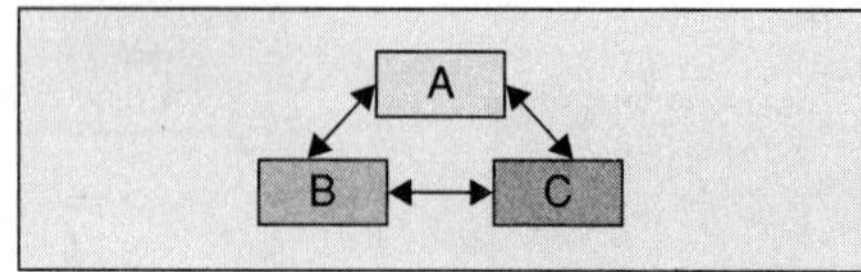

Figure 4.3c Reciprocal Resources

The dyeing department cannot start their task before the cleaning unit finishes cleaning the fibre. Conflict potential is fairly high in sequential interdependence as one individual's/group's performance is dependent on another individual's/group's performance. Careful planning is required with a provision for creating adequate buffer to avoid conflicts between groups or individuals.

– *Reciprocal resources* commands the highest level of interdependence among the members where any one's performance will affect each other's. This is a team performance scenario, where the possibility of conflict is quite high.

- **Scarce resources:** If organizational resources are limited, there will be competitions among the members to get hold of the resources. Even when the limited available resources—such as money, space, labour and materials—are to be shared among the members, conflicts will ensue, primarily because of a higher level of dependence among the members.
- **Differences in goals:** The different subunits or departments within an organization often have their unique goals or targets to achieve. With increased specialization, the differentiations increase further. This results in dissimilar or even incompatible goals among the departments. Thus, while cost control becomes the primary objective of the accounts department, excessive funding is the primary objective of the R&D department, resulting in a friction or conflict among them.
- **Ambiguous rules:** If organizational rules and policies are not crystal clear and leave room for interpretations, conflict will occur as the 'interpretation' and enforcement of the rules will be perceived as biased by the people, particularly by those who feel they are discriminated. If, for example, one faculty member in a teaching institute is given a sabbatical of one year, and when after a year another faculty member applies for the same he is denied on some flimsy ground, a feeling of conflict will naturally take place. If, on the other hand, rules are clear cut (such as specific years of services to be completed before one becomes entitled for such a privilege), there will be less chances of misunderstanding and conflicts. Thus, when even a legitimate privilege is viewed as a favour and depends on the discretion of the authority, people will try to keep the authority in good humour (read *buttering the boss*). This will result in organizational politics. Ambiguous rules will also create problems in setting and achieving targets by individuals or groups in an organization, because of the confusion in understanding one's responsibility.
- **Problems in communication:** If the communication process is not free and open across the organization, it will tend to create stereotyping, and individuals will be judged on the basis of their belongingness to certain groups. People will tend to develop wrong perceptions about certain subgroups, and this will tend to increase even more as the lack of communication will not allow lessening the misconception. On the other hand, the less people communicate among themselves, particularly

with the individuals against whom there is already a negative feeling, the misperception, mistrust and apathy would grow even more against those people. This would lead to a vicious cycle.

- **Organizational changes:** Conflict would be rife particularly during the times of transition and organizational change. A general confusion and a feeling of mistrust will tend to prevail at these times. The air of uncertainty and a feeling of fear will spark conflicts more easily as people will tend to be rather high-strung.

Perceptual Factors

- **Incompatible goals:** If one party's goals are perceived to be incompatible with the goals of another party, naturally conflicts will arise among them. If one group believes that they would be harmed by the other party, no matter it is true or false, conflict will definitely arise. Traditionally, the accounts departments are known for their detailed scrutiny of every single figure (this is their job and professional orientation). But this often creates misunderstanding with other departments who believe that the inordinate delays are deliberate attempts to harass them.
- **Differentiation:** If people are from different backgrounds and value systems, there will be difficulty in understanding and appreciating each other's views. This would often lead to conflict among individuals and groups. The problem may become even more acute when people are to work across cultures. The lack of understanding would basically lead to conflict. The conflict would also be pronounced when people of different age groups are to work together. The generation gap will also be a basis for developing conflict.
- **Communication problems:** Communication, or rather lack of it, can play a powerful role in creating conflict. A point to note in this context is that in communication, it does not matter too much as to *what* is being communicated but *how* that is communicated, which is of critical importance. The same content, when conveyed arrogantly will create conflict. For example, the superior officer may ask his subordinate to do a task either politely or demand arrogantly. There will be heaven and hell difference between the two. In the former case, the subordinate would willingly do the job, but in the latter instance, there will be unnecessary hostility and ill feelings that will be created between the two.
- **Contrasting perceptions:** Even when somebody tells something nice to his colleague, it may not always be taken in the same spirit. For example, some body may appreciate your work genuinely, but you might feel that he/she is being sarcastic and ridiculing you. This will undoubtedly result in a conflict.

Manager's Essence: Fight Between Accounts Department and Faculty Coordinator

Offering management development programmes for the executives of various corporate houses is one of the standard activities of the management faculty, which is also considered prestigious. However, there is quite often a misunderstanding between the accounts department and the concerned faculty coordinator for the programme. While the faculty coordinator feels impatient, even insulted for the inordinate delay in passing the bills, the chief accounts officer considers it his sacred duty to scan every bill and voucher and prefers 'sitting on them' for being extra cautious. How could this be addressed?

- **Threats to status:** Conflict is often a result of comparative analysis in the organizational hierarchy. Even within the same level, some departments traditionally seem to enjoy a better status. That apart, some changes in the organization might pose a potential threat to some group and thus would lead to conflict. When young and bright professionals are newly recruited by the company, old timers might feel intimidated and would develop a feeling of resentment towards the group as they would be a potential threat to their status.

CONSEQUENCES OF DYSFUNCTIONAL CONFLICT WITHIN AN ORGANIZATION

As noted earlier, consequences of dysfunctional conflicts in an organization are detrimental to the organization. In particular, the effect of such conflicts affects the group functioning significantly. Most commonly, people tend to lose reality orientation and develop *distorted perception* regarding the other group. This could range from attaching inordinate importance to their own functioning and dismissing the contributions of the other group to the organizational effectiveness ('only *we* work so hard!'). For example, the faculty members in a teaching institute would not appreciate the effort of non-teaching staff or the doctors would hardly acknowledge the contribution of hospital administrative staff in running the hospital. The dysfunctional conflict between groups would also give rise to *negative stereotyping* and a 'we vs. them' feeling. This, however, might generate better cohesion within the group, and an urge to excel in their own performance though this might also result in sticking only to the group's own views and ignoring others' altogether thereby further *decreasing communication* between groups and reinforcing the negative stereotyping even more.

OUTCOMES OF CONFLICT

Outcomes of conflict could be any one of the four as depicted in Figure 4.4. The first quadrant denotes the situation when one of the party wins and the other party submits or loses. Though apparently this may end the conflict, this is certainly not the ideal option, as the losing party will nurture a feeling of resentment and would wait for an opportunity to 'fix them up' at the opportune time. The second quadrant is slightly better than the first one as both of them are losing, which in a way is a better option than the previous one. The third quadrant depicts a situation where we lose, conceding the other party a chance to win. This apparently looks fine, but has a potential danger, in that if it is taken for granted that one particular party would always accept the demands of the other party, a sudden revolt may occur, perhaps when it is expected the least.

Win–Lose	Win–Win
Lose–Lose	Lose–Win

Figure 4.4 Conflict Outcomes

MANAGEMENT OF CONFLICTS

There is hardly any doubt that one of the major responsibilities of a manager, irrespective of his functional role, is to take care of the people in an organization. Ask anyone in a managerial position, and he will vouch that a considerable amount of his time goes in to managing interpersonal conflict. The issue of conflict management can be seen vis-à-vis in the following two dimensions: cooperativeness and assertiveness. There can be five possible strategies of conflict management in an organization which are described in Figure 4.5.

1. *Avoiding* is a strategy that is lowest in terms of both cooperativeness and assertiveness, as is evident from Figure 4.5. When avoidance is adopted as a strategy by an individual, she/he withdraws herself/himself from the conflict situation. Avoidance may work well in reducing conflict only when the issue is of low concern for either party. If, for example, I borrowed ₹100 from you and since then start avoiding you, you might, at some point of time, decide to forego the amount altogether as it is not really a big sum. However, the same would not be the case if the amount is considerable, say, ₹10,000. In that case, as much as I may try to avoid meeting you, you would surely catch hold of me and demand the amount back. Nevertheless, avoidance might work as a good strategy in buying time (avoiding you till I get some money to pay you back), though it would only be temporary in nature. Avoidance, thus, might be called 'no strategy'!
2. *Yielding*, as a strategy, is high in cooperation but low in assertiveness. It is accommodating the other party without any concern for self-interest and represents the 'lose–win' outcome. It might look as an effective strategy in removing conflict, but there are two strong points against yielding. *Firstly*, over the long run, the person foregoing self-interest might feel wronged and resentful, particularly when he feels that he is being taken for granted. *Secondly*, in an organizational context, one party usually represents the group or the entire organization where it is neither ethical nor possible to ignore self-interest completely.
3. *Forcing* is aggressively achieving personal goals at the expense of others' concern. Understandably, it is high in assertiveness and low in cooperativeness and corresponds to the 'win–lose' strategy, with all the associated problems as mentioned earlier.

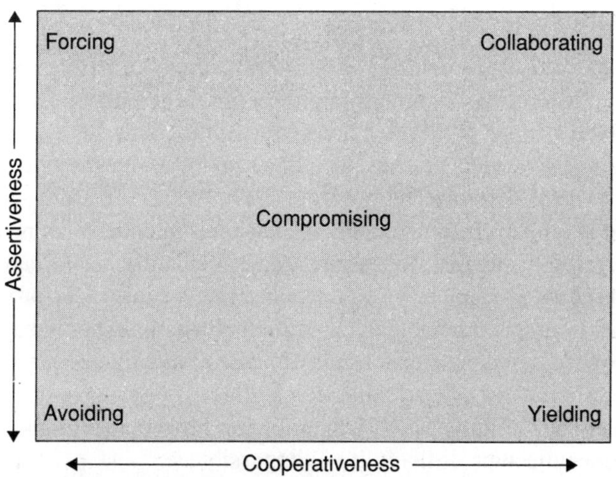

Figure 4.5 Conflict Management Strategies

Source: de Dreu, Evers, Beersma, Kluwer, and Nauta, A. (2001).

4. *Compromising*, which is moderate on both cooperativeness and assertiveness, is an effort for searching the middle ground. It is a strategy when one gives up some in order to gain some. For example, when the boss wants you to come to the office early tomorrow, he also has to grant you to leave early. It is a 'lose–lose' strategy, and is what might be called the best of the worse options.
5. *Collaborating*, which is also referred to as 'confronting' or 'problem solving', is high on both cooperativeness and assertiveness. This takes place when both the conflicting parties acknowledge the existence of conflict in the first place, and face the problem squarely instead of shoving the hostility under the carpet. Once the existence of conflict is acknowledged, only then the concerned parties may commit themselves to resolve it and explore all the possible options to reach a mutually satisfactory resolution. This is the best strategy for resolution of conflict as it satisfies both the parties as much as possible and represents a 'win–win' strategy. It may be noted that it is never easy to adopt this strategy where the concerned parties must focus solely on the issues at hand without being too personally involved. In other words, it makes an effort to keep the conflict at the 'task level' without allowing it to slip in to the 'socio-emotional' level.

As noted in the previous section, collaboration or win–win solution is the best that can happen to any conflict situation. It is not scaling down from what an individual party strives to achieve but to achieve much bigger. It has been established beyond doubt that the collaborative strategy is a far superior strategy than the traditional competitive strategy. Perhaps the most serious allegation against competition is it generates a general negative attitude among the involved parties. The problem of collaborative strategy is that the possibility of it is often overlooked. People, in general, seem to have only the traditional 'either–or' option, that is, either we get what we want or you fulfil your demand, whereas the collaborative strategy is about increasing the 'pie' so that each warring party will not only gets her/his share but often more than that. However, the trick actually lies in generating options which would increase the 'pie' and thus make both parties happy. A few simple guidelines of collaborating are:

- **Commit to solution:** This is the first step. It is of prime importance that both parties commit themselves in arriving at a solution. Though it might seem so obvious, in reality resolution of conflict is not what it is always aimed at. Many a times, one of the parties or even both may actually wish the conflict to linger for various reasons. The trade union leader may really want the impasse to continue so that he enjoys his powerful position!
- **Stop arguing and listen carefully:** Actually the trick lies in understanding and gauging others for which listening carefully is a must. When one argues, he hardly listens carefully and all his attention is focused on refuting the other. So valuable insights are lost in the process.
- **Control emotions:** In order to achieve collaboration, the parties should be careful enough to keep the emotions in control. Otherwise distortions of perception will take place in addition to viewing any different suggestion more as a personal attack.
- **Be frank and open:** If the information which is vital for the resolution of conflict is held back, reaching an agreement become difficult, if not impossible.
- **Be flexible:** Sticking to what you first said throughout will be a very poor tactics. It is enhancing the socio-emotional or the dysfunctional conflicts which will make an agreement almost impossible.
- **Be courteous:** Showing respect to the other party will leave room for further interaction, which is essential.

Manager's Essence: Collaboration Between Two Sworn-in Enemies

Kishore Biyani, the founder of the Future Group retail enterprise was in deep trouble at the beginning of 2012 as he incurred a debt as heavy as ₹5,800 crore. Biyani thought a possible way out could be to ally with a rival retailer at the back end and exploit synergies in the supply chain. He sought a meeting with Kumar Mangalam Birla, the Chairman of Aditya Birla group, who was also in the fashion apparel business as Future Group's Pantaloon. Though things did not take shape exactly the way it was planned, later on Biyani had to withstand the pressure to part with a controlling stake in the business he pioneered, the very idea itself was indeed unique, joining hand with rival!

NEGOTIATION

Negotiation is an effort to resolve conflict in a collaborative way where both the parties agree to jointly explore the possibility of various options and generate alternatives. Needless to say, it can happen only when both parties are keen to resolve the conflict. To arrive at a mutually acceptable agreement through negotiation requires time and continuous interaction and open dialogues between the parties in order to understand the needs, demands and points beyond which either of the parties cannot be pushed.

Five essential steps of a negotiation process may be identified as follows:

1. **Unfreezing:** Concerned parties must feel an urge to reach a solution for the problem they are facing. Until and unless both the parties feel it is essential to resolve the issue, nothing will come out.
2. **Being open:** Once committed to resolve the issue, the next essential step is to be open and candid to each other and not hold back the information that is important for reaching the solution.
3. **Learning empathy:** It is of vital importance to understand the other party's position, their needs, strengths and shortcomings, the bottom lines or the points beyond which they cannot be pushed any further. It is essential to understand the other party's position in order to strike a deal.
4. **Searching for common theme:** It gives a good start to the process of negotiation by identifying common issues and concerns which both the parties strongly share.
5. **Generating alternatives:** Once they could be brought into a common platform, then it would be easy for them to commit to the problem and search for alternatives.

EFFECT OF CULTURE ON NEGOTIATION PROCESS

In today's era of international business transactions across the world, it often necessitates to engage in cross cultural business negotiations. In such cases, it is important to note that any negotiation strategies adopted by any individual or group are highly culture-specific. Many a times an international negotiation falls through because of the cultural incompatibility and not so much about the contents of negotiation. Thus, while most of the Asian cultures are more contextual in nature, Western cultures are found to emphasize more on the contents. Low-context cultures pay more attention on individualistic values and stresses on verbal communication. In contrast, high-context cultures stress more on group orientation and non-verbal communication such as a slight nod or avoiding the eye contact. People from Western cultural background put more emphasis on talking, clarifying points and so on, people from the Asian origin tend to be more observing and reflecting of the processes involved. In short, to get a clue regarding the nature of cross-cultural communications, Hofstede's cultural framework would be a good starting point (refer to Chapter 3). Apart from the cultural background of the negotiators, the language barrier between them is indeed a major point of concern in cross-cultural communication.

Exercise: What is Your Style

Read the statements given below. Give your response against each statement following the given guidelines as below:

1. Rarely or never
2. Once in a while
3. Sometimes
4. Fairly often
5. Very frequently or always

_______ 1. I like to discuss the issue openly
_______ 2. I don't like arguments
_______ 3. I see to it that my view is respected
_______ 4. I try hard to reduce differences and work towards a common goal
_______ 5. I believe in a give-and-take solution
_______ 6. I persist till the issue is solved
_______ 7. I usually keep away from confrontation
_______ 8. I do not accept no for an answer
_______ 9. I believe in minimizing the differences
_______ 10. I believe if one has to get something one has to give something in return

Scoring

After giving your responses, total the number assigned to each statement according to the set of statements as given below.

A	B	C	D	E
1:	2:	3:	4:	5:
6:	7:	8:	9:	10:
Total:				

Your Conflict Management Style

The highest score indicates your style in resolving conflict. There may be more than one style to resolve conflicts.

A. You have a win–win approach to problem solving. You recognize the abilities and expertise of yourself and others. The focus is on solution to the problem and not on winning or losing.
B. You attempt to withdraw from the situation. As the conflict does not dissipate, it grows to the point where it becomes unmanageable.
C. You use your authority or position. Power strategy results in winners and losers.
D. You try to play down differences and do not recognize the positive aspects of handling the conflict openly.
E. You compromise.

QUESTIONS

1. Give examples of intra-individual conflict from your personal experience.
2. 'Conflict is necessary to bring in change'. Do you agree?
3. How can a manager diagnose intergroup conflicts?
4. Is competition for better marks among the students functional or dysfunctional? Explain.
5. Think of the conflict your group had with the other group in your workplace. How did your group respond? Analyse the strategy.

REFERENCES

1. J. Greenberg, and R.A. Baron, *Behaviour in Organizations* (PHI, 2008).
2. J.L. Gibson, J.M. Ivancevich, *Organizations: Behavior, Structure, Process* (McGraw-Hill International Edition, 2009).
3. S.L. McShane, M.A.V. Glinow, and R.R. Sharma (Tata McGraw-Hill, 2006).
4. S.P. Robbins, *Organizational Behavior* (PHI, 2005).
5. H. Witteman, 'Analyzing interpersonal conflict: nature of awareness, type of initiating event, situational perceptions, and management styles'. *Western Journal of Communications*, 1992, **56**, 248–280.
6. Luthans, F. (1998). *Organizational Behavior* (McGraw-Hill).
7. Gibson, J. L., Ivancevich, J. M., Donnelly Jr., J. H. and Konopaske, R. (2006). *Organizations, Behavior, Structures, Process* (McGraw-Hill).
8. McShane, S. L., Glinow, M. A.V. and Sharma, R. R. (2006) "*Organizational Behavior*" (Tata McGraw-Hill).
9. de Dreu, C. K.W., Evers, A., Beersma, B., Kluwer, E. S., and Nauta, A. (2001). "*A Theory-Based Nature of Conflict Management Strategies in the Workplace*", Journal of Organizational Behavior, 22.

Case Study: War at Work

Dr C.K. Mozumdar, the Chairman of a Japanese multinational company producing inks, lacquers, pigments, industrial tapes, resins, fluorochemical products, and degassing materials, was looking out from his stylishly done office at the top floor of the administrative block. The office is situated in what was once known as the industrial hub at the eastern fringe of the city. The area used to be dotted with a number of manufacturing and heavy engineering companies, all bustling with activities throughout the day and night. Streams of workmen coming in and going out from the factories at different shifts, heavy trucks being loaded and unloaded all the time, and so many different kinds of people all around associated in some way or other with the factory life making the place lively always. But presently the place has worn almost a haunted look. Most of the companies, except this one and only a few more, have pulled down the shutters one after the other over the past decade or so. It makes Dr Mozumdar sad to see the desolated look the locality down. The main culprit for this is the ravaging war between managements and the militant trade unions, often strongly backed by political parties, which blindly pursued short-term gains at the cost of sustainability and well-being of the organizations they are part of. The whole situation was hopeless and foolish, like, mercilessly killing the proverbial goose that laid the golden eggs.

Dr Mozumdar, the son of a revered professor in chemistry whose books on physical chemistry were bible to generations of students, was a brilliant student himself. After doing his Ph.D in chemistry from a top German university, Mozumdar Jr. joined the industry instead of becoming an academician like his father. He did very well in his career in the Japanese multinational company from the very beginning and soon took charge of its European operations. He was well settled in England, and was not interested to come back to India. But fate had other plans. When the Indian operations of the MNC developed some problems, Mozumdar was asked to trouble shoot. Thus, he came back and took charge of the plant and the entire Indian operations as the chairman cum managing director.

Mozumdar's technical brilliance has been established long time back. But, the main problem in the Indian operation was the manpower, and not a technical glitch. Given the raj of militant trade unionism, the constant strife between management and trade unions used to take its tolls in the entire eastern region, where the head office of the company was situated. In addition, there were often more than one registered unions, backed by the political parties, with an open and violent hostility towards each other. Thus, resolving conflicts between the management and the trade unions and arriving at an agreement were an uphill task.

In spite of holding the topmost position and having a plush office, Dr Mozumdar was a very down-to-earth kind of a person who used to enjoy working in the factory, to have the smells of paint and liked to smear his hands with dirt and paints. He used to take number of rounds in the plant during the day, used to know each and every worker in the shop floor by his first name. Not only that, he used to know their family and personal problems like his own family members, and treated them just like that—a family. And this was what actually provided him with the clue to succeed. His closeness with the workmen, his warmth and spontaneity towards them and a natural respect for them as individuals won him such a huge acceptance and a great respect that he could make them do whatever he wanted. And he actually did what he wanted to do, to bring back some reason and rhyme to the stubborn mindset of the people who were actually digging their own graves. Dr Mozumdar used to tell the workers, 'What do you people want? Four square meals a day and taking care of your children, or being jobless and just beg in the streets? Look at the closed-down companies around this goddamn place and be careful. Do not let this happen to your company, because the first casualties will be people like you. The company will hardly suffer; it will simply wind up the operation and move out. You will be suffering like hell for the rest of your life'. He forced the two unions to sit together and prepare one set of common agenda, instead of two, to which the management would negotiate. And this proved to be a winning strategy. There were two unions, yes, but practically they were one, with a good rapport among all the members.

Questions

1. How could Dr Mozumdar manage the two warring unions and play them to his tune to ensure organizational effectiveness?
2. How could he stop the conflicts between the unions as well as between the management and the unions?
3. Why was he successful? What was his trick?

Chapter 5

Management of Group Processes

After reading this chapter, you will be able to understand that how groups are formed, deliberately or spontaneously, and influence the general functioning of an organization. Today, more emphasis is being given on understanding of the formation and maintenance of groups in an organization as the functioning of an organization actually depends on the functioning of organizational members, who more often than not are in groups. But just putting a number of assorted individuals together does not make a group or team. It is never the arithmetic summation of individual skills or efforts, and a lot of subtle things always happen within a group. If that is not fully comprehended, it will not be possible to form or maintain one in an organization.

More specifically, you will learn the following:

LEARNING OBJECTIVES

- Definition of groups
- Groups and teams
- Process of group formation
- Reasons for formation of groups
- Different models of group development
- Group norms and roles
- Group cohesiveness—strengths and weaknesses
- Group decision making

DEFINITION OF GROUPS

A group is a collection of two or more individuals, interacting and interdependent, who have come together to achieve a common objective/s.

Now, what we really mean by a group? Traditionally, a group is defined as *a collection of two or more individuals, interacting and interdependent, who have come together to achieve a common objective/s*.

The important characteristics of groups are as follows:

- **Social interaction:** The members of a group affect each other and there is a definite pattern of interaction among them.

- **Stability:** Groups also must possess a stable structure. Although groups can change, which often they do, there must be some stable relationship that keeps the group members together and functioning as a unit.
- **Common interests or goals:** Members of a group must share some common interests or goals that bind them together.
- **Recognition as being a group:** It is not just being together that would ensure the formation of a proper group. The members of the group must also perceive themselves as members of a group. They must recognize each other as a member of their group and distinguish them from non-members.

REASONS FOR JOINING A GROUP

People may join groups chiefly to achieve their personal objectives and to satisfy their mutual interests. As long as they are getting a chance to get these fulfilled, joining a group would make some sense for them. The following reasons are often found to influence one's decisions to join a group:

- **Security:** By joining a group and having the '*we-feeling*', people feel more secured and confident to fight potential threats. Forming unions are examples of such case.
- **Status:** Getting entry into an elite group will enhance an individual's status. Getting the membership of a prestigious club may be considered as an elevated status for the individual.
- **Self-esteem:** Groups can provide people with a feeling of self-worth. For example, an individual's getting into the core committee will enhance his self-esteem.
- **Affiliation:** Groups often fulfil the social needs of its members. To be able to relate to others is a basic human nature.
- **Power:** Joining an influential group often enhances an individual's power. Being a union member or gaining membership of a political party can substantially increase one's power.
- **Goal achievement:** Sometimes to achieve a desired objective, it requires joining hands with like-minded people so as to pool talents, knowledge and power. For example, when fighting a social evil like practice of child labour you need to form a group, as the objective can never be attained single handedly.

Concept Check

1. What is a group?
2. What are the typical characteristics of a group?
3. Why do people join a group?

TYPES OF GROUPS

Groups can be of different types. The basic categories of groups could be primary vs. secondary groups. In primary groups, members interact face to face with other members of the group. Examples include families, friends, classmates and so on. In secondary groups, members may not have the opportunity to interact face to face with other members. But still they feel they belong to the same group. Examples of secondary groups may be 'the management students in the country'. You may never be able to interact with each one of them. Still you will strongly feel that you are part of them.

Another way of looking at groups would be in terms of formal or informal groups. The formal groups are those that are deliberately formed within an organization with a definite purpose, whereas the informal ones are those that evolve spontaneously without anybody's active initiation. There are again different types within each of these categories. Figure 5.1 shows the different types of groups that are found within any organization.

There are various types of *formal groups* that are found in an organization. These are:

- **Command groups,** which are determined by the organizational chart depicting the approved formal connections between individuals in an organization. Examples of command group are director and the faculty members in a business school, school principal and teachers, production manager and supervisors, etc.
- **Task groups,** comprising some individuals with special interest or expertise, are created by the organizational authorities to work together in order to complete a specific task. Task groups are often not restricted to the organizational hierarchy and can be cross-functional in nature. Examples of task group might be people working on a particular project.
- **Standing committee** is a permanent committee in an organization to deal with some specific types of problems that may arise more or less on a regular basis. Examples of standing committees include the standing committee in a university to discuss various academic and administrative issues.
- **Task force/ad hoc committee,** in contrast, is a temporary committee formed by organizational members from across various functional areas for a special purpose. Meetings can also come under this category.

As noted above, formal groups are deliberately created at the organization for various reasons ranging from task accomplishment to maximum utilization of resources. However, organizations may not always be aware about the emergence and existence of informal groups that are formed spontaneously within the formal structure of the organization. Organizations are best understood as socio-technical entities where people come and join, but not only for the purpose of goal accomplishment. The existence of informal groups was first acknowledged during the Hawthorne experiments conducted by Sir Elton Mayo and his colleagues at Hawthorne plant of Western Electric Company and triggered the human relations school. Various types of *informal* groups are:

- **Interest groups** are formed when a group of employees band together to seek some common objectives, like protesting some organizational policy or joining the union to achieve a higher amount of bonus.

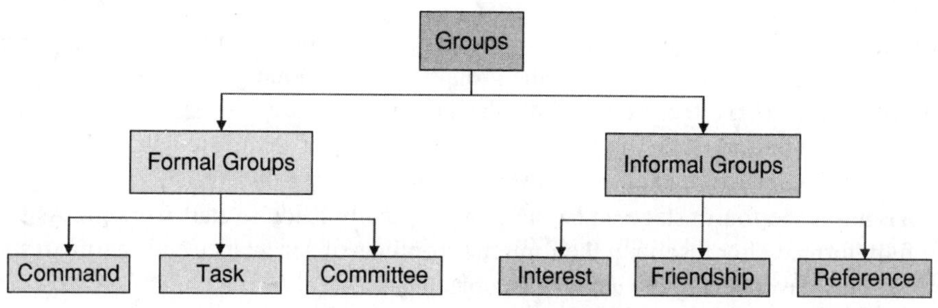

Figure 5.1 Types of Groups

- **Friendship groups** develop among the organizational members when they share some common interest like participating in some sports activities or staging the office drama, etc.
- **Reference groups** are those groups, with which individuals identify and compare themselves. These could be within the organization when a middle-level executive compares himself with the higher-level executive and longs for the perks and benefits enjoyed by the latter. The reference group might exist outside the organization as well when an individual compares himself with his batchmates working in other organizations or an ideal group of people he likes to become.

Concept Check

1. What are different types of groups?
2. Differentiate primary groups from secondary groups.
3. Distinguish between formal and informal groups.

HOW ARE GROUPS FORMED?

Groups are not just an assembly of few people together. In fact, it takes a considerable amount of time before a group really starts functioning and is usually found to go through some definite stages before actually taking the shape of a true group and is expected to start performing. Two models of group development have been offered by the researchers in the field of social sciences to explain how groups are formed. These are:

1. Five-stage model
2. Punctuated equilibrium model

According to the *five-stage model* of group development, proposed by Tuckman (1965), groups go through five distinct stages during the process of its development. These are as follows:

1. **Forming** is the initial stage of group development when the group members first come in contact with others and get acquainted with each other. This stage is characterized predominantly by a feeling of uncertainty among the group members as they now try to establish ground rules and patterns of relationship among themselves.
2. **Storming** is the next stage that is characterized by a high degree of conflict among the members. Members often show hostility towards each other and resist the leader's control. If these conflicts are not adequately resolved, the group may even be disbanded. But, usually the group eventually comes to terms with each other and accepts the leadership role as well as other members' role at the end of this stage.
3. **Norming** is the third stage of the group development process during which the group members become closer to each other and the group starts functioning as a cohesive unit. The group members now identify themselves with the group and share responsibility for achieving the desired level of performance of the group. Norming stage is complete when the group members can set a common target and agree on the means in achieving this.
4. **Performing** is the fourth stage when the group is finally ready to start working. As the group is now fully formed after resolving their internal conflicts of acceptance and sharing responsibility, they can now devote energy to achieve its objectives.
5. **Adjourning** is the final stage when the group, after achieving the objectives for which it was created, starts to gradually dissolve itself.

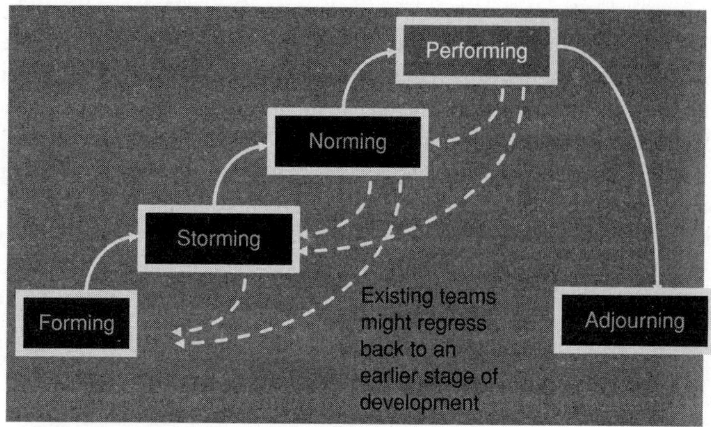

Figure 5.2 Tuckman's Five-stage Model of Group Development

Source: Tuckman (1965)

It is important to note the backward direction of the dotted arrows in the figure. Thus, there is always a chance for the group to slip back from a particular stage to the previous one. For the progression of the group to the right direction and reach the stage to perform, it is essential to manage the smooth transition of one stage to the next one.

The *punctuated equilibrium model* (Chang et al., 2003) questions the five-stage model of group development and claims that though the stages of group development model may not be followed universally for all the groups, groups are almost always found to follow a definite pattern. This pattern is described as the *punctuated equilibrium* model of group development as it is found that groups progress through alternative phases of inertia, followed by a phase of vigorous activities. The *Phase I* of the group's life stretches from the beginning to almost the half of the entire life of the group. Though during this period, at usually the first meeting, the group defines its tasks, and sets the missions for the group, this phase is marked by group

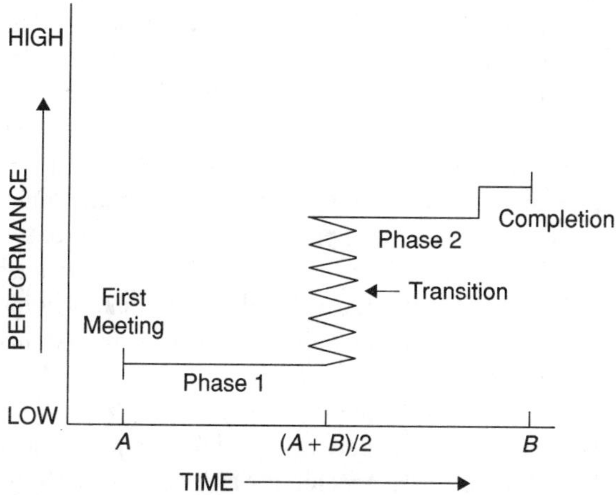

Figure 5.3 Punctuated Equilibrium Model

Source: Robbins, S.P. (2005).

inertia. Nothing seems to move the group towards its goal achievement. The transition takes place at the end of the first phase at a point when the group has consumed almost half of its allotted time. The group now seems to face some sort of alarm or crisis by recognizing that they have to redefine the premises on which they were working till then. It generates a lot of renewed vigour in the group's activities and the group drops its old way of thinking and adopts new ways. Groups then carry out its objectives until they reach the end of *Phase 2*, when there is again a spur in their activities. This marks the *Phase 2* of the group's life.

Although the punctuated equilibrium model is a relatively new approach to understand groups, it seems to offer a good explanation of the process of group development. If you refer to your experiences during working in, say, the groups you had participated for your project in organizational behaviour, you will find that this was the way you had worked. Remember the amount of frustration you felt when you suddenly realized that the date of submission and presentation was nearby, and your group's progress is almost nothing. Eventually, came a period when all of you started working in a frenzy and finally completed the task that had looked enormous in the beginning.

TEAMS AND GROUPS

Are these two the same? Though these two terms are often used interchangeably, they in the true sense are not the same, though the difference between the two is often rather thin. A team can be defined as a special type of group whose members have complementary skills and are committed to a common purpose or set of goals for which they hold themselves mutually accountable. Moreover, the amount of interdependence is much pronounced in teams than in groups. *Indian cricket team,* that is certainly *not* a group, is an example of team. While selecting the players for the team, they typically select a desired proportion of batsmen, bowler with variations of bowling skills, such as fast bowler or spinners or all rounders, and so on and so forth. The importance of teams has long been appreciated in the world of sports, and now it is being used increasingly in the realm of business and industry as well. Though there are similarities between groups and teams, there are a few clear differences between the two.

Table 5.1 will help to summarize this. Thus, even when the members of a group are together with the objective of accomplishing a specific task, the emphasis would still be on the individual level of performance or effort, which may eventually result in the group's performance. But in a team, the collective performance is of far better importance than individual member's performance. Even when an individual player in a national cricket team makes superior performance, this would get far less importance if the team's collective performance is not excellent. In the same way, the accountability of a group would be rather individualistic while in a team this is mutual. The purpose of joining a group also differs from that of joining a team. In group, members would look forward to sharing information in order to achieve the goals better, whereas in teams the focus is on collective and not individual performance.

The concept of synergy is very relevant in the present context. By the term 'synergy' we mean that the output or the performance of a team or group is never the arithmetic summation of individual effort or performance and this could be positive (when the output is greater than individual effort or performance), negative (when the output is less than individual effort or performance) or neutral when there is hardly any difference between the summation of individual outputs and the overall output of the group or team. In teams, there would always be a positive synergy, while in groups this may be neutral or even negative.

People in organizations are often deliberately assigned in groups to accomplish an objective more efficiently, but these groups will report to the person in charge of the group. But teams can also be self-managed, when they would be highly autonomous and responsible for their own actions. They would not report to any supervisor and would have the freedom of choosing the team members, procure the resources they would require, deciding their own pace of work and so on, only with one condition

Table 5.1 Groups and Teams

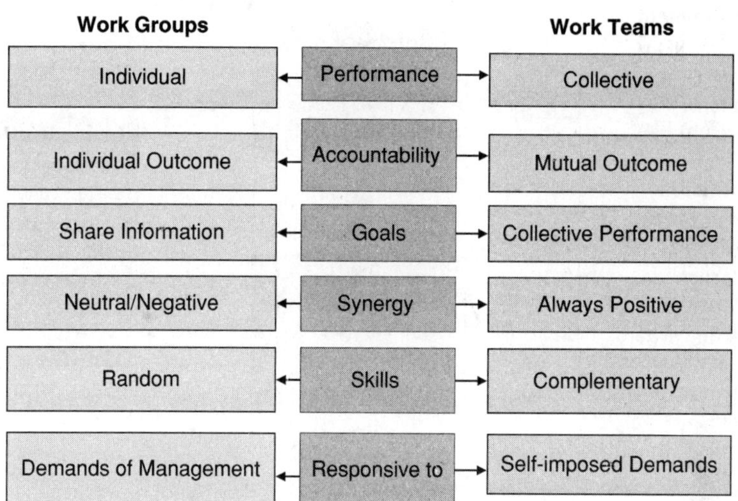

Work Groups		Work Teams
Individual	Performance	Collective
Individual Outcome	Accountability	Mutual Outcome
Share Information	Goals	Collective Performance
Neutral/Negative	Synergy	Always Positive
Random	Skills	Complementary
Demands of Management	Responsive to	Self-imposed Demands

being imposed upon them—they would have to deliver what they have been asked within the given period of time. The case of team for making the small car Tata Nano in Tata Motors is an example of self-managed high performance team. The extremely able group members were given all the freedom, they could do whatever they wanted to, as long as they would deliver the blue print of a 'safe, fuel efficient car at an affordable price', and the Nano team really did accomplish it.

Real World Focus: Senior vs. Junior Managers in a Large PSU

In a large public sector company that was conceived during the country's first five-year plans and was set up afterwards with strong government support and encouragement, things apparently seem to move fine. The organization could really boast of a highly qualified and efficient workforce who is quite devoted to their organization. But when the senior and very junior managers were asked to participate in a management training programme at the organization's picturesque training resort situated amidst a vast lake, a fallout of creating a huge dam over a once fearsome river, sparks started flying! During an informal discussion, older employees seem to take serious offence at the slightest question regarding the company culture. The divide was clear to the facilitator who is a professor of a management institute of repute.

Question

If you were to work in this organization, what step could you take to lessen the 'divide'?

TEAM EFFECTIVENESS MODEL

The effectiveness of a team, however, depends on many inter-related and interdependent factors. Figure 5.3 depicts these in a rather simple way, though in actuality, it may be fairly complex.

Organizational and Team Environment

First and foremost, we need to understand that the functioning and effectiveness of a team depends on the typical organizational and team environment as these doubtlessly exert significant influence on the

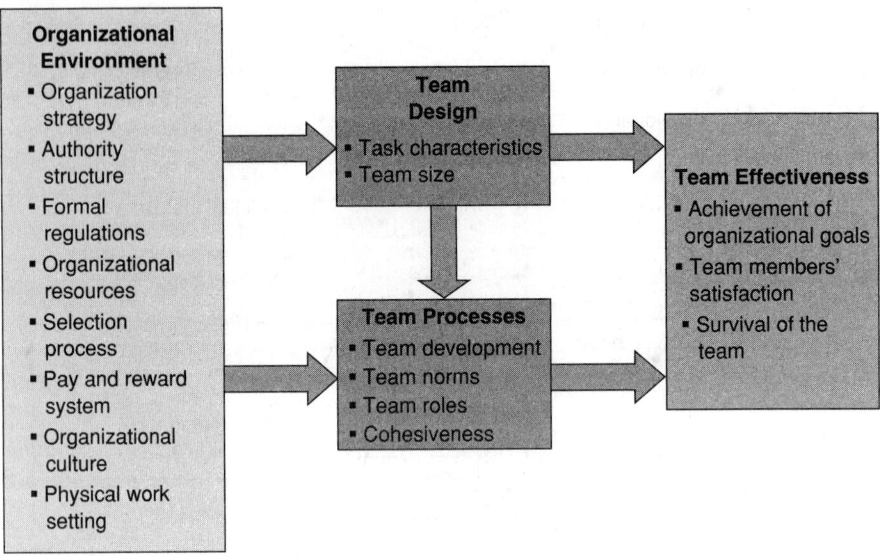

Figure 5.4 Team Effectiveness Model

team performance. Organizational rewards system and communication process play a crucial role in initiating and maintaining the team spirit in the organization. Organizational infrastructure and physical layout are also responsible in setting the tone and culture of the organization to inculcate the team feeling. What may happen in one organization may hardly be expected to take place in another because of these organization-related factors.

We may summarize all these as follows:

- Organization strategy
- Authority structure
- Formal regulations
- Organizational resources
- Selection process
- Pay and reward system
- Organizational culture
- Physical work setting

In addition to all these, one of the most critical factors to consider in this context is doubtlessly the organizational leadership. Leadership is possibly the single-most critical factor in setting the tone or climate within the organization.

Team Design

This refers to the two specific factors, viz., team size and nature of task the team would be engaging in. The size of the team, that is, the number of members present in a team, would have a strong impact on the team performance. A team should have at least the requisite number of people to carry out the task. But if it is too large, then it will be difficult to make all the members adequately involved in the team process. This would result in what is called social loafing, when individual members feel that it is not mandatory to put in their maximum effort as there will always be 'others' who would take care of the task. And the ultimate outcome could be disastrous, if everybody thinks this way and shirks from the personal responsibility. This is known as '*social loafing*', which refers to the tendency of individual team members to put in less efforts than what they would have put while working alone. Thus, the size of the group has some direct impact on the group's performance. While a larger group has in its disposal more resources, and is more likely to have formalized communication processes and bureaucratic practices; smaller groups give people the opportunity to interact frequently, facilitate the free flow of information, and provide a setting in which it is easier to reach agreement. All these points are to be kept in mind in determining the optimum size of a team.

The functioning of the team varies considerably depending on the task the team would be engaged in and would set the tone of the team. The way a football team functions is different from what would be expected from the board of directors of a company.

The models of team formation, viz., the five-stage model and punctuated equilibrium model of group development, have been discussed in the previous section. Presently, we would discuss the other three components of team processes, that is, team norms, team roles and team cohesiveness.

Norms

They are the rules and mutual expectations that develop within the group. Norms have profound effect on members' behaviour as it ensures conformity among them. In fact, social norms regulate the relationships among individuals in groups and can guide the behaviour of the team members on a number of issues ranging from how tasks are done and level of output to levels of tardiness (Blau, 1995).

Though norms regulate behaviour in groups, some norms may be viewed more seriously than others simply because the sanctions associated with violating them are more stringent. For example, to win the work group's acceptance, members may sometimes violate the organizational rules and policies. Usually, pressures are created on the deviants who violate the group norms and conform to the expected patterns of behaviour. The findings of the famous Hawthorne studies may be cited here when the group members had to obey the norms set by the members as well as those imposed by the emergent leaders in the group.

- The *internally imposed norms* refer to the situations when deviation from a group norm would not activate any significant sanctions apart from the inner anxiety.
- *Externally imposed norms*, in contrast, take various forms of disciplines taken by the authority for violating the expected patterns of behaviour, as is prevalent in say military groups.

Norms can also be of two types—*prescriptive* when it dictates behaviours that should be performed and *proscriptive* when it dictates specific behaviours that should be avoided by the group members.

Roles

The typical part played by an individual group member in accordance with the expectations of other members from him. The term role can be defined as a set of expected patterns of behaviour attributable to a person occupying a particular position.

The person holding the role is known as the *role incumbent*.

- *Role expectations* refer to the behaviours that are expected from the person playing the role. Thus, a professor is expected to teach, guide and evaluate his students. This often leads to what is known as the 'psychological contract', which refers to an unwritten agreement that exists between employers and their employees. These contracts define the expectations that accompany each role. The management is expected to treat employees fairly, offer a realistic workload and provide feedback on the employees' performance. Employees, in turn, are expected to display a positive attitude, fulfil his duties and obligations and show loyalty to the organization. If the role expectations are not adequately met, lower productivity on the part of the employees and disciplinary measures to be taken by the management. At times, there might be some gap between the *perceived role* and the *enacted role* of an individual. The individual develops his perceived role from the expected roles and on that basis he starts playing or enacting the role.

- *Role ambiguity* takes place when the person holding the role feels confused and does not know what is being expected from him. More specifically, role ambiguity arises when people are uncertain about their duties, responsibilities, or authority or all three (Peterson et al., 1995). It can result from lack of sufficient guidance in job descriptions or explanations by superiors and may lead to confusion, conflict and lower levels of performance. The role incumbent is said to suffer from the problem of *role identity* when he faces difficulty in accepting the assigned role.
- *Role conflict* arises when a person performs more than one role, and performance in one role makes performance in the other role difficult (Peterson et al., 1995). Take the example of a lady executive striving to play the part of a superwoman when she tries to balance her professional life with the personal and family life. Most of us at some time or the other have faced the problem of role conflict in our life.
- *Role problems*, if these continue for long, may cause serious amount of stress in the individual. It is, therefore, advisable to take adequate steps to minimize these. In the event of role ambiguity, the person may approach his superior seeking clarification of his jobs and responsibilities. In the case of role conflict, several possible steps may be taken. For example, where conflict occurs due to *role overload* (when the person feels it is almost impossible to perform the expected roles), one can try to prioritize the activities or delegate some part of it to the subordinates. If one experiences the *person–role conflict* (when a person's values are incompatible with the expected behaviour/performance of the role), he can look for organization's code of ethics or simply refuse to engage in activities contrary to one's personal values or ethics. Where *inter-role conflict* is experienced, it is important to appreciate the need to function in a number of areas and seek the support and advice of others in performing and unpalatable task.

Status

Status or the relative prestige or social position given to groups or individuals by others. It can be defined as the social ranking given to an individual because of the position she/he occupies in a group. Various factors may contribute to status, such as seniority, title, salary and power, and any of these factors could be critical in bestowing status. It is important to note here that status must exist in the eyes of those who confer it. In the olden society, status used to be acquired by birthright (as the son of the *zamindar* of the village has a much higher status than others). In modern times, one's position in the organization hierarchy often determines the status of a person. However, there are people in groups whose status is influenced by their personal attribute though understandably the powerful combinations are both position and personality.

Two common problems with status are 'status incongruency' and 'status discrepancy'. Status discrepancy happens when people engage in activities considered to be out of keeping with their status. For example, if the COO of a corporate house was to lunch with operatives in the factory canteen, this could be viewed as a discrepant behaviour by some people. Status incongruency arises when there is a disagreement among members of the group about an individual's status. If a particular employee draws a salary less than his colleagues, he will be perceived to have lower status than others.

Composition of a Group: A group may be homogeneous or heterogeneous in terms of its composition. A homogeneous group is said to exist when the profile of members (i.e. age, education, experience, specialization and cultural backgrounds) is similar in one or more ways that are relevant to the functioning of the group. In the heterogeneous group, the profile of the members is dissimilar.

Table 5.2 Differences Between Homogeneous and Heterogeneous Group

Homogeneous Groups	Heterogeneous Groups
There will be less conflicts among the members.	There will be more conflicts faced among the group members.
The process of group development is quick and fast.	Developing the groups take a much longer time.
They work better on tasks requiring a high degree of cooperation among the members.	They are found to perform in complex tasks.
The coordination among the members is found to be better.	They are found to be much more creative.
The level of satisfaction among the members are found to be high.	They have a better representation in the outside world.

Cohesiveness

Group cohesiveness referring to the strength of group members' desires to remain a part of the group. This also refers to the degree of attraction of the group members for each other and the 'we-feeling' among the members. Cohesiveness is likely to exist when there is high level of agreement among group members with respect to values, beliefs and objectives. This promotes the sharing of similar ideas and the mutual acceptance of such ideas. Cohesiveness increases the attractiveness of the group to members, motivates the members to remain in the group and decreases their tendency to leave the group.

The degree of cohesiveness has been found to depend on external threats, the difficulty in getting included in the group, the amount of time spent by the group members with each other and the success of the group. These are described in more detail below.

- **Similarity of attitudes and goals:** People with similar attitudes and goals like each other's company satisfying.
- **Time spent together:** As people spend more time together, they tend to form closer relationship with each other.
- **Isolation:** Groups that are isolated from other groups may perceive themselves as special and develop more dependence on each other to counter possible threats from outside.
- **Threats:** The group cohesiveness increases dramatically when the group faces external threats or competitions from outside. We all remember the 'we-feeling' and grand level of patriotism during the Kargil war in Kashmir.
- **Size:** The smaller the size of a group, the higher is the group cohesiveness as with larger size; the group induces more bureaucracy and lack of face-to-face communication among the group members.
- **Stringent entry norms:** The more difficult it is to get into a group, the greater the likelihood that the group is cohesive. This is found in professional courses which have very tough admission criteria (like in IIT's or IIM's or the National Defence Academy).
- **Rewards:** It is sometimes argued that incentives based on group performance enhance group participation and group performance.

It is, however, to note in this context that group cohesiveness may not necessarily be always a boon. Group cohesiveness is good as long as the objectives of the group is aligned with the organizational objectives, and in those cases, cohesive groups are indeed assets for the organization. But they are not always such. Figure 5.4 will illustrate the effect of cohesive groups on organizational effectiveness in terms of groups' performance.

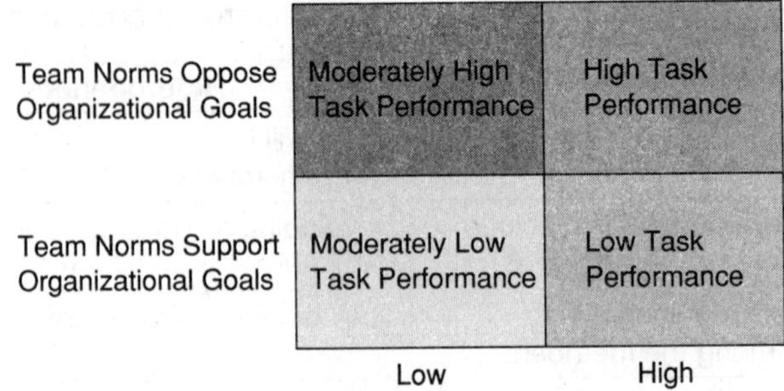

Figure 5.5 Team Cohesiveness and Performance

*Source:*McShane, S. L, Von Glinow, M. A., and Sharma (2006)

TEAM BUILDING

Much of the emphasis is being given to work teams for various reasons. If a self-managed team of committed members can be created within the organization, the accomplishment of the organizational objectives becomes rather easy. But it requires a lot of hard work and sensitivity to create successful teams within an organization. Team building is the process of enhancing the effectiveness of a team. A model proposed by Hackman (1987) provides some useful guidance on how to design an effective work team. The steps of team building may be described as follows:

- **Pre-work:** One of the most important objectives of this stage is to determine whether a team is to be created or not. This requires identifying the exact nature of the work that needs to be done, the objectives of the team and an inventory of the skills that are necessary to accomplish the task. In addition, decisions should be made in advance about what authority the team should have. They may be advisory to the manager, or they may be given full responsibility and authority to execute the task (i.e. self-regulatory).
- **Creating performance conditions:** At this stage, the organization's authority is to ensure that the team has proper conditions necessary to execute their task. Resources (including human, material, physical and financial) necessary for the team's success should be provided. In addition, the support from the organization, that is, the willingness to let the team do its own work and function in the way it feels necessary, is essential.
- **Forming and building the team:** At this stage, it is required for the managers to set the boundary of the team, that is, to ascertain who is and who is not a member of the team. Sometimes teams fail because of the confusion and ambiguity in establishing the member's identity. *Secondly*, the members must accept the team's overall mission and purpose. Unless they do, failure of the team is almost inevitable. *Thirdly*, organizational officials should clarify the team's missions, responsibilities and expectations.
- **Provide ongoing support:** Although once the teams start operating, they often guide themselves; managers may be able to support by providing opportunities for the team to eliminate problems and perform even better. For example, the disruptive team member be either counselled or eliminated from the team, material resources may be replenished or upgraded, etc.

It is clear that creating and managing well-functioning teams are not easy. This requires considerable managerial skills and hard work on the part of the managers. As Hackman points out, 'the considerable investment required to learn how to use work teams well can pay substantial dividends…'

The technique of team building also refers to the application of sensitivity training to work groups. The approach attempts to get members of a group to diagnose how they work together, and to plan how this may be improved. More specifically, team building begins when members of a group admit that they have a problem and gather data to provide insight into it. The problems that are identified may come from sensitivity training sessions, or more objective sources, such as production or sales figure or attitude surveys. These data are then shared, in a diagnostic session, to develop a consensus regarding the group's current strengths and weaknesses. From this, a list of desired changes is created, along with some plans for implementing these changes. This step is known as the action plan. Next, the plan is carried out and the progress is evaluated to determine whether the originally defined problems remain. If the problems are solved, the process is completed. If these still persist, the entire process should be restarted.

OUTBOUND EXPERIENTIAL LEARNING

Outbound experiential learning, also known as wilderness training or adventure learning, is an effort of building teams and is particularly applicable when the purpose of the team building is to enhance skills related to interpersonal effectiveness, including self-awareness, problem solving, conflict management and risk taking. There may be variations of how the typical exercises take place, but the basic pattern remains more or less the same. The whole programme takes place away from the workplace, usually in a resort or a hill station or somewhere where there are scopes for adventure and at least some amount of risk or threat, enough to challenge the capabilities of the team members. The team is assigned

various tasks or exercises, according to the capabilities of the members, but that certainly stretches their abilities and resources. It may vary from finding to survive in an unknown territory, without money or cell phones, or climbing a steep terrain or accomplishing a difficult feat, such as rafting or rappelling in turbulent streams or walking on ropes at a great height. There are of course experts who can ensure the safety of the participants so that no mishaps may happen, but the participants do not get to know that always and experience the thrills of danger. After the exercises are over, during the day, the team gathers together in the evening with the facilitator and discusses the happenings of the day, recounting their experiences and feelings towards other team members. The discussions basically revolve around the following lines:

- What happened in the exercise?
- What was learned?
- How events in the exercise relate to job situation?
- How to apply what was learned on the job?

Apart from the learning, these types of exercises enhance the team cohesiveness enormously.

GROUP DECISION MAKING

Decision making is essentially the process of choosing from among several alternatives. However, the decisions taken in an organization are often taken in a group and are hardly individualistic. Various groups or committees or task forces usually take decisions in an organizational set up. There are certainly a number of positive points in favour of group decision making, along with some weaknesses of the process as well.

- **Strengths of group decision making:** Groups generate more information and ideas by pulling in the individual member resources, which is essentially richer than individual inputs. There are increased chances of diversity of views, thus helping to evolve high-quality decisions. Moreover, the level of acceptance of the group is always high.
- **Inherent weaknesses of group decision making:** The process of group decisionmaking is notoriously time consuming. In addition, there are pressures of conformity on the group members that result in the members agreeing on some decisions when they really are not convinced. It is also a common occurrence in a group situation that one or a few members dominate the other group members. Group decisions also tend to suffer from ambiguous responsibility where nobody seems to own up the personal responsibility and feels accountable for the consequences.
- **Group think:** Group think is an interesting phenomenon where pressure for conformity inhibits the individual members from critically appraising each of the views generated within the group including unpopular, unusual or even absurd views. In doing so, the group loses its effectiveness considerably by ignoring rich and often potentially effective decisions. As noted earlier, too much of cohesiveness within the group may prove to be dangerous for the group.

Techniques for Improving Group Decision Making

Brainstorming

This is the process of generating creative solutions to a particular problem after overcoming the pressures of conformity within the group. The specific aim of brainstorming is generation of ideas, encouraging diverse alternatives and withholding criticisms of these alternatives at this stage.

Usually brainstorming sessions are held with not more than 10–15 members who sit around a table facing each other. The group leader states the problem before the group in a clear manner, and members are requested to think as many alternative solutions as possible. No criticism is allowed even with the most bizarre and weirdest ideas, and all the alternatives are recorded on flip charts for later analysis. The encouragement to think and absence of criticism helps the individual members to think creatively. Thus, brainstorming is a powerful tool for generating creative alternatives from the group.

Delphi Technique

Delphi technique is a method of systematically collecting and organizing opinions of experts regarding some particular problem or issue. This is a method of improving group decisions using the opinions of experts in the field in order to get the best possible solution, which are solicited by mail (or electronic mail today for increased speed) and then compiled. The expert consensus of opinions is used to make a decision. The steps of Delphi technique are as follows. First a list of experts who agree to cooperate is generated. Then the particular problem or issue on which their opinion is sought is sent to them either by post or through e-mail. Each expert then proposes what he believes is the most appropriate solution. The group leader then compiles all the individual responses and shares them with the other experts (through e-mail or by post). At this point, each expert comments on other's ideas and usually proposes some altered solution. These individual solutions are then returned to the leader who compiles these again and looks for a consensus of opinions. If a consensus is made, the decision is reached. If not, the process of sharing reactions with others is repeated until a consensus is eventually reached. This is an effective group decision technique as it minimizes the influence of some members over other members in the group.

Nominal Group Technique

Here small groups of individuals systematically present and discuss their ideas before privately voting on their preferred solution. The most preferred solution is accepted as the group's decision. The steps of nominal groups are as follows:

- Members meet in a group and the group leader presents the problem to them.
- Before any discussion takes place, each member writes down his opinion or idea about the problem privately in a piece of paper.
- After this period of individual analysis is over, each member presents her/his opinion or idea that is duly recorded. No discussion is allowed until all ideas are presented and recorded.
- The group now discusses these ideas and evaluates them.
- Each group member privately ranks each idea and submits it to the group leader. The idea with highest ranking is considered as the group's decision.

Stepladder Technique

This technique is useful for improving the quality of group decisions, and reducing the possible biases and unwillingness of the members while presenting their ideas before a larger group. Thus, in a step-ladder technique of group decision making, new members are introduced in the group one at a time, after the group has already discussed the problem. It starts with a two-member group who have discussed the problem independently and then come together, present their views to each other and come to a joint solution. While these two individuals work together, a third individual is presented with the problem on which he starts working alone, he later joins the group and presents his view to them, and starts working on the problem jointly. In this manner, after introducing a new member to the group, the group discusses the problem jointly to arrive to a solution.

The basic rationale behind the stepladder technique is that each new member is forced to present his view or ideas regarding a problem without being influenced by other members. The group also gets exposed to a continuous inflow of new ideas all the time and is forced to consider these.

Interactive Exercise

Ask the participants to recount their experience in working in groups. Ask them to share the experience and analyse it in the light of the group development model as described in the chapter. Individual students will later present their experience before the entire class.

GLOSSARY

- **A group:** A collection of two or more individuals, interactive and interdependent, who have come together to achieve a common objective/s.
- **Formal groups:** Deliberately created by the organization in order to help the organizational members achieve some of the important organizational goals.
- **Informal groups:** Develop spontaneously among an organization's members without any direction from the organizational authorities.
- **Command groups:** Determined by the organizational chart depicting the approved formal connections between individuals in an organization.
- **Task groups:** Comprises some individuals with special interest or expertise, created by the organizational authorities to work together in order to complete a specific task.
- **Standing committee:** A permanent committee in an organization to deal with some specific types of problems that may arise more or less on a regular basis.
- **Task force/ad hoc committee:** A temporary committee formed by organizational members from across various functional areas for a special purpose.
- **Interest groups:** Formed when a group of employees band together to seek some common objectives.
- **Friendship groups:** Develop among the organizational members when they share some common interests.
- **Reference groups:** Groups, with which individuals identify and compare themselves.
- **Teams:** A special type of group whose members have complementary skills and are committed to a common purpose or set of goals for which they hold themselves mutually accountable.
- **Team building:** The process of enhancing the effectiveness of teams.

QUESTIONS

1. Define a group. Give examples of different groups.
2. What do you understand by the term 'group norms'? Distinguish between externally and internally imposed group norms. In which category would you place a production target?
3. What do you understand by group cohesiveness? Identify the factors that increase group cohesiveness.

4. What are the reasons behind people's joining a group? Discuss with examples from your personal experience.
5. Distinguish formal groups from informal groups. Describe various types of formal and informal groups that are found to exist in organizational setup.

REFERENCES

1. R.M. Belbin, *Management teams* (London: Heinmann Educational Books, 1981).
2. G. Blau, 'Influence of group lateness on individual lateness: A cross-level examination'. *Academy of Management Journal*, October, 1995, 1483–96.
3. A. Chang, P. Bordia, and J. Duck, 'Punctuated equilibrium and linear progression: Toward a new understanding of group development'. *Academy of Management Journal*, February, 2003, 106–117.
4. J.R. Hackman, 'The design of work teams' in J. W. Lorsch (Ed.), *Handbook of organizational behaviour* (Englewood Cliffs, NJ: Prentice Hall, 1987, 315–342).
5. B.W. Tuckman, '*Development sequence in small groups*'. *Psychological Bulletin*, 1965, 63, 384–399.
6. Tuckman, B. W. (1965). "*Developmental Sequences in Small Groups*," Psychological Bulletin," June.
7. McShane, S. L, Von Glinow, M. A., and Sharma, R. R. (2006). *Organizational Behavior*, 3rd Ed (Tata McGraw-Hill, New Delhi).
8. Robbins, S.P. (2005). *Organizational Behaviour*. (Prentice-Hall, inc. NJ).

Case Study: The Team Building Effort of the New Director

Mr K. Roychoudhury had worked in East India Paper Mill for around 15 years before he became the executive director of the company. The company used to manufacture parts of paper machinery and catered to all the paper mills across the country. The company is a fairly old one, started by Mr Aurobindo Basu, an enterprising Bengali who was a refugee from the then East Pakistan. He lost his father during partition and reached India with his mother without as much as ₹ 10 in his pocket. He started his life from a scratch and struggled tremendously. After trying his hands in various areas, he eventually started to supply waste paper and related materials to paper mills where these were recycled in making paper. Basu did not get a chance to acquire formal education, but he was very intelligent. He soon understood that manufacturing of paper machinery was a very good prospect as most of these were imported from Western countries at a considerable high price. He initially started a small engineering firm in Howrah with the help of local artisans. Over the next 10 years, the business flourished and Basu established his 'state-of-the-art' factory at the northern fringes of Calcutta with a turnover of ₹ 300 crores.

Roychoudhury, a mechanical engineer from a regional engineering college, had worked in several companies before joining East India. His family had huge land and property in north Bengal, and he could have spent his life in style without doing anything like his other two brothers. But Roychoudhury preferred to work. He is an intelligent and sensitive person and rather a silent worker who would never show off. The last executive director of the company was Mr R. N. Chatterjee, who was pompous and arrogant and a tyrant. He use to bulldoze on the employees' morale and never bothered to show any respect to anybody. The employees and the entire work force became so hostile that eventually the board of directors had to remove Chatterjee from his position and elevated Roychoudhury to replace him.

Roychoudhury himself had suffered a good deal in Chatterjee's regime. He had been humiliated on several occasions even in front of his juniors by Chatterjee who used to consider these as his tools of controlling others. As an insider, Roychoudhury knew every story of humiliation and mental tortures that most of the people had endured during Chatterjee's time. After assuming the position, Roychoudhury concentrated on restoring people's morale first. He used to meet the unit heads every fortnight to discuss the future plans and prospects of the company. He also adopted a transparent process of administration and took active effort in stopping backbiting and maligning people, a favourite practice of his predecessor to cow down the people. During the last Convention of Paper Machinery Equipment Manufacturers, East India Paper Mill acted as the host. Hundreds of delegates from India and abroad participated in the convention, which was a grand success. It took a lot of hard work and precise coordination among various teams within the company for a period of time. Roychoudhury delegated the authorities completely, and after delegation and establishing the accountability of each group, he withdrew himself almost completely. But everybody knew that he was there and would help them out whenever there would be any trouble.

The convention was hugely successful and got great media coverage, with East India Paper Mill's name everywhere. But what was more important was that he could really cement the 'we- feeling' among the people in the organization.

Question

Comment on the team building effort of Roychoudhury.

Chapter 6

Leadership and Change

Opening Case: Two Men in the Early Morning

It was early morning. Two men were driving a chariot through a huge field. The one who was driving and also looked the older of the two glanced at his co-passenger, who seemed to be sad, gloomy and confused.

—'What's the matter with you? Why are you so uncomfortable?' the driver asked.

—'I ... I don't know. But I am sure I will not be able to do what you want me to. It is absolutely impossible! Let me go away', pleaded the younger one.

'Look Partha, do what I have asked you to do. Kill all these men who are already dead and win the war'. The elder one told firmly though at the same time he was genuinely concerned. 'Do what I have asked you to do, Partha!' he urged again.

A series of long argument and counter argument between the two followed hereafter. Partha, the younger one, seemed to be rather obstinate at one point of time. He won't do anything at this stage, come whatever may be. The elder one was his dearest friend, though senior to him in age and of course in terms of experience and wisdom. He was his dear friend, but at the same time more than just a friend. He was his mentor. But what he was now telling him to do was impossible for him!

The elder one was answering all the questions of Partha patiently to quell his doubts. But when Partha was still not convinced and wavering, his companion seemed to be rather exasperated!

—'Look Partha, look at me carefully. Can't you recognize me? I am the whole world and beyond! I am holding all the forms of life in me! What I say is truth, the absolute truth! I am the destiny; I am the fate of everything! You can't escape me! Do what I say!'

Partha was now looking at his friend in awe. Who is he? What he saw then in his friend made him realize that he still had lots of doubts but to disobey him was beyond his capability. He would have to perform what his friend would ask him to do, because his friend was the leader.

By now, you must have identified both the men. Yes, the elder one was Shree Krishna, the leader of leaders ever born and the other one Arjuna, the third Pandava! The scene is surely the field of the great war of Kurukshetra, and the famous dialogue that took place between Lord Shree Krishna and Partha i.e. Arjuna, had been recorded in the sacred Hindu scripture 'Srimad Bhagavad Geeta.

Shree Krishna is considered the greatest leader because of his clear vision, his ability to transform his followers into contributing their maximum and his ability to keep himself detached and distanced from what was going on around him, and yet clearly focused on the goal. His remarkable flexibility and playfulness enhanced his repertoire and charm infinitely.

In the present chapter, the importance of leadership and its possible impact on the organizational effectiveness has been discussed. Various viewpoints of the concept of leadership have been given to enhance the comprehensive understanding of the concept. After reading this chapter, the reader should be able to understand the basic nature of leadership in the context of work in general. More specifically, you will learn the following:

LEARNING OBJECTIVES

- Meaning and importance of leadership in the context of work environment
- Distinguish between leadership and management
- Recognize the role of power and influence
- Main approaches to the study of leadership

LEADERSHIP

Leadership is a topic that has traditionally fascinated researchers through out ages. It evokes the image of powerful personalities who can inspire and conquer the hearts of many in the world of business, and it is a well-recognized fact that organizational leadership is very critical for the performance of the organization. The person at the helm of an organization may take it either to an unprecedented height or mar it completely. There is ample evidence to suggest that the well-led organizations performs much better as compared to the not-so-well-led organizations. As noted by Bennis (1999), corporations that are perceived to be well led have been found to increase their stock value over 90 per cent as compared to 78 per cent for firms perceived as poorly led. The same holds true in terms of the general goodwill of the company in the market. Although many factors go into being an admired company, the single most important factor, according to Bennis, is leadership. The concept of leadership is particularly important in the context of change and developing the organization.

The concept of leadership is rather tricky. Identifying a leader when you see one seems to be quite obvious, but defining the term 'leadership' is not easy. There is a strong disagreement among the researchers regarding this term. Different authors have defined leadership in their own way, which prompted Stogdill (1974), a noted researcher in this field, to comment with some amount of vexation that probably there are 'almost as many definitions of leadership as there are persons who have attempted to define the concept'.

However, as a thumb rule, we may say that a leader is the one who exerts the maximum amount of influence over other members in a group. Organizational leadership may thus be defined as *the process of directing and influencing the task-related activities of group members.* Mullins (2002) defines leadership essentially as *a relationship through which one person influences the behaviour or actions of other people.*

Leadership is the process of directing and influencing the task-related activities of group members.

It is important to note that leadership is a dynamic process that involves changes in the relationship between the leader and the followers. It is a two-way process and essentially a reciprocal one in nature. Shree Krishna could not have function or achieve his objectives of establishing the supremacy of good over evil without Arjuna. He also needed Arjuna as much as Arjuna needed him as a guide. Leadership is also about possession of power and requires an unequal distribution of the same. Shree Krishna clearly was far more powerful than Arjuna in terms of knowledge, experience, expertise, vision and wisdom. The same holds true for any leader.

Leadership is related to someone's ability to motivate others and managing interpersonal behaviour. Shree Krishna became a leader who is whole-heartedly accepted by his followers. In the present context, it was Arjuna, but as everybody knows, he had scores of followers who would die willingly for him at any point of time just to make him happy. Evidently leadership relies heavily on the process of effective communication. Shree Krishna was undeniably an eminently effective communicator as well.

It is to be noted that leaders inspire the followers to act in a desired way by generating a consensus from the latter. The influence exerted by the leader is in turn gets modified by the influence the followers in turn exert on the leader. The entire process is certainly reciprocal in nature though the influence exerted by the follower often remains less visible or apparent.

Thus, if we examine the term 'leadership' more minutely, it will be found that it has the following implications as presented in Table 6.1.

As noted earlier, the concept of power is inherently implied in the process of leadership. *Power*, as we understand the term in this context, is *one's ability to exert influence, that is, to change the attitude or behaviour of individuals and the groups*. There are five possible bases of power as identified by French and Raven (1968), which are: *reward power, coercive power, legitimate power, referent power and expert power*. The greater the number of these power sources available to an individual, the higher is his potential for effective leadership.

Let us now try to understand each of these power sources as summarized in Table 6.2.

Figure 6.1 Relationship between the leader and the followers as proposed by Greenberg & Baron (2008).

Table 6.1 Implications of Leadership Concept

Involves others	In the absence of followers or employees to be led, the whole idea of leadership does not make any sense.
Unequal distribution of power	There is always an unequal distribution of power between leaders and other group members.

Table 6.2 Different Sources of Power

Reward power	This is based on the subordinate's perception that the leader has the ability to control rewards that the followers are looking for; for example, leader's ability to influence the decisions regarding pay, promotion, praise, recognition, increased responsibilities, allocation and arrangement of work, granting of privileges, etc.
Coercive power	This is based on fear and the subordinate's perception that the leader has the ability to punish or to cause an unpleasant experience for those who do not comply with directives. Examples include withholding pay raises, promotion or privileges; allocation of undesirable duties or responsibilities; withdrawal of friendship or support; formal reprimands or possibly dismissal. This is in effect the opposite of reward power.
Legitimate power	This is based on subordinate's perception that the leader has a right to exercise influence because of holding a particular position in the hierarchy of organizational structure. Legitimate power is thus based on authority and not on the nature of personal relationship with others.
Referent power	This is based on the subordinate's identification with the leader. The leader is able to influence the followers because of the interpersonal attraction and his personal charisma. The followers obey the leader because of their respect and esteem towards him.
Expert power	This is derived from the subordinate's perception of the leader as someone who has access to information and relevant knowledge.

Concept Check

1. What is leadership?
2. What are the implications of leadership concept?

Now refer to the opening case: What were the sources of power for Shree Krishna? Clearly they were referent power or *personal charm* and expert power or what we may say, *wisdom*. People used to be simply charmed by Him, be it as their guide, friend, philosopher or beloved and would take immense pleasure to please Him!

Critical Exercise

Look around and check the lesser mortals! Why do we consider somebody more powerful than us and try to find out that individual's sources of power.

Leadership is one of the most important processes in an organization. It may not be *seen* and seem to be rather intangible in nature, but you surely would always *feel* it. It is all around each of the organizational members and clearly sets the tone for the organization. Most usually, organizational leadership is responsible for the culture and climate of an organization.

LEADERSHIP AND CHANGE

Guiding organizational members, especially during the turbulent time, is one of the most critical and demanding responsibilities of a leader. In fact, this is the acid test for a leader's success and effectiveness. As noted by Yukl (2007), 'It is the essence of leadership and everything else is secondary'. Organizational changes for betterment are usually planned at the top. However, no matter how well designed and meticulously these changes are planned its success depends on the implementation of the same in the organization. Normally, a change is faced with stiff resistance from the ones for whom the change is meant. This is an innate and universal human tendency and leaders in an organization have to convince others in order to effectively implement the change process.

Manager's Essence: Organizational Insight

Indian IT companies like Infosys or erstwhile Satyam were giants in their own fields. But the destiny of these companies was dramatically different which was a result of the personal profiles of the respective founders. Narayana murthy, the founder and past chief mentor of Infosys, was known for a high level of personal integrity and strong work ethics, which skyrocketed the organization to an almost dizzying height. In contrast, the tainted CEO of Satyam, Ramalinga Raju, is perishing behind the bars for unbridled level of corruption in the company. Thus, a lot depends on the nature of leadership of the top person in the organization.

LEADERS vs MANAGERS: SOME FUNDAMENTAL DIFFERENCES

Do we commonly find the post of 'leader' in the organizational chart of any company? Rarely. We find the post of 'manager' aplenty. Why do we then require leaders in the organization? When are they required most? What are the differences between these two terms? Let us try to address this issue.

As we know, managers are those who get the work done through people. Their main objective is to help subordinates to work smoothly towards attaining the organizational goals by virtue of their legal and coercive power. A manager's focus is primarily to maintain the 'status quo' to ensure that everything is done according to the laid down rules and policies of the organization. And there is no denying that they usually do a good job. But it is to be noted in this context that they work best in a stable and predictable environment where sticking to the laid down rules will deliver the desired outcome. To achieve this, the primary requirement is of course well-laid organizational systems and reliable procedure in the first place. However, the role of managers is thus basically of maintenance.

__Managers__ are those who are responsible for achieving those goals and implementing the ways to attain those set objectives efficiently.
__Leaders__ are primarily responsible for defining (and sometimes redefining) organizational goals and objectives or what is known as the mission of the organization.

But a leader in a business organization is the one who can cope with changes that an organization compels to go through when faced with uncertain external environmental situations. This is a time when the safety of sticking to a known and tested course of action is harshly denied. There is hardly a set precedent to refer to and the person in charge now will have to curve new paths and develop new guidelines to survive in the ensuing chaos. If he can make the

Table 6.3 Major Differences Between a Leader and a Manager

Manager	Leader
Administers	Innovates
Maintains	Develops
Focuses on systems and structures	Focuses on people
Relies on control	Inspires
Does things right	Does the right thing

organization survive this moment, chances are high that the organization will catapult to a never-before height of glory. The main source of strength is his referent power or personal charisma. He hardly wields his status or position power. He is the one who inspires.

The major differences between a leader and a manager may thus be summarized as in Table 6.3. The last point mentioned in Table 6.3 is a much-appreciated quote of Peter Drucker, the revered management guru of all ages. The author would like to share a small story to illustrate the point. Once upon a time there was a clerk in an office who was well recognized for his high level of efficiency in his work. One day his boss called him and gave him a simple task of copying content from one old ledger book to a new one for the purpose of keeping records (usage of computers were not prevalent those days). Normally, the task should not have taken more than two working days. However, a whole week went by but the clerk did not complete the work. The impatient boss called the clerk and asked what the matter was. The clerk said, 'sir, I have finished copying everything from the old ledger to this new one. But, have a look at page number 15. There is a dead fly stuck at the right hand corner of that page. I am frantically looking for a fly, which after killing I will stick exactly in the same place. But I am still not getting it and that is the reason for the delay, sir'.

We all tend to laugh at the unfortunate clerk here, because though he was doing things quite rightly, he could not differentiate between what is relevant and important from what is not. Even though he is working hard, he is incapable of applying his mind and thus remains ineffective. The terms 'efficient' and 'effective' are never inclusive of each other. To be effective, one has to be efficient, but being efficient does not guarantee effectiveness. The leader has to be *effective* and have the capability to look beyond.

Concept Check

1. Distinguish between a leader and a manager.
2. When would an organization require a leader rather than a manager?

THEORIES OF LEADERSHIP

We noted earlier that leadership seems to be too vast a topic with noted distinctive approaches. Nevertheless, all the theories that had been offered to explain leadership may be neatly put under few rather distinct heads, viz. *traits theory*, *behaviouristic theory*, *contingency theory* and *charismatic theories* of leadership. We will now have a brief look at each of these.

Traits Theory

In early 20th century, the researchers were trying to identify leaders from non-leaders on the basis of the individual's possession of certain skills and personality, social, physical and intellectual traits. With the rapid development of psychological tests during this time, a serious effort was made to assess these characteristics through psychometric measurements. In a typical study, Terman (1904) asked teachers to describe the typical playgroup leaders in schools for young children. The identified playgroup leaders were reported to be active, quick and skilful in devising and playing games. Bavelas (1960) found quickness of decision, courage to take risks, coolness even under stress, intuition and even luck as crucial factors for determining effective leadership qualities. Thus, the popular way of defining a leader often includes the possession of the such traits as intelligence, attractiveness, self-confidence, confidence on others, honesty and integrity, vision, warmth and conviction. They are also believed to be energetic, ambitious, having task-related knowledge, creative, flexible and having a desire to lead others.

Traits theory attempts to identify leaders from non-leaders on the basis of the individual's possession of certain skills and personality, social, physical and intellectual traits.

But there were a number of problems inherent in the trait approach. Stogdill (1948), on the basis of an extensive survey of literature on leadership, pointed out that a person does not become a leader by virtue of the possession of some combination of personality traits alone. What is actually important in this context is that the leader's personality must be compatible with the personal characteristics, activities and goals of the followers. House et al. (1997) supported this view in their leadership theory known as the *culturally implicit leadership theory* (CLT).

Thus, the main criticism against trait theory is that though few traits have been identified as responsible for increasing the probability of leader's success, none of these traits guarantee success (Robbins 2002). More specifically, the reasons behind the failure of trait approach are presented in Table 6.4.

Behaviouristic Theory

The inability of traits approach in providing a comprehensive list of leadership traits as a basis of identifying leaders from non-leaders led the researchers to look for the *ways* the effective leaders are found to behave. This gave rise to the behavioural theories of leadership, which aim at identifying the effective styles of leadership. In contrast to the traits approach, which insists that *leaders are born*, the basic premises

Table 6.4 Criticisms Against Trait Theory

Subjectivity of judgement	There is bound to be some subjective judgement in determining the effectiveness of a leader.
Too long list of traits	The lists of possible traits tend to be very long.
Absence of relative importance of the traits	It generally fails to clarify the relative importance of various traits.
Followers' needs ignored	It overlooks the needs of the followers.
Difficult to establish causal relationship	It cannot discriminate between the causes and their effects.
Situational factors not considered	It ignores the impact of situational factors, which is found to be critical in determining leadership effectiveness.

of behavioural theories are that if specific behaviours can be identified as effective styles of leadership, people can be *trained* to imbibe those behaviours and become successful leaders.

Behavioural theories of leadership aim at identifying the effective styles of leadership.

Of the various behavioural studies, we will discuss a few here, viz., Ohio studies, University of Michigan studies and managerial grid theories.

Ohio State Leadership Studies

During the later part of the 1940s, the Bureau of Business Research at the Ohio State University undertook an extensive amount of research studies in order to identify the effective styles of leadership. Starting with a huge and almost baffling number of leadership styles they finally identified two distinct and mutually exclusive categories of leader behaviour: *initiating structure and consideration.*

- **Initiating structure** refers to the extent to which the leader defines and structures group interactions and group activities in order to attain formal goals. It includes those aspects of leader behaviour that are concerned with organizing work, work relationships and goals. Leaders high in initiating structure are those who would insist on the attainment of goals and meeting the deadlines.
- **Consideration** refers to the extent to which the leader establishes trust, mutual respect and rapport with the group and shows concern, warmth, support and consideration for the subordinates. This dimension is associated with the two-way communication, participation and the human relations approach to leadership. Leaders high in consideration are those who tend to help the subordinates with personal problems and show respect for the subordinates' ideas and suggestions.

Available research evidence seems to suggest that a leader high in both these dimensions, consideration and initiating structure, are found to be more effective. However, the evidence is not entirely conclusive and much seems to depend upon the situational factors.

University of Michigan Studies

When the Ohio studies took place, another major research was conducted by the University of Michigan Institute for Social Research. Likert, who summarized the findings of the University of Michigan Studies, used the terms *employee-centred* and *production-centred* leaders that are similar to dimensions of consideration and task structure. Thus, employee-centred leaders were described as those emphasizing interpersonal relations and tend to take a personal interest in the needs of their subordinates. The production-oriented leaders in contrast were identified as those whose main concern tended to be the task aspect of the job. Achieving the group objectives was their sole concern and the group members were a means to that end. The employee-centred leaders, according to the Michigan researchers, were associated with higher group productivity and higher job satisfaction while the production-centred leaders tended to be associated with low-group productivity and lower-worker satisfaction.

Managerial Grid

Blake and Mouton (1985) tried to show an individual's style of leadership on a 9 × 9 grid consisting of two separate dimensions, viz. concern for production and concern for people which are similar to the concept of employee-centred and production-centred styles of leadership as mentioned earlier. The grid has nine possible positions along each axis creating a total of 81 possible styles of leader behaviour. The managerial grid, thus, identifies the propensity of a leader to act in a particular way. The (9, 1) style is known as *task management*, which focuses wholly on production. Managers with this style are exceptionally competent with the technicalities of a particular job but are miserable failures in dealing

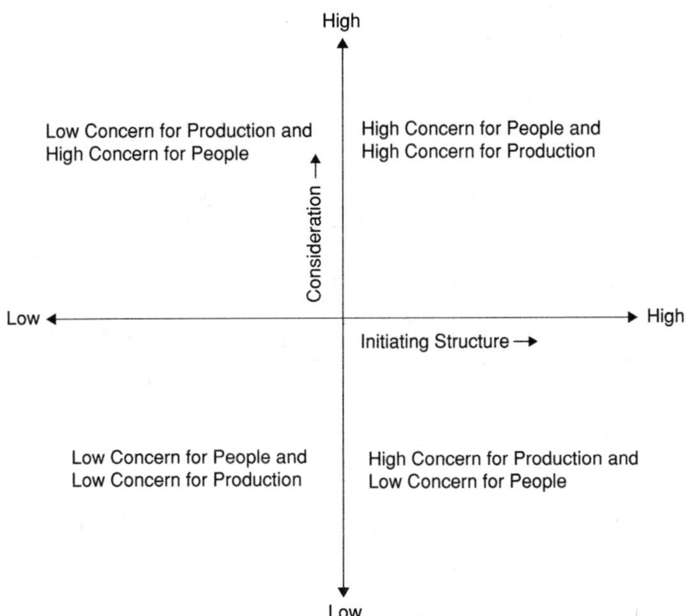

Figure 6.2 Two Dimensions of Leader Behaviour

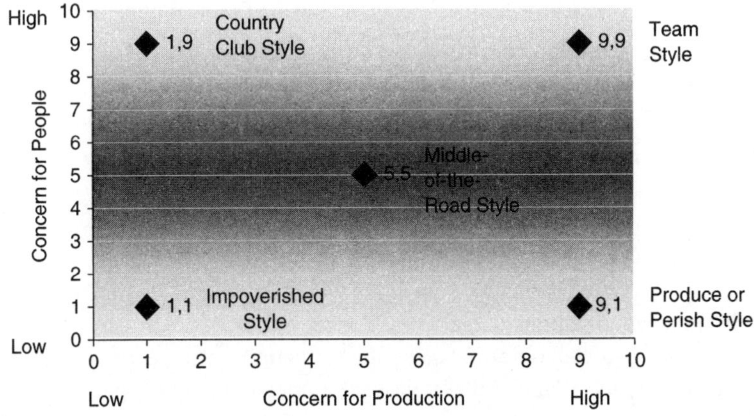

Figure 6.3 Managerial Grid

with people. The (1, 9) style in contrast emphasizes people to the exclusion of task performance and is known as *country club style of management.*

The ideal style of leadership, as envisioned by the theory of managerial grid is the (9, 9) style or *team management style* where there is maximum concern for both people and production. The research evidence in favour of the view that managers perform best under (9, 9) style is, however, scanty.

The behaviouristic theories too have its share of criticisms. The basic criticisms against the behaviouristic theories are as follows:

Table 6.5 Criticisms Against Behaviouristic Theories

Lack of generalizations	It is difficult to generalize the findings as they are found to vary widely from one organization to the other or from task to task.
Overlooking the situational factors	More or less in the same vein, the behaviouristic theories fail to take into consideration the significant influence of the situational factors on leadership effectiveness.

LEADER–MEMBER EXCHANGE (LMX) MODEL

It is a fact that leaders hardly treat all their subordinates equally. For various reasons, leaders do form varying relationships with different subordinate groups and in the process some members are treated more favourably than some others. Graen and Wakabayashi (1994) pointed out this phenomenon and proposed the leader–member exchange (LMX) model, which suggests that two distinct groups are generally created—the in-group and the out-group. The discrimination in the leader's behaviour takes place rather early in their relation and often on the basis of few tangible sources of information ranging from leader's perception of the personal characteristics and/or competence of the followers.

Leaders tend to create in-group and out-groups. Members of in-group are found to have higher performance ratings, greater satisfaction and remain longer with the organization.

Members of the in-group, who are generally favoured and encouraged by the leader, perceive the leader in better light, whereas those belonging to the out-group are not receiving the leaders' favour and are entitled to fewer organizational resources. As a consequence, they tend to perceive the leader in a less favourable light. Thus, the leader–member relationship within a group is hardly uniform and that forms the basis of their mutual perception of each other. The in-group members are found to be more satisfied with their jobs and are usually better performers. They hold more positive attitude towards their jobs and also tend to stay in their jobs longer. Available research evidence seems to support the theory.

Contingency Theories

By early 1960s, researchers in the area of leadership studies came to acknowledge the importance of situational factors in identifying a successful leader behaviour. Contingency theories are based on the assumption that there is no single style of leadership appropriate to *all* situations. Here we will review three contingency theories, which have attracted serious attention from the researchers in this area, viz., the Fiedler's model, Hersey and Blanchard's situational model and House's path-goal theory.

Contingency theories are based on the assumption that there is no single style *of leadership appropriate to* all *situations.*

Fiedler's Model

Based on an extensive study of various group behaviours under different situations, Fiedler (1967) proposed a model that asserts that effective performance of a group depends on the appropriate match between the leader's style of interacting with his/her subordinates and the degree of control and influence that the situation provides the leader. He developed a measuring tool (*least-preferred co-worker* or *LPC* questionnaire) to discern the attitude of the leader, that is, whether he is task-oriented or people-oriented. Fiedler suggested that leadership behaviour is dependent on the favourability of the situation. According to him, there are three major variables determining the situation and affect the leader's role and influence as summarized in Table 6.6.

Table 6.6 Factors Determining Situation

Leader–member relations	This refers to the degree to which the leader is trusted and liked by group members, and their willingness to follow the leader's guidance.
Task structure	This refers to the degree to which the task is clearly defined for the group and the extent to which it can be carried out by detailed guidelines.
Position power	This refers to the power of the leader by virtue of position in the organization, and the degree to which the leader can exercise authority to influence, say, rewards and punishments.
According to Fiedler, when the situation is	
Very favourable	Good leader–member relations, structured task, strong position power.
Very unfavourable	Poor leader–member relations, unstructured task, weak position power), a task-oriented leader (with low LPC score) with a directive, controlling style will be more effective.
Moderately favourable	Moderately favourable and the variables are mixed, the leader with an interpersonal relationship orientation (with high LPC score) and a participative approach will be more effective.

With knowledge of an individual's LPC score and an assessment of the three contingency variables, the Fiedler's model proposes matching these up to attain maximum leadership effectiveness. Thus, one can choose the leader who best fits the situation. The other alternative would be to change the situation to fit the leader, which could be done by restructuring the task or increasing/decreasing the control power of the leader.

Hersey and Blanchard's Situational Model

The situational leadership model, developed by Paul Hersey and Kenneth Blanchard (1982), suggests that the leader's behaviour should be adjusted according to the maturity level of the followers. The level of maturity or the readiness of the followers were assessed to the extent the followers have the ability and willingness to accomplish a specific task. Four possible categories of followers' maturity were identified as in Table 6.7.

The leaders' behaviour was determined by the same dimensions as used in the Ohio studies, viz. production orientation and people orientation. According to the situational model, a leader should use a *telling style* (high concern for task and low concern for people) with the least matured group of followers who are neither able nor willing to perform (R1). A *selling style* of leadership (high concern for both task and relationship) is required for dealing with the followers with the next higher level of maturity, that is, those who are willing, but unable to perform the task at the required level (R2). The able, but unwilling followers are the next matured group and require a *participating style* from the leader, characterized by high concern for consideration and low emphasis on task orientation. Finally, the most matured followers who are both able and willing require a *delegating style* of leadership. The leader working with this kind of followers must learn to restrain himself from showing too much concern for either task or relationship as the followers themselves do accept the responsibility for their performance.

Telling style: *High concern for task and low concern for people.*
Selling style: *High concern for both task and relationship.*
Participating style: *High concern for consideration and low emphasis on task orientation.*
Delegating style: *Low concern for task and relationship.*

Though this theory is difficult to be tested empirically, it has its intuitive appeal and is widely used for training and development in organizations. In addition, the theory focuses attention on followers as a significant determinant of any leadership process.

Concept Check

1. What is situational theory of leadership?
2. 'Leader's flexibility is the key to his success'. Why?

LIKERT'S FOUR STYLES OF MANAGEMENT

Likert (1967) put forward four specific styles of leadership that may usually be found in an organization. These are explained in Table 6.8.

According to Likert, each of the four styles of leadership has relative advantages and disadvantages of its own. It is also important to note that the relative success of each depends heavily on conditions existing within its specific stage of development.

Table 6.7 Different Categories of Followers' Levels of Maturity

R1	Unable and Unwilling
R2	Unable but Willing
R3	Able but Unwilling
R4	Able and Willing

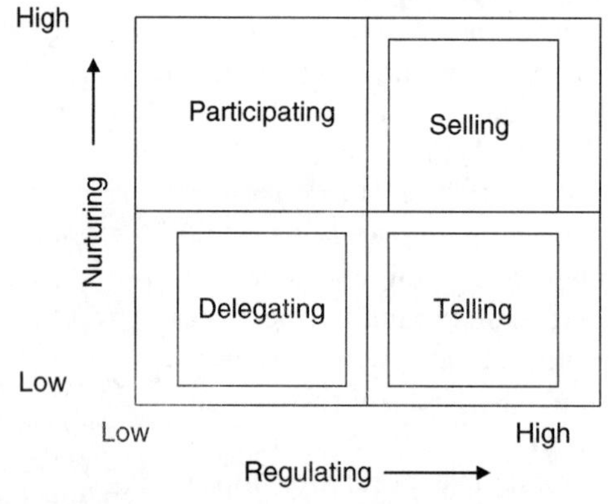

Figure 6.4 Different Styles of Management

THE PATH–GOAL THEORY

In the recent time, one of the most appreciated theories of leadership is the path-goal theory as introduced by Robert House (1979), which is based on the expectancy theory of motivation. According to this theory, the effectiveness of a leader depends on the following propositions:

Manager's Essence: How to Deal with Them?

S. Mahadevan is the general manager of a multi-speciality hospital in Chennai, where a group of highly qualified medical professionals are engaged. Each one of them is extremely good in their fields of specialization. In addition to that, they are devoted to their job. Today there is a scheduled brain surgery where a team of doctors will have to operate on a small boy. What should Mahadevan do now? Should he call the team of doctors and give them some special instructions before the operation starts?

- Leader behaviour is acceptable and satisfying to followers to the extent that they see it as an immediate source of satisfaction or as instrumental to future satisfaction.
- Leader behaviour is motivational to the extent that
  - It makes the followers' needs satisfaction contingent or dependent on effective performance
  - It complements the followers' environment by providing coaching, guidance, supports and rewards necessary for realizing the linkage between the level of their performance and the attainment of the rewards available.

Table 6.8 Likert's Four Styles of Management

Exploitive authoritative	The leader uses fear and threats, communication is downwards, the psychological distance between superior and subordinates is wide, and almost all decisions are taken by the management at the top.
Benevolent authoritative	The leader uses rewards to encourage performance, the upward flow of communication is limited to what the superior wants to hear, subservience to superiors is widespread, and although most decisions are taken at the top echelon of organizational hierarchy, there is some delegation of authority to the subordinates.
Consultative	The leader uses appropriate rewards, communication may be two-way, though upward communication is more guarded, employee involvement is more and subordinates have a moderate amount of influence in some decisions, though the more important decisions are taken by the top management only.
Participative	The leader discusses economic rewards and makes full use of group participation and involvement in fixing high performance goals and improving work methods and procedures. The emphasis is on a network of accurate information; subordinates and superiors are psychologically close, and group decision making is widely spread throughout the organization.

The leader selects from any of the four styles of behaviour, which is most suitable for the followers at a given point of time. These are directive, supportive, participative and achievement-oriented according to the need and expectations of the followers. In other words, the path-goal theory assumes that leaders adapt their behaviour and style to fit the characteristics of the followers and the environment in which they work. Actual tests of the path-goal theory provide conflicting evidence and therefore it is premature to either fully accept or reject the theory at this point. Nevertheless, the path-goal theory does have intuitive appeal and offers a number of constructive ideas for leaders who lead in a variety of followers in a variety of work environments.

TRANSFORMATIONAL LEADERSHIP

Transformational or charismatic leaders are those who could inspire their followers to transcend their own self-interests for the good of the organizations or for a greater objective. Thus, leaders like Netaji Subhas Chandra Bose or Gandhiji could inspire their followers to submit their own personal goals of pursuing lucrative academic or professional careers and sacrifice everything else for the sake of the freedom of their motherland from the British rules. By the force of their personal abilities they transformed their followers by raising the sense of the importance and value of their tasks. Five leadership attributes have been identified as important in this context, which are self-confidence, a vision, strong conviction in that vision, extraordinary or novel behaviour and ability to create an image of a change agent.

It is, however, important to note that the effect of cultural difference in the context of leadership must be considered in order to understand and identify the effective leadership behaviour. An extensive project has been undertaken jointly by GLOBE foundation and Wharton Business School to identify the impact of culture on leadership across the world, which concluded only recently. The study has identified lists of both positive and negative leader attributes, which have been universally accepted across culture. The findings from the completed phases of the study, however, suggest the presence of a strong influence of cultural bias on the success and effectiveness of the leaders.

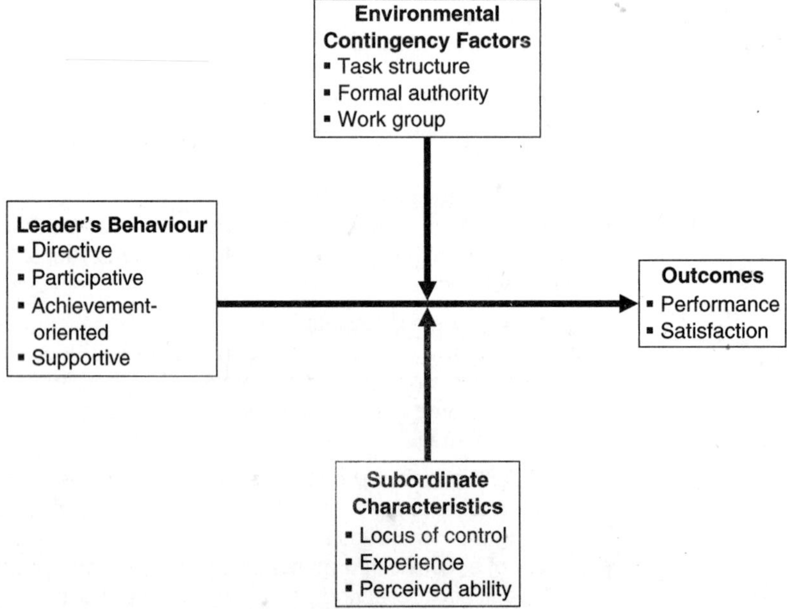

Figure 6.5 House's Path-goal Theory

SUMMARY

Leadership is basically the process of directing and influencing the task-related activities of group members. Power is an essential prerequisite of leadership that emerges primarily in the situation of unequal distribution of power. Power could be derived from various sources, viz. reward power, coercive power, legitimate power, expert power and referent power.

There are three distinctly different approaches to leadership theories which give rise to traits theory, behavioural theory and situational theory. In *traits* theory of leadership, an effort is made to identify leaders from non-leaders on the basis of the individual's possession of certain skills and personality, social, physical and intellectual traits. The basic problems with the trait theory are that it offers a list of traits too long for application purpose and these are never found to apply uniformly. In contrast to the traits approach, which insists that *leaders are born*, the basic premises of *behavioural theories* are that if specific behaviours can be identified as effective styles of leadership, people can be *trained* to become leaders. The behaviouristic theory basically aims at identifying the effective *styles* of leadership. Contingency theories or situational theories are based on the assumption that there is no single style of leadership appropriate to *all* situations.

Transformational or charismatic leaders are those who could inspire their followers to transcend their own self-interests for the good of the organizations or for a greater objective.

GLOSSARY

- **Leadership:** A relationship through which one person influences the behaviour or actions of other people.
- **Power:** One's ability to exert influence, that is, to change the attitude or behaviour of individuals and the groups.
- **Traits approach:** Effort to identify leaders from non-leaders on the basis of the individual's possession of certain skills and personality, social, physical and intellectual traits.
- **Behaviouristic approach:** Effort to identify effective styles of leadership.
- **Initiating structure:** The extent to which the leader defines and structures group interactions and group activities in order to attain formal goals.
- **Consideration:** The extent to which the leader establishes trust, mutual respect and rapport with the group and shows concern, warmth, support and consideration for the subordinates.
- **Employee-centred leaders:** Are those emphasizing interpersonal relations and tend to take a personal interest in the needs of their subordinates.
- **Production-oriented leaders:** Are those whose main concern tends to be the task aspect of the job.

QUESTIONS

1. Define leadership. Distinguish it from management. Why do you think leadership is important for the organization's well-being?
2. Describe the strengths and weaknesses in the traits approach of leadership.
3. What is managerial grid? Contrast its approach to leadership with the approaches of Ohio State and Michigan groups.
4. Describe leader–member exchange theory. What are its implications for leadership practices?

REFERENCES

1. A. Bavelas, 'Leadership: Man and function'. *Administrative Science Quarterly*, 1960, 4, 344–360.
2. W. Bennis, 'Five Competencies of New Leaders'. *Executive Excellence*, September, 1999, 4–5.
3. R.R. Blake, and J.S. Mouton, *The Managerial Grid III* (Rev. ed.)(Houston, TX: Gulf Publishing Co, 1985).
4. F.E. Fiedler, *Theory of Leadership Effectiveness* (New York: McGraw-Hill, 1967).
5. G.B. Graen, and M. Wakabayashi, 'Cross-cultural Leadership-making: Bridging American and Japanese Diversity for Team Advantage' in H.C. Triandis, M.D. Dunnette, and L.M. Hough (Eds.) *Handbook of Industrial and Organizational Psychology* (2nd ed.) Vol. 4, (Palo Alto, CA: Consulting Psychologists Press, 1994).
6. P. Hersey, and K. Blanchard, *Management of Organizational Behaviour* (New York: Prentice Hall, 1982).
7. R.J. House, and M.L. Baetz, 'Leadership: Some Empirical Generalizations and New Research Directions' in B.M. Staw (Ed.), Research in Organizational Behaviour Vol.1, (Greenwich, CT: JAI Press, 1979).
8. R.J. House, and R.N. Aditya, 'The Social Scientific Study of Leadership: Quo Vadis?', *Journal of Management,* 1997, 23(3), 409–73.
9. R. Likert, *The Human Organization* (New York: McGraw-Hill, 1967).
10. R.M. Stogdill, 'Personal Factors Associated Leadership: A Review of the Literature', *Journal of Psychology*, 1948, 25, 35–71.
11. L.W. Terman, 'A Preliminary Study of the Psychology and Pedagogy of Leadership', *Journal of Genetic Psychology*, 1904, 11, 413–51.

Students' Activity: Identify Great Leaders

Directions

- The entire class may be divided into small groups containing not more than five members.
- Each group will identify a leader, preferably from the present day scenario, and justify why they have selected the particular leader.
- After deciding the leader, they will then conduct extensive research in order to define her/his leadership.
- They will also try to identify the source/s of power of that leader.
- If it possible for them to secure an appointment with the leader, the students should be encouraged to interview the leader.
- The groups will then present their findings before the entire class.

Issues to address

- To identify the list of traits possessed by a leader and after comparison with the entire class to come up with a list of common traits that are found to exist in all the leaders.
- To note the possible impact of followers' expectation and perceived compatibility with the leader.

Case study: The New MD at Indian Metallurgical

In March 2009, Srinivas became the managing director of Indian Metallurgical Works, a heavy engineering firm worth ₹3000 crore. He joined the organization in 2000, after serving at various other organizations. An engineer who has also done his MBA from a premiere management institute, Srinivas had always been known for his courage and straightforwardness. He had been at the helm of several industries and is generally credited for turning at least a couple of them around from rather sorry states of affairs when he joined them. Quite a few of these were rather notorious for their militant trade unionism during the early 1980s and Srini showed the courage of matching them fearlessly. One thing that Srinivas believed in ardently was total transparency while dealing with people.

When Srini joined his present organization, R. N. Srivastava was the managing director. He was a qualified and gifted individual, but was terribly moody and temperamental. He was known for his arrogance and high-handedness. People were usually in awe of Srivastava as he was very unpredictable and would often come down on somebody and blast him, usually in the presence of others. In all probability, Srivastava was possibly an insecure person himself who never trusted anyone. As a departmental head, Srini himself was often at the receiving end of Srivastava's tantrum and fury. He had been humiliated in public on more than one occasion, even in front of his juniors. Evidently, Srivastava's reputation with the board was diminishing fast. In addition, there were allegations of financial irregularities against him, which eventually sealed his fate. Towards the end of 2008, the decision to replace Srivastava was finalized and he was given the graceful option to resign. It was decided that instead of bringing somebody from outside, this time it would be someone from within the organization. Getting somebody from outside, the usual practice, particularly for the top positions, had its share of problems. To get attuned to the organization's ethos and practices as well as the general culture, takes too long a time from an outsider. Srini was a good choice for several reasons. He has been in the organization for quite some time now. He was middle aged, and not too old. He was capable and intelligent. Only doubt that was there in the mind of the board members was the acceptability of Srini. Would he be accepted by his colleagues as the person in charge? He was their equal only the other day and moreover, they have witnessed his harassments in the hands of the predecessor. It is true that majority of them had been harassed quite often in the previous regime, but to accept him at the top person might not be easy.

During the interview, when the board members asked Srini what he thought were his strengths, Srini simply said honesty and conviction. He said he knew this place like the back of his palm and knew each and every individual there. He was very confident that if given a chance he would certainly be able to bring in some positive changes in the organization.

He was appointed as the Managing Director of Indian Metallurgical in March 2009. In the history of Indian Metallurgical, Srini was the first MD recruited from within. Once in the chair, Srini took care to make a fresh start. As one of the victims of humiliation in the earlier regime, with the pain still raw and fresh in mind, Srini made an effort of win back people's trust and goodwill. He called a general meeting of all managers from both junior and senior levels. It was certainly a very candid affair from Srini's side. He addressed the gathering by way of opening up the self. He stressed on the need for total transparency in each and every aspect of running the organization—from sharing information and taking decisions to interpersonal relationships. He admitted his drawbacks as well. He was never a great orator nor is he known for his placidity. But his strength lied in his honesty and transparency. He subtly hinted at the mental trauma suffered by most in the previous regime and vowed not to let it happen anymore.

The acid test of his acceptance came a few months later when Indian Metallurgical hosted an International Conference of Metallurgical Engineers at a famous beach resort. That the programme was a grand success attended by a number of participants from India and abroad is besides the point. The major success for holding the conference successfully was that it helped to integrate the members of Indian Metallurgical to a great extent. And the double boon for Srini did certainly count. As an able strategist, Srini grabbed the opportunity of hosting the programme at the auspices of Indian Metallurgical, which is usually been hosted in turn by various metallurgical houses in the country, and subsequently withdrew himself from the nitty-gritty of the various activities, but left everything to the organizing committees set up from members across the organization. Indian Metallurgical, like so many other big houses, was fraught with inter-departmental rivalry and people hardly knew each other in a 500-plus workforce organization. The setting up of different committees and sub-committees with full working authority bestowed on them was something that had never happened to Indian Metallurgical before. The previous MD never used to trust anybody and used to always impose himself, even at the most trivial issues, in an effort of what he thought to retain his own authority and supremacy. The complete absence of any direct intervention of the new MD in the present activities and an assurance of support all the while from him triggered two things—faith in the MD and a faith in their own capability. And all this, certainly cemented the acceptance of Srini at the top.

Questions

1. Comment on Srini's style of leadership.
2. What would be your advice to Srini to improve his effectiveness?

Chapter 7

Power and Politics

Opening Case: Invisible Strings

When the director of one of the premier management institutes in eastern India resigned, the board of directors selected Dr Chaturvedi, one of the senior-most professors who had been serving the institute for more than a decade, as a replacement. The reasons for selecting him were cogent and realistic. He knew the people around and the organizational culture like the back of his hand. He was qualified and well-mannered and was generally accepted by his colleagues. However, within a year of him joining the office, he got ousted. One of the main reasons being his straightforwardness in dealing with the day-to-day activities as well as tackling the all-powerful board members. Dr Chaturvedi was a no-nonsense individual with an impeccably honest background. Either he was incapable of understanding the various intricacies of the transactions taking place within the organization (specifically those that were financial in nature) or he was decidedly against all types of 'shady' deals. Though he was reasonably well-accepted by his colleagues and staff and he was trying to lead the organization in the right direction, he was no more perceived as 'the blue-eyed boy' as the board thought him to be. He had to put in his papers before he could complete a full year in his chair.

What do you think are the reasons for the change at the helm? Of course, you can sense the various underlying pulls and strains within the organization that culminated in the resignation of Dr Chaturvedi. After going through this chapter, you would understand how things really function in an organization and how individuals become powerful or how they lose the power they possess.

LEARNING OBJECTIVES

- Dynamics of power within an organizational setting
- Structural vs. personal sources of power
- Effective and ineffective use of power
- Factors that foster politics in an organization
- Effects of power and politics in an organization

What happened to Dr Chaturvedi is not something unheard of. Like him, people often become prey to power game within an organization. Closely related to the concept of power is organizational politics which is, you like it or not, a hardcore reality of organizational life. Nevertheless, people are reluctant to discuss power and politics openly as these two terms seem to carry a negative overtone.

WHAT IS POWER?

Power refers to the ability to influence others.

Simply put, power refers to the ability to influence others. Power signifies the situation when one compels an individual to submit to his wishes and behave accordingly. The ones who are powerful may not necessarily exert the power they possess. Sometimes people may be unaware that they have any power over others. A person, for instance, with charming personality, may not know about his power to others.

Although power denotes the ability to influence others, the two terms—power and influence—are not the same. Thus, when your teacher compels you to study for your project, he is certainly influencing you! This refers to the fact that possession of power by your professor is indeed necessary to influence you positively.

POWER DYNAMICS

There are variations in the possession of power by an individual, group, organization or even a country that are found all around us. Not everyone enjoys the same amount of power, and this may happen within the same organization and even sometimes with the same hierarchical position. Within an organization, some groups are found to be more powerful than others. For example, faculty members in a teaching institute are traditionally found to yield more power than the non-teaching staff. Similarly, some organizations too are found to be more powerful than some others, such as Tata group of companies in India is evidently more powerful than a smaller business house. In the global context, countries like the United Kingdom or the United States are more powerful than some others like Greece or Holland. It is to be noted in this context that power equations keep on changing over time. Countries like India or China, who were traditionally lower in the power order, have recently emerged as more powerful than before for various reasons. The same thing also does happen within the organization with changing situations and/or individuals gaining or losing power over time.

Power and Dependency

The concept of power is essentially social in nature, in the sense that it requires other individuals to manifest power, and cannot happen in isolation. Nevertheless, an individual will be able to exert power on another individual as long as he depends on him for something or the other. Like your boss will be all powerful as long as you work under him and depend upon him for attaining your desired objectives such as performance appraisal report, recommendations for pay hike or promotion and the like. The boss can easily influence or mould you as he likes. But the moment you leave the job or have a good job offer in hand, the person in question would hardly be able to influence you anymore. The more the dependence of person B has on the other person A, quite evidently the more is the power of A over B. However, the concept of dependence is largely the perception of the individual.

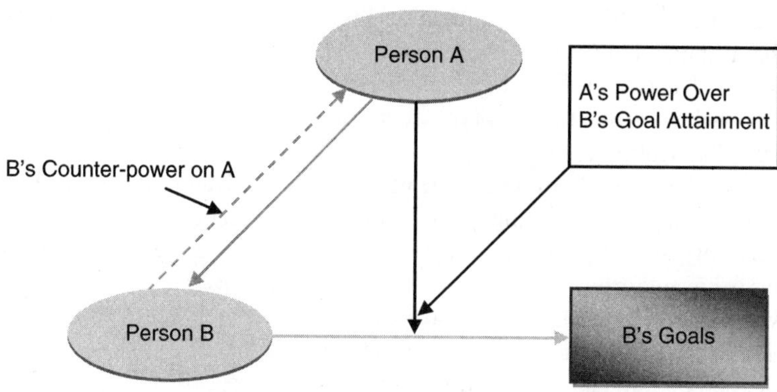

Figure 7.1 Power and Counter-power

Source: McShane and Glinow (2005).

Concept Check

1. What is power?
2. How does dependency control power play?

Power and Counter-power

It is interesting to note that when A has power over B, it is hardly unidirectional and B also found to exert a 'counter-power' on A. For example, a manager with higher designation can indeed fire an employee when he is angry with the latter's behaviours, but if the same employee is dedicated and hard working then the manager will not be be able to act likewise. Thus, counter-power puts a stop and motivates the manager to use power more judiciously.

SOURCE OF POWER

Where does one get the power in an organization? Sources of power in the organization can be broadly categorized into—*interpersonal power* and *structural power*.

Interpersonal Power

According to French and Raven, there are five sources of interpersonal power, viz. legitimate power, reward power, coercive power, expert power and referent power. A brief description of these sources of power is given below.

- **Legitimate power:** This refers to one's ability to influence others on the virtue of his position in the organizational hierarchy. This is also known as the positional power, which indicates that the power that one enjoys is due to his 'chair' or the position within the organization. This is, in other words, the *authority* or the formal power that is bestowed upon an individual, by which an individual can legitimately command obedience from his subordinates. If a subordinate refuses to obey the

Legitimate power refers to one's ability to influence others on the virtue of his position in the organizational hierarchy.

authority of a superior, this would be held as insubordination, and consequently disciplinary actions can be initiated against the subordinate.

Authority typically has the following characteristics:

- It is due to the position of an individual within the organization, and is not dependent on his personal characteristics.
- It is accepted by the subordinates. The person in power enjoys a legitimate or legal authority to command and achieve compliance from the subordinates.
- The authority flows from top to down. The higher, one is in the organizational hierarchy, the greater is his authority.

- **Reward power:** This refers to an individual's ability to reward a follower for compliance. *Firstly*, it is actually the followers' perception that the superior may give them what they want, though in reality it might not necessarily be so. *Secondly*, it has to match the expectations of the followers. As long as the followers perceive that the superior is in a position to give what they want, such as pay raise, promotion, recognition, challenging job assignments, etc., the superior will yield the power over the subordinates. But, if the superior can give the rewards that are not too important for the followers, the magic will certainly cease to work so effectively. The reward power in an organizational set up is clearly linked to the individual's legitimate or position power.

__Reward power__ refers to an individual's ability to reward a follower for compliance.

- **Coercive power:** Coercive power is the opposite of reward power. Here the compliance is attained on the basis of fear of punishment. A manager may write unfavourable report about the subordinate's performance, thus denying him a chance of promotion. The subordinate complies to avoid the negative consequence. The punishments include denying some privilege or inflicting some negative consequences.

__Coercive power__ ensures compliance on the basis of fear of punishment.

- **Expert power:** This refers to the power that one achieves due to his knowledge or expertise. Expert power is not necessarily related to legitimate or a position power. A senior machinist may exert more power than a young engineer in the shop floor, in spite of the fact that the latter's designation and qualification are much higher than the machinist. Thus, expert power is a personal characteristic while the legitimate, reward or coercive powers are because of organizational characteristics.

__Expert power__ refers to the power that one achieves due to his knowledge or expertise.

- **Referent power:** It is an individual's personal power or charisma that attracts people towards him. People are inspired by the individual and obey him primarily because of the fact that they adore him and want to be like him.

__Referent power__ is an individual's personal power or charisma that attracts people towards him.

It is evident that these five power sources are often interdependent. As noted earlier, reward power and coercive power are found to be closely associated with the legitimate or position power of an individual within an organization. It is also to be noted in this context that some forms of power are accepted more favourably than some others. Thus, reward power or notably the referent power evokes strong positive response from the followers while too much use of coercive power tends to make people resentful and rather hostile.

Structural Power

Structural powers are those that are derived from the organizational structure and the existing social subsystems rather than the personal characteristics of the individual concerned. Thus, the CEO of a company would evidently exert more power than an individual in a lower position. We have already discussed this in the section on legitimate power. However, even individuals in the same hierarchical level may have differences in the power sources. Some departments traditionally enjoy more prominence and power than others in an organization. For example, the development team could be more powerful than the quality assurance team in a software firm. Some important sources of structural power are as follows:

- **Resources:** An individual becomes powerful when he has free access to resources, including money, people, technology, material, etc. and support and cooperation from people in getting something done. The higher one goes up the organizational hierarchy, more access he gets to resources. In addition to one's job designation or the 'legitimate power' as mentioned earlier, it also includes the degree of support and cooperation he could command within the organization. Some individuals seem to enjoy more obedience by virtue of the complex networking and organizational dynamics that prevail in the organization.
- **Decision making:** The extent to which individuals or groups can influence decision-making process in an organization, with or even without the formal authority vested upon him. It also might refer to the amount of discretion that one can make in his job, which usually increases with higher positions though the reverse may not always hold good. For example, when Dr B. C. Roy was the chief minister of Bengal he could take major decisions for the state, not all the time seeking approval from the Centre. Not all the chief ministers could enjoy the same status as him.
- **Information power:** Knowledge or information is considered to be a key factor in determining the power of an individual or group within an organization. Having access to relevant and important information in time matters a lot within an organization, and an individual or group or department can gain considerable power and control by achieving that. We have noticed how powerful is the accounts department in most organizations, which is clearly not because of their personal power (often found to be rather dismally low!), but because of their access and control over the crucial information regarding the financial health of the organization.

Concept Check

Distinguish between personal and structural sources of power.

EFFECTIVE USE OF POWER: VARIOUS INFLUENCE STRATEGIES

There are various possible ways to influence people and exert power over others which vary in terms of their effectiveness. The effective managers are those who not only have access to various personal and structural power sources but can also use the power tactics judiciously to achieve their objectives. It is important to note that not all the tactics are equally effective in all the situations and often it pays to combine more than one strategy rather than relying on a single one.

A brief outline of these is given below:

- **Use of reason:** This is a form of logical persuasion with extensive use of data and factual evidence. Though it is considered as one of most effective influence strategies in the organizational set up, recent research evidence seem to point out that it would be more effective when used with emotional appeal.
- **Friendliness:** Here, the person wishing to influence first creates a positive ambience by praising or pointing a mutual likeness or similarity. Supporting the boss in an important departmental meeting helps to create a positive feeling and paves the way to earn his favour later.
- **Coalition:** This happens when people join a group with individual power bases and resources to exert influence to bring in change. Creating a coalition in itself may pose some considerable amount of pressure and may well legitimize the issue.
- **Bargaining:** Bargaining or negotiating is essentially creating options for dialogues and searching for a mutually acceptable common ground. It may also act as a tactic promising some desired benefits in exchange of compliance.
- **Silent authority:** It works really well with individuals having considerable position power. A polite request is enough for the people who would certainly oblige.
- **Appealing to higher authority:** When people are in conflict that are not readily resolved, one party may resort to appealing to the higher authority.
- **Assertiveness:** This is the extreme opposite to silent authority where the person trying to influence is crying hoarse like 'You know, I am the boss and not you!' this is an effort to establish the authority explicitly. It is an open threat and relies heavily on punishment or the fear of it.
- **Sanctions:** This tactic relies on the use of organizational rewards and/or punishment to regulate someone's behaviour.

It is perhaps wise to remember that too much use of 'hard' tactics such as assertiveness or sanctioning may not be very effective as these breed resentment and hostility and worst, these tend to become ineffective as people sort of 'get used to' these.

Managers' Issue: Mismatch Between Exertion of Power and Its After Effect

Once there was an aborted attempt of political coup against the Odisha Chief Minister Naveen Patnaik while he was away on an official visit to the United Kingdom. This was engineered by his close political advisor Piyari Mohan Mohapatra. Piyari Mohan, known as the 'Chanakya' of Odisha because of his sharp political brain, used to enjoy the confidence of the chief minister till he tried to portray himself larger than Naveen. Naveen stopped depending on Piyari less and less and started to take all important political decisions himself, thus cutting Piyari to his size. This evidently angered Piyari immensely and he plotted the coup against the chief minister with a number of MLAs and ministers one night at his house. But there was a gross mistake in calculating the support as hardly any of the 'discontent' MLAs and ministers were with Piyari in the morning. Worse even, they already sent the information to Naveen who came down immediately, cutting short his visit. On arriving, Naveen reshuffled his cabinet thoroughly and threw away the conspirators including Piyari.

PROBABLE EFFECTS OF POWER

People may have power but that does not mean that they can always use it at their will. Before applying power you have to assess the possible repercussions of applying it. Figure 7.2 may describe the contingencies of using power.

Whether it is possible to exert power or not depends on the following factors:

- **Substitutability:** If what an individual or group does can be easily performed by others, then it would be easy to exert power, as the replacement would be easy. If, on the other hand, the individual or the group cannot be readily replaced by others, it is not so easy to exert power. Thus, if it is possible to get alternative sources of skill, information or resources, the concerned individual or the group will have less power.
- **Centrality:** The department or the subunits that are most central to the flow of work will possess more power than other. Thus, the software development team in an IT company will wield more power than perhaps the HR group.
- **Visibility:** Even someone having access to power is not enough. It has to be seen by the people around to be able to appreciate the degree of power he enjoys. Thus, a back office service provider often tends to be overlooked. People who stay longer time in the office (irrespective of the real contribution made) have more chances of being noticed by the superiors.
- **Discretion:** People who enjoy greater freedom of deciding the pace or flow of their work or other resources (irrespective of their designation or positional power) are believed to have more power than others.

Manager's Essence: Misjudgement About the Power Balance

The most visible group of employees in an airline is undoubtedly the pilots. As a natural consequence, they wield a lot of power in the industry. But their calculation of their own importance proved to be grossly inflated, as was seen in the recent agitation of the Air India pilots. Not only the strike was declared illegal by the ministry of civil aviation, AI, the national carrier of India, sacked a number of striking pilots, and their association was also derecognized by the government. The power balance in this case was certainly tilted against the agitating pilots.

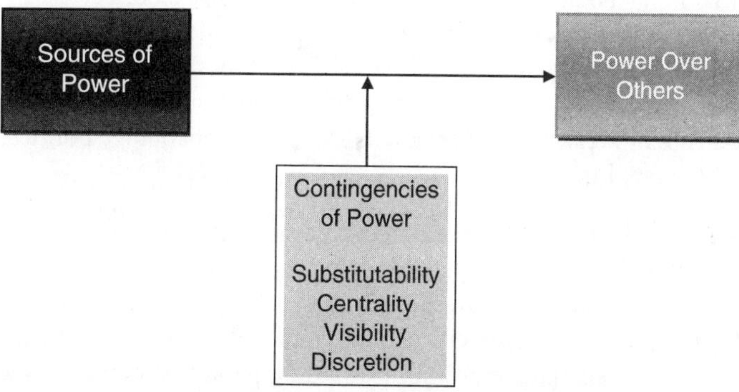

Figure 7.2 Contingencies of Power

ORGANIZATIONAL POLITICS

What is politics? The difference between the so-called 'effectiveness' and organizational politics often seems to be rather thin. However, most authors agree on the following as the behavioural syndrome of organizational politics, which employ different forms of influencing as discussed in the previous section.

- Behaviour that is beyond the legitimate role expectations.
- Behaviour that facilitates distribution of organizational rewards, even at the expense of organizational well-being.
- Behaviour that is deliberately adopted to capture and maintain power.
- Behaviour that others perceive as self-serving or for personal gain, even harming others' interest.

The amount of organizational politics that will take place in an organization depends on various factors, which can be put into two broad categories: individual and organizational.

Individual Factors

Some of the personal characteristics are found to be associated with political behaviour. These are:

- *High need for power* is the driving force of some type of people who would always seek to acquire power wherever they go. These people would always indulge in organizational politics as they crave for power.
- Individuals *high in Machiavellianism* or those who believe deceit is an acceptable and legitimate way to influence others. These people will have fewer scruples and would start politics wherever they go because such is their nature.
- People with *high internal locus of control* tend to believe that they are responsible for their fate and believe in their ability to achieve anything under the sun, or almost. The internals are, therefore, found to use influence tactics more than the externals, who tend to resign on their destiny instead.

Organizational Factors

- **Ambiguous job expectations:** If the job expectations are not clearly spelt out, there might be a lot of organizational politics at play. As a result, the individual may often feel harassed as whatever he does or strives to do may be dismissed as 'useless' without any clue.
- **Bottlenecks in the communication process:** If the communication channels are not free flowing and have bottlenecks to restrict or even distort the flow, this would surely result in organizational politics as some people having access to more information would certainly enjoy a better position.
- **Absence of good role models:** If the individuals at the helm encourage politics, it would be almost impossible not to have politics.

If the authority honestly wishes to curb politics in an organization, they should *firstly* start the selection process very carefully, trying to eliminate people who have a tendency to create politics in the workplace. *Secondly*, they should scrutinize the internal process and check the organizational climate for keeping it free from politics. More specifically, they should try to be clear and transparent in their policies and take a vow not to encourage politics. Providing good role models, especially at the higher level, would help establishing a positive and politics-free culture in the organization.

QUESTIONS

1. Define power in the context of an organization. Identify the different sources of power. Suggest an effective use of power in a service industry.
2. Think of two situations from your personal experience: (a) when you had power to influence the behaviour of your junior colleague; (b) when he has the power to influence you. In each case, list down the probable source power for both the individuals.
3. Performance appraisal process is often believed to create political behaviour in an organization. Suggest ways to minimize politics in this instance.
4. Based on your experience in being part of a teaching organization, describe a situation when a student had the power to influence the professor and his fellow students. Identify the sources of power bases.
5. Describe and discuss the influence tactics that are usually employed in an organization.

REFERENCES

1. J.R.P. French, and B. Raven, 'The Basis of Social Power' in D. Cartwright (ed.), *Studies in Social Power* (Ann Arbour: Institute for Social Research, University of Michigan, 1959).
2. D. Hellriegel, J.W. Slocum (Jr.), and R.W. Woodman, *Organizational Behavior* (South-Western, 2001).
3. J.M. Ivancevich, R. Konopaske, and M.T. Matteson, *Organizational Behavior* (Tata McGraw-Hill, 2005).
4. S.L. McShane, M.A.V. Glinow, and R. Sharma, *Organizational Behavior* (Tata McGraw-Hill, 2005).
5. McShane, S. L. and Glinow, M. A. V. (2005). *Organizational Behaviour: Emerging Realities for the Workplace Revolution* (McGraw-Hill).

Case Study: At Daggers' End!

Rajeev Malhotra was moving up and down in his room chewing the cigar. He had really come to his wit's end as to what he should do with the director of his group of companies. He has never seen a more laidback fellow in his life! What he initially felt as the cool expertise of the person was nothing but plain and simple lethargy! But he knows that as he himself found the man out and went almost overboard to appoint him as the director of the entire group no one but he should be blamed. But he did not have any clue that it would backfire against him. Shuvendu Goswami had an impeccable track record and had been at the helm of a number of renowned companies in the country. He was an engineer by profession and had a management degree from USA. Shuvendu was definitely a highly intelligent and capable person, but the main charm of his personality was that he had a very congenial and relaxed temperament and was a perfect gentleman. These were the two qualities that attracted Rajeev to Shuvendu from the very first meeting, though he meticulously checked all the background information of Shuvendu before finally offering him the position in the group. Shuvendu also, in his turn, did not exactly jump with joy with the offer and took considerable time to finally accept the offer. But after he took charge, Rajeev felt relieved.

Rajeev had built up his business empire right from scratch. He had nobody to lean on. His father left his mother when he was only four. His mother taught in a school and raised him single handedly. The life they led was absolutely without frills. Two square meals a day were all that she could manage for them. The school fees were requited as he studied in his mom's school. Only thing that was not given to him in limited amount was his intelligence. He was terribly sharp from the very beginning though he never stood first or second because he was never studious. He put just that amount of effort in his studies that would pass him through. That was precisely the reason behind his opting for the commerce stream in graduation, though in his time with the scores that he secured in the school leaving exams anybody would certainly have opted for science. But Rajeev had his own plans for life. He knew that pursuing a science subject would eat up all his energy and he was certain that with just a minimum amount of effort he would easily get good score in graduation if he took commerce. And he did exactly that, saving his energy for something, which he knew he would be doing in his life. His classes in the college were in the morning and he had enough time in his hand during the day to start a small business of trading of his own from his graduation days.

That was the beginning. It is a long story how Rajeev built up his business of manufacturing paper mill equipment over time. His only asset was his intellect and a burning desire to rise to the top. And his driving force was his past. He could never forget the hardship he had to go through during his childhood days, nor could he ever forget the silent stigma he and his mother had to put up with as his father had deserted them. There was hardly any outward sign of all these, but Rajeev became a hard nut to crack. He was thoroughly disillusioned from the beginning of his life and was determined to live life on his own terms. His route to success was not always straight, but he never landed up into any big trouble, as he was intelligent enough to read the situations and assess the future. He started his business in a rather modest way and was thoroughly down to earth in his approach. He eventually set up his plant in the eastern suburb of the city, which was a 'state-of-the-art' manufacturing plant that employed nearly 500 people. That he was not from an engineering background never deterred Rajeev as he had an innate business sense and an ability to hunt talent. He was soft spoken and suave in his manner, but beneath his politeness lay a person who was ruthless, shrewd and exacting. Over the years Rajeev had come to be recognized as a pioneer in manufacturing paper mill machinery in the eastern region and became the sole supplier to the top paper mills.

His success in professional life, however, was not matched with his personal life. His mother died quite early at an age of 60 when Rajeev was just trying to establish himself. It always made Rajeev sad that his mother could not see the success that he eventually earned in life. In the family front, Rajeev was also not too lucky. He had a failed marriage and though he later settled down with his wife of the second marriage, it was only a lukewarm relationship that he had with her. In fact, he was a loner throughout his life.

When he first met Shuvendu he sensed that he is a person whom he can implicitly trust. Though their natures were poles apart, there was nevertheless a feeling of mutual admiration for each other. Shuvendu's background was diametrically opposite to Rajeev's. Shuvendu was the eldest son of a scrupulously honest school teacher who worked hard to instil in his children the basic

Indian value system of honesty and sacrifice and not to value materialistic prosperity too much. Simple living and high thinking was the motto of the family. And that was perhaps the reason why Shuvendu returned back to India after completing his MBA from a prestigious B-school in the United States without accepting lucrative job offers there. Back home, Shuvendu was always well recognized for his contributions wherever he worked. But he never was a showy type and would always rather underplay his achievements and success. Shuvendu was a methodical worker who loves to plan before he leaps. He did not like to take chance or live in any make-believe world. He likes to rely on his senses far more than any vague and brilliant ideas. It was in sharp contrast with Rajeev's outlook to the world. Rajeev was a dreamer and used to loathe working out the smallest details of anything he would think of.

When Shuvendu joined the group, the first thing he took up was to restructure the entire organization in a rational manner. Though he consulted Rajeev at every step, he was quite firm in his objective. Rajeev did not like this at all, particularly when Shuvendu suggested to remove one or two very 'trusted' men from the main office to a distant location, he objected vehemently. These two trusted men were used to actually feed Rajeev with all kinds of information and were in fact part of glorified 'organizational espionage system'. Needless to mention that these people were not too scrupulous and could use their closeness to the chairman in more ways than one. They used to brag about their closeness to the chairman and often terrorized the employees in various ways. Shuvendu could sense the undercurrents and did not press any more. But that was the point when the chasm between the two was first created. Next was the issue of managing the daily show. Rajeev had developed the habit of micromanaging and being into everything himself as he was used to take all the decisions single handedly. After he joined, Shuvendu tried to streamline the entire running in such a systematic way that it could take care of itself without the chairman's presence in petty matters. All these certainly relieved Rajeev from the unnecessary burden that he was shouldering for so long and left room for concentrating into real-important aspects such as policy-making and planning. But still Rajeev was not exactly happy. He felt like his power is being curbed by the 'intruder' who seemed to have his own independent way of functioning. He knew it was silly of him to think like that as Shuvendu was nobody than a hired hand in his company. Still he could not get over the feeling of insecurity.

The actual root of the chasm between the two was perhaps deeper than it looked. In fact, they both belonged to different schools of thought. Shuvendu thought it was his duty to relieve his boss who was paying him so much for running the show without disturbing him in any way. But Rajeev considered this rather an intrusion into his empire. In addition to this, as mentioned earlier, Rajeev was also a dreamer and used to have lofty ideas about the future. And he certainly liked to have 'yes men' around him who would adore his every word. Shuvendu was never near this group of people. He never seemed to be excited so much about any of the tall word plays that Rajeev liked to use. Even when he actually appreciated any of these, he would always play the devil's advocate and would rather ask very practical questions about those grand plans, as he was more concerned about the implementation of the same. These, however, irritated Rajeev the most. He was looking for someone who would appreciate him continuously. Whenever Shuvendu argued or wanted some clarifications from him, Rajeev never took it kindly.

The relation between the two deterioted further over the appraisal of an old timer in the company. Shuvendu wanted to transfer him to another office and did not recommend a raise in his salary as he considered him as a worthless employee. He was lazy and thrived in the organization only because of his closeness with the chairman with whom he was associated for a long time. He was also known to feed the chairman with lots of inside information. Rajeev was furious. He wished Shuvendu had minded his own business and told that too. Shuvendu stood up and left the boardroom where the two were having the close door meeting. Next day he sent his resignation letter through courier.

Questions

1. Why was Rajeev so angry with Shuvendu?
2. How could the final estrangement be avoided?

SKILLS AND COMPETENCIES REQUIRED OF EFFECTIVE CHANGE AGENTS

Following skills and competencies have been identified as essential qualities of change agents.

- **Diagnosing the problem:** The change agents must have an adequate understanding of both the business and the organization in order to identify the key performance issues and the possible impacts of these on both the long-term and short-term functioning of the organization.
- **Developing trusting relationship:** One of the most critical tasks of the change agent is to create an ambience of faith and mutual respect and to develop a trusting relationship with the client and the organizational members. It is evident that without this, there will be absolutely no progress.
- **Articulating organizational vision:** It is the task of the change agent not only to articulate and interpret the vision of the organization to the people but also to align their aspirations and motivate them.
- **Create teams and define leadership roles:** The change agents must be able to define the ongoing processes in the organization including communication, role modelling, reinforcement of desired behaviour in the context of the past history of the organization and the group dynamics in order to create and sustain effective teams and leaders.
- **Problem solving:** One essential skill of the change agent is to decipher the emotional and political overtones of the problems that arise in organizations. The task of a successful change agent is to enhance the sensitivity of the organizational members and involve them in collaborative problem solving as opposed to the prescriptive one.
- **Managing resistance to change and conflict:** As when the change agents would initiate changes in the organization in a deliberate and planned manner, people would instinctively try to resist those changes. These would also disrupt the old status quo and result in increased conflicts among people. The change agents must have the ability to tackle these change-induced problems effectively.
- **Risk taking:** The change agent must be able to take risks and tolerate ambiguity, as in changed situations things will have to chalk out anew and often without any cut and dried solutions.
- **Ability to change himself:** It would never work to urge others to change and maintain one's own status intact. The change agent must have the flexibility to change himself if that is required.

Chapter 8

Process of Employee Empowerment

Opening Case: The Valour of Employees that Saved Lives on a Day of Carnage

On 26 November 2008, during a high-profile corporate dinner party thrown at the second floor banquet hall of the Taj Mahal Palace Hotel in Mumbai, a young manager in charge of the party and her staff heard some gunshots. They initially thought that probably the sounds were coming from the crackers bursting at a nearby weeding, but soon they realized that something was terribly wrong. They realized that those were gunshots of the terrorists that had stormed into the Taj hotel. Sensing trouble, the manager and the staff took immediate charge of the guests' safety. Getting the doors locked and lights turned off, the manager asked the guests to lie on the floor under the tables and switch off their cell phones. She also insisted that husbands separate from wives to reduce the risk to families. The group stayed there all night, listening to the terrorists rampaging through the hotel, firing automatic weapons, hurling grenades and tearing down the place in the most savage manner. The staff and the young manager, hardly 24 in number, kept their cool and helped the guests the whole night. Early in the morning when a huge fire started engulfing the hotel, the group was forced to climb out the window. A fire crew located them, and helped them to be rescued quickly. The manager and the staff members evacuated the guests first, and were the last ones to leave. The manager later told that though she was the youngest, she still 'did her job'.

What is most striking in the above incident? Certainly the courage and ownership of the employees of the hotel! They took the decisions themselves regarding the safety of the guests and risked their own life. Nobody told them to do this, it was not written anywhere in the work manual, as the incident was indeed an unprecedented (and horrible!) one. But they did what *they* thought was right at the moment. They were, in fact felt, empowered to decide what was the need of the hour and simply did it. The result—the lives of so many innocent people getting saved and, in addition, they are the ones who put the name of the hotel in the league of 'caring' companies forever.

After reading this chapter, the reader will appreciate the need for employee empowerment and its impact on the organization. More specifically, he will understand the following:

LEARNING OBJECTIVES

- What is empowerment?
- Needs for employee empowerment
- Importance of employee empowerment
- Steps for employee empowerment
- Effects of employee empowerment

WHAT IS EMPOWERMENT?

Employee empowerment is viewed by researchers as an effort at creating a working environment where an employee is allowed to make his own decisions in specific work-related situations. Various scholars have concluded that employee empowerment steers the company to a winning position in the present day harsh and competitive corporate environment. The magnitude of the decisions taken by the employees can be big or small, but the employer ideally should stand by the employees and take the responsibility of the possible fallout of the decisions. The logic behind employee empowerment is to increase the level of employee involvement and participation and enhance their sense of responsibility and ownership towards the company. This helps in building employee morale and improve the quality of employees' work life. It seems rational to believe that when an employee feels involved and thinks he has the power to make some impact in the decision-making process of an organization, he will be more productive, loyal and more confident.

The concept of employee empowerment may be viewed as the legacy of the human relations movement in and around the 1930s. More specifically, it may be related to Douglas McGregor's 'Theory Y', which is essentially a manager's assumptions regarding human nature. Thus, while the more traditional approach seems to emphasize the general workforce's innate unwillingness to work and getting involved along with their inability to think properly and the take right decisions, Theory Y assumptions are found to be diametrically opposite. Here, we find the general belief that people across the organizational hierarchy do have intelligence, which is not necessarily lesser than their counterparts in the elevated positions in the organization. People, irrespective of their positions in the organizational hierarchy, are keen, alert, willing to work and accept responsibility. In fact, if they are deprived of taking responsibility and intellectually stimulating work assignments, they would feel bored and disinterested in the affairs of the organization. The situation today is even more so with more educated and qualified individuals coming to work than yesteryears' workforce. They certainly can take decisions within their area of operation and expertise, often much better than the higher-up individuals who are far away from the actual fields of operation. It is therefore imperative that people in charge of running the organization should never forget that the individuals they hire are not just an extra pair of hands but they also possess brains, and it would indeed be a great loss not to utilize those. On the contrary, if the minds of people would have been harnessed and engaged, it would have been much easier for organizations to achieve the projected goals and objectives, as there would have been more people truly working towards those. Not just that, allowing people assuming more responsibility would free their superiors to devote more time in solving bigger issues and problems rather than being engaged in day-to-day routine activities.

DEFINITION OF EMPLOYEE EMPOWERMENT

Employee empowerment is allowing the employees more discretion, that is, more power, authority, responsibility, resource and freedom to take decisions as well as solving work-related problems.

Employee empowerment is defined as allowing the employees more discretion, that is, more power, authority, responsibility, resource and freedom to take decisions as well as solving work-related problems. Rephrased differently, empowerment refers to the process of providing greater autonomy through sharing relevant information and provision of control over performance.

CHARACTERISTICS OF EMPLOYEE EMPOWERMENT

Some of the typical criteria of empowerment are perceived control over the work situation, self-efficacy or competence, sense of purpose and the meaningfulness of the job performed, scope for increased use of talent and trust.

- **Control over the work situation:** When employees feel that they can control their immediate work environment, it is easier for them to develop a sense of ownership and involvement than otherwise.
- **Self-efficacy:** Unless employees are confident of their ability to perform a job excellently, they would hardly come forward to face the challenge of doing it in the first place. But when they know they can, they would look forward to perform and would be willing to face the consequences, if any.
- **Sense of purpose:** The empowered employees know the significance of their job in the context of the entire organization as well as its impact on other related tasks. This would make him rightfully proud of his own input and thus more responsible.
- **Scope for increased use of talent:** The empowered employees, who have control over their work environment and the pace and way of doing their job, can use their talent which may have remained untapped so far. This would indeed enhance the happiness quotient of the individual employee, and the entire organization would naturally reap the benefit of increased and better levels of production.
- **Trust:** The organizational climate and the general ambience of trust are essential for the process of empowerment. People must have a faith in the system and their superiors that even if they fail in their effort and initiatives, they will get the required support from them. They must believe that the entire process would never turn out to be a blame game.

Concept Check

1. What is employee empowerment?
2. How would you understand whether the employees in an organization are truly empowered or not?

Manager's Essence: Red Rickshaw Revolution

Red Rickshaw Revolution at Vodafone is a unique effort to celebrate the achievements of inspirational women across the country and raise crucial funds for the NGOs which are working to empower women. On 9 March 2013, a day after the 'women's day', Laura, Carina and Sunita embarked on a nine-day rickshaw journey from Delhi to Mumbai, traveling over 1500 km spanning five states. Along the route, they discovered and encountered ordinary women doing extraordinary things across India, celebrating the achievements of amazing women and sharing their story with everybody. From learning self-defense to setting up new enterprises, Vodafone Foundation offers dynamic programmes to empower women in both Delhi and Mumbai and has pledged to match up to ₹85 lakhs of donations.

Vodafone Foundation in India is combining skills, resources and funding to build a brighter future for people who are currently unable to fulfill their potential. They recognize the power of mobile technology to address some of India's most pressing challenges and are using it to encourage innovation, share knowledge and improve lives. They focus on areas of greatest need and at a grand scale. They seek to empower women so that they can compete on an equal footing, to reach rural areas and support the people living there, and to provide new opportunities for education.

PROCESS OF EMPLOYEE EMPOWERMENT

It is, however, important to note that to enable employees to take initiatives and make decisions in the organization, it is imperative to bestow them with adequate authority and power. Before we progress any further, it is necessary to check the concept of power and delegation to fully understand the process of employee empowerment. The term *authority* refers to the rights inherent in any organizational position to give orders to the subordinates and expect that to be obeyed (Mukherjee, 2006). Delegation is imperative for empowerment, which is closely related to the concept of authority. Delegation refers to the process of assigning a portion of the managers' workload to their subordinates. This would work only if the manager gives his subordinates the required authority to enable them to accomplish the task. The basic purpose of delegation is to get more work done in lesser time. Delegation also helps to develop the subordinates as they are given more opportunity to exercise their decision-making ability and gain more access to relevant information. The process of delegation, however, is never an easy one. Potential barriers to delegation may be two-fold. In the first place, managers are often found to be reluctant to delegate because they are either too unorganized to decide what to delegate or they are apprehensive of the fact that the subordinates may perform the task better than them and thus would pose a threat on their status. Another reason for their unwillingness may be their lack of trust on the subordinates. The subordinates themselves might often resist delegation as they may view it as extra responsibility without any additional tangible reward. They would want to avoid taking risks and may fear the reprimands from the superiors for any mistakes they might commit in the process.

Delegation refers to the process of assigning a portion of the managers' workload to their subordinates.

However, it is to be kept in mind that empowerment is not simply the delegation of tasks only. It refers to a trusting relationship between the management and employees, which is the offshoot of a continuous process built over time. The empowered employees do not need a prod from higher authorities for their initiatives. They are self-directed and self-controlled. Empowerment is aimed at developing and actualizing the potential of the employees by handing over to them the power of control. Thus, they are the ones who are allowed to choose their goals and make decisions regarding the accomplishment of tasks, including setting the pace of work.

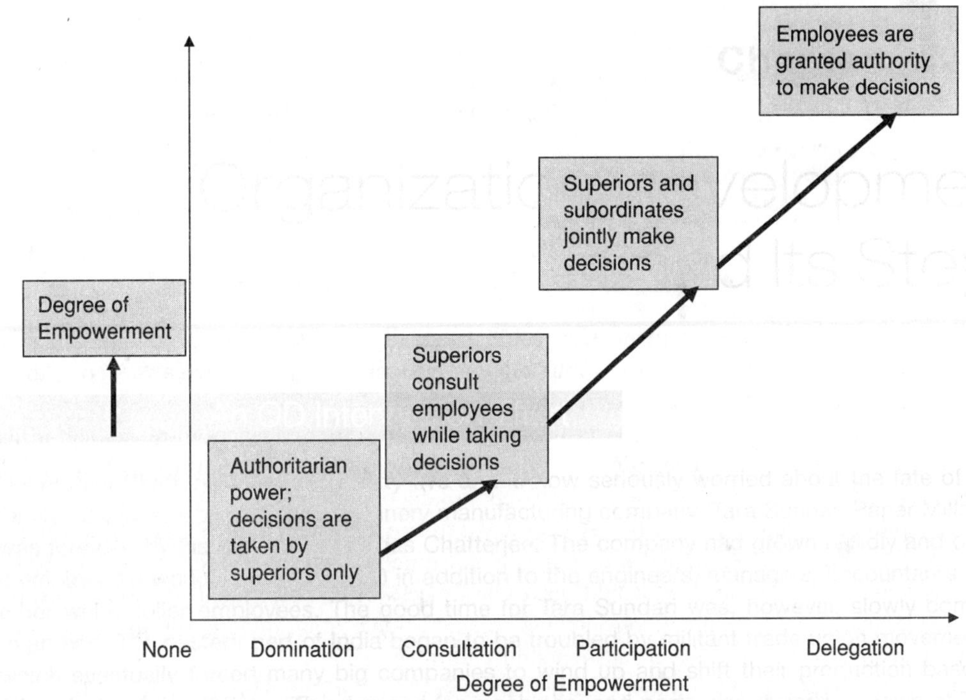

Figure 8.1 Phases of Employee Empowerment

In an organizational setting, the process of employee empowerment is usually found to go through different phases. Thus, from absolute control or domination by the superiors, employees may move towards delegation through phases such as consultation and participation, as shown in Figure 8.1.

One has to note that employee empowerment does not take place overnight neither it is a magical process. It has to be created with a lot of genuine effort on the part of the management. It has to be kept in mind that not every employee can be empowered, as it is a function of the perceived feeling of self-efficacy on the part of the employee and a sense of control over the ways of the work environment. However, the self-efficacy of the employees can certainly be enhanced in the organization by providing the scope for excellent training. If these two factors—feeling of self-efficacy, which is directly related to the amount and quality of training provided by the organization, and some degree of controlling power to determine the way and pace of their functioning—were found to be absent, no amount of effort would result in employee empowerment in an organization. When these two factors are found to be present, it will lead to the perception of empowerment in the mind of the employees. They will now believe that they can truly make an impact on the organizational environment and can take charge of the situation. This would eventually result in enhanced performance and a sense of commitment towards the organization.

The first step towards employee empowerment, as Figure 8.2 suggests, is to remove the conditions that might lead to the feeling of powerlessness among the employees. If the employees feel they can hardly make any impact in the organizational life, they would naturally refrain from taking any initiative. The role of the organization is of immense importance in this context. More specifically, it depends on the nature of leadership that is prevalent in the organization. If the leaders or people in the top positions of the organization genuinely want the employees to feel empowered, they would certainly

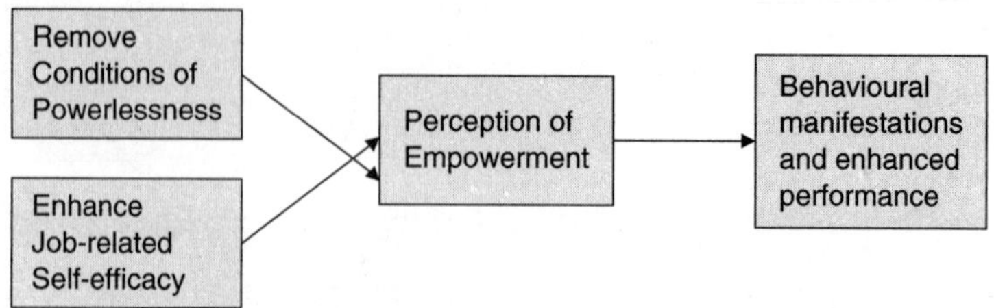

Figure 8.2 Process of Employee Empowerment

encourage the practice of empowerment. This would eventually be reflected in the major organizational policies such as the reward and compensation policy or designing the job in such a way so as to allow more scope for individual discretion and freedom.

The next step towards employee empowerment is to make an effort to enhance job-related self-efficacy. The enhanced competence and capability would instil a sense of confidence in the employees. These can only be possible with the provision of increased training opportunities in the organization. In addition, the employees should also be provided with good role models within the organization whom they should ideally follow. These, along with adequate and timely feedback regarding their performance and support from the organization, would make the process of empowerment possible. Needless to say, empowerment would require a considerable amount of delegation of authority to be given to the employees, with a strong emphasis on accountability for their actions.

Apart from delegation and employee participation in the organizational decision-making process, true empowerment also encourages employee self-management. These are independent work groups with the full responsibility of managing the entire activities of the group, right from selecting the members, identifying the resources, deciding on the pace and pattern of working, everything lying with them only. The sole objective of the self-managed teams is to achieve the stated goals set for them, with a considerable amount of discretion being given to them. However, self-managed teams can never be formed with people who lack self-motivation, a high level of competency and a sense of commitment and self-discipline.

Effort should also be made to enrich the jobs with more scope for utilizing one's talents. It would encourage the employees if they can have frequent and relevant feedback vis-à-vis their performance.

But above all, it is the culture and ambience of the organization that would ultimately decide whether employees truly feel empowered or not. Organizational culture plays a decidedly critical role in making empowerment possible. It certainly requires a supportive and trusting organizational culture, where employees would try out things on their own without a nagging suspicion and a feeling of possible 'blame game' and 'fixing' people up syndromes that they might have to face later.

Thus, to sum up, following are some specific actions that might encourage the process of employee empowerment in an organization:

- Delegation of authority
- Accountability
- Quality of leadership
- Reward system
- Job design
- Participative decision making and goal setting
- Employee training and development

- Encouragement to create self-managed work teams
- Job enrichment and intrinsic feedback
- Supportive and trusting organizational culture with less amount of formalities

CHARACTERISTICS OF EMPOWERED ORGANIZATIONS

Empowered organizations are typically different from traditional organizations in more ways than one. The following section gives a broad overview of the major characteristics of empowered organizations.

- **Organizational structure:** Organizations that encourage empowerment are mostly found to have flatter organizational structure. Unlike organizations with tall bureaucratic structure, today's organizations have fewer layers or hierarchies, which enable them to adapt to changes faster and more effectively. In addition, this lessens the degree of formality and the so-called red tapism, thus allowing more discretion and flexibility to the employees.
- **Organizational culture:** As mentioned earlier, the culture of the organization stands out most. Organizations where employee empowerment is found to thrive well seem to be quite different. More teamwork is found there, with an environment of trust and openness. People do not hesitate to disagree with an open mind to search for common ground and to look beyond narrow individual and often conflicting goals, but rather focus on superordinate goals. Employees are committed and do not hesitate to own up the consequences of their decisions. Employee creativity is hugely appreciated and encouraged.
- **Recruitment and selection:** The recruitment and final selection processes in organizations where employee empowerment is practised are conducted with extra care so that new recruits' mindsets match with those of the existing employees' and they respond favourably to the process and culture of empowerment.
- **Focus on goal achievement:** In empowered organizations, emphasis is given on goal achievement and the binding nitty-gritty of the processes are far too less compared to the traditional organizations. Flexibility in the pace and schedule of work are often encouraged.

The resultant effects of employee empowerment are manifold. The level of employee satisfaction is higher with a significantly lower rate of employee turnover. The productivity is usually higher with uniform good quality products or services rendered by the organization, and people in general tend to show uncompromising integrity and unflinching loyalty towards the organization.

BENEFITS OF EMPOWERMENT

The effect of employee empowerment is multifaceted. Empowered employees take initiatives and ownership and stand by their own actions and decisions, become more responsible and feel committed to the organization. They become more capable and can contribute to the development of the organization often in a significant way. Employee participation in the goal-setting process also increases in an organization that believes in employee empowerment. This may result in obtaining valuable inputs from the employees and enhancing employee commitment. In addition, the level of self-respect of the empowered employees is certainly higher and they do command respect from others as well.

The impact of employee empowerment on the overall organizational outcomes is indeed positive. Empowered employees are often found to be more satisfied with their jobs in general, and as a consequence employee absenteeism and turnover both tend to drop. The level of conflicts with superiors is also found to decrease considerably and the overall productivity tends to go up because of increased levels of competence of the employees.

Concept Check

1. What are the benefits of employee empowerment for the organization?
2. Which one would you consider most important?

PROBLEMS OF EMPLOYEE EMPOWERMENT

Employee empowerment, however, is not without its flip sides. There could be several disadvantages of employee empowerment in the organizations. More specifically, these are as follows:

- **Potential abuse of increased power:** As noted earlier, empowered employees are given more power and allowed more amount of discretion in their job. Now, if they are not truly conscientious and fail to exert adequate self-control, the increased power might be misused for personal gains.
- **Chances for focusing on one's own success:** The empowered employee may tend to focus all its effort towards his own success rather than ensuring the success of the team of which he is a part. At the same time, it may require spending too much time with the group, with a possibility of hampering the regular workflow.
- **Support and cooperation of the superiors:** The process of empowerment depends, to a great extent, on delegation of authority. In addition to the amount of authority bestowed upon them, the superior manager must always stand by them, particularly in the time of any difficulty as might be faced by the employees.
- **Increased training cost:** Since empowerment demands increased skills and competencies of the individual employees, more training has to be provided to them, and that certainly entails an increased cost for the organization.
- **Increased conflict and power struggle:** As empowered employees enjoy a considerable amount of freedom, the possibility of conflict with the superiors and peers may increase because of each one's independent ways of functioning.
- **Lack of knowledge:** Not every group of employees can be empowered as only the capable ones may do justice to the enhanced status. If their knowledge base is not sound enough and their capability is questionable, then they would certainly not be worth of the empowered situation.
- **Employees must accept the concept first:** The concept of empowerment is relatively new and might not be exactly compatible with the existing ideas of the employees. Imposing it on them and rushing them through the process would never be a good idea and would certainly not help implement effective empowerment. This should first be explained to them and expectations from them should be spelt out clearly. This would help them understand and accept the idea.
- **Too much responsibility for the employees:** Employee empowerment requires shouldering more responsibility by the employees, which may not be directly related to the enhancement of pay or other tangible benefits. It would be a mistake to presume that every employee would exactly look forward to be empowered.
- **Decisions on the basis of personality:** Decisions taken by the empowered employees may be taken on the basis of their personality, with the associated risks of possible bias.

Concept Check

1. What are the potential problems of employee empowerment?
2. Suggest ways to overcome these in an organizational set-up.

STEPS OF EMPOWERMENT

The process of empowerment is never easy and requires careful planning before effective implementation. The most challenging step of empowerment is preparing the people to accept the change in mindset. The various steps of empowerment may be described as follows:

- **To explain the needs for change to the concerned employees:** The first step towards implementing empowerment is to convince the people regarding the need for change. As noted earlier, people generally resist change and want to maintain the status quo.
- **To bring in changes in senior managers' behaviour too:** Change is essentially a two-way process. If the employees change their pattern of work behaviour and accept more responsibility, people at the top would also have to change their behaviour accordingly. They should be ready to support the changed behaviour and respect their effort.
- **To determine the areas where employees can take better decisions:** The areas where employees are directly related would be the areas they can offer most valuable inputs. These would have to be identified before any attempt towards empowerment is made.
- **To establish natural work teams:** It is always better to allow individuals to work with people of their choice. The mutual bonding and likeability will help enhance their performance.
- **To share relevant information:** Information is power today. If employees have difficulty in accessing relevant information, all their efforts would be futile, and the entire process of empowerment will remain at the very superficial level only.
- **To select the right people:** Not everyone can be empowered. Those who have adequate skills and competencies and have a sense of commitment can be considered for empowerment. So there has to be a judicious selection of the people who can be entrusted with empowerment.
- **To provide adequate training:** Employees' skills and competencies should always be updated through frequent and rigorous training processes.
- **To communicate expectations:** Expectations from employees should always be clearly spelt out. They should be clearly told what they must accomplish and what should be the changed patterns of behaviour.
- **To align reward and recognition policies:** Employees must be given an impetus if the organization really wishes them to be truly empowered. To sustain their effort, their performance should be properly rewarded.
- **To have patience and expect problems:** Empowerment is indeed an attempt to change. As in every change scenario, the effort would hardly be foolproof, at least at the beginning. So senior people in charge of the organization must be patient and willing to pitch in whenever some problems crop up.

EMPOWERMENT AND ORGANIZATION DEVELOPMENT

Any effort of organization development depends primarily on the extent of individual development that may take place in the organization. As discussed in the earlier chapter, OD is essentially a planned change initiative that addresses the issues of the belief and value system prevailing in the organization as well as the individual attitudes. The establishment of employee empowerment in an organization brings in the changes that encompass the entire organization and indeed puts it in the path of development. In this context, employee empowerment may certainly be viewed as a step towards organization development.

GLOSSARY

- **Employee empowerment:** The process of providing greater autonomy through sharing relevant information and provision of control over performance.
- **Authority:** The formal power that is bestowed upon an individual by which they can legitimately command obedience from their subordinates.
- **Delegation:** The process of assigning a portion of the managers' workload to their subordinates.
- **Self-managed teams:** Independent work groups with the full responsibility of managing the entire activities of the group.
- **Self-efficacy:** A sense of confidence in the employees that results from increased competence and capability of an individual.
- **Employee participation:** Allowing the employees to take part in the organizational decision-making process.
- **Organizational culture:** A system of shared meaning held by the majority of members that distinguishes the organization from others.

QUESTIONS

1. What is meant by employee empowerment?
2. Do you think employee empowerment is necessary for the organization? Support your views.
3. What are the benefits of employee empowerment? What are its potential problems?
4. Identify the steps of employee empowerment.
5. Describe the typical characteristics of an empowered organization.

REFERENCES

1. D. McGregor, *Human Side of the Enterprise* (McGraw-Hill, 1960, New York).
2. K. Mukherjee, *Principles of Management and Organizational Behavior*, Second Edition (Tata McGraw-Hill, 2006, New Delhi).
3. R. S. Rao, *Essentials of HR and IR: Texts, Cases and Games* (Mumbai, Himalayan Publishing House, 2008).

Case Study: 'Whose Job Is It Anyway?'

Ajay Ghosh graduated in mechanical engineering from one of the premier engineering colleges in Eastern India. Ajay has always been a very good student right from his school days and secured a high rank in the entrance examination for studying engineering. He moved out of his native village in a southern district in Bengal to take admission in the famous engineering college near Kolkata. He was from a middle-income Bengali family. His father was a teacher in a primary school from which he retired as an assistant headmaster. His mother, a homemaker, used to toil from morning to night to keep everyone happy in the family. Ajay's younger sister is in Class VIII in the local school.

Ajay got a job in a manufacturing company in the outskirts of Delhi as a shop floor supervisor. Ajay is a slightly built, mild natured, decent person who strongly believes in respecting people and treating them as equals wherever they came from. He disliked bullying others and genuinely appreciated individuality. His first day at the shop floor however was indeed an experience, perhaps a bit scary too. There were around 100 people when he entered the factory shed at 8 a.m. All of them were tall and strongly built, with a number of them being rather hefty. They were a mix of skilled and non-skilled workers with a low level of formal education. The practice in the shop floor was to start the day after allocating the required resources to the workers along with setting their day's target in line with the overall weekly targets. The jobs were largely assembling and needless to say bit monotonous. He asked the team leaders of each work to come forward, meet him and take the material and the work chart. True to his tradition, he certainly requested them in a polite and civil language, and addressed them 'aap' and certainly not 'tu'! The people, junior and senior ones alike, looked genuinely surprised. They were listening to Ajay quietly when he distributed the materials to them and then moved to the individual workstations, without a word or even a nod. Then they all started talking among themselves across their workstations in booming voices, which drowned the noise in the shop floor. Ajay could hardly follow what they were talking as they were speaking in their local dialect, but he nevertheless had a sneaking suspicion that they were discussing him only and that too perhaps not very kindly. However, things settled down later and there were no further incidents that day. The days went on the same way. Ajay used to come to the factory sharp at 8 a.m., allot the day's work to the workers who in turn would take these without a single word or a nod, go back to their work stations and have a huge uproar and loud laughter among themselves before starting the day's work. They all were good and sincere workers. They would never shark from their duties and work-related responsibilities. But they would hardly talk to Ajay. They were never rude or abusive, but it seemed that they preferred to maintain a distance from him. Ajay certainly felt a bit low. This was his first job, he had left his native state to come so far for work, but the apparent coldness at the workplace was sitting heavily on him.

So one day Ajay came to the factory with an idea of involving the workers in the day's job more whole-heartedly. Before distributing the day's work and the target for the day, he called the team leaders. He asked them what they would like to do that day. He explained that they could have a choice and decide what they would start with and how would they like to progress through the day. There was absolute silence! They did not speak a word and looked incredulously at him. If Ajay was not wrong, there was indeed a look of contempt in their eyes. For that day, Ajay did not press the matter any further and distributed their job and materials to the team leaders as was the usual practice. But he was determined to involve the people in the day-to-day functioning of the organization more. He believed that they were certainly a capable workgroup and quite loyal to the organization, as indicated by the low rate of turnover in the company. The next day he called them again and repeated the same question, 'What do you want to do today and how would you go about that? Please decide yourself.' This time, the looks of the people slowly became more menacing. They slowly closed around Ajay before they answered anything. The 5 feet 6 inches frail figure of the first class engineer could hardly be seen as the 6-feet tall, heavy built Northern people surrounded him. Baldeb, the most senior among them, pointed a finger to Ajay and burst out, 'What do you mean, "decide what you would do today?" That's your job Sab to tell us what is to be done a day. You are paid a hefty sum of money for doing just that, don't ya know that? Why should we do your job?' Though none of them touched him, the entire scene nevertheless was so menacing and nerve racking that when Ajay came to his quarter that evening, he had a very high temperature. He had to take leave for a week, and after recovering he tendered his resignation letter to the plant manager, Mr Singh. Mr Singh looked at him for some time before responding. He said at last, 'I was fearing this from the time you joined. I knew you would not be able to work in this place. Go back to your place and find a job that would suit your nature.'

Questions

1. Why did Ajay's attempt to empowerment fail?
2. What could Ajay try differently?

Chapter **9**

Management of Diversity Including Gender Issues and Cross-cultural Dynamics

Opening Case: Surviving in a Melting Pot of Culture

Sankaran was born in a middle-class orthodox Tamil Brahmin family. His father, Shibaraman, was a school teacher and his mother, Sabitri, a homemaker. Sankaran's two elder sisters were married rather early, right after their graduation. Sankaran was the youngest in the family. Though they were never rich, Sankaran's every need was well taken care of. He never had to do anything except study. After his senior school leaving examination from the local school, Sankaran enrolled in the Department of Computer Engineering at the university engineering college. Before he wrote his final semester examination, he was selected by a reputed multinational company. He was trained for three months in Mumbai before getting a posting in Hyderabad. Sankaran was learning a lot on the job, not only about programming and designing, but also about how to work with the diverse work group he was with. His team consisted of people from all corners of the country. There were only two girls in the team of 11, one from Delhi and another from UP, under team leader Roy, who was from Bengal. Sankaran was doing very well as he was intelligent, hard-working and sincere. In less than a year, Sankaran found himself working in a team with people much elder to him. Before he completed his second year on the job, Sankaran was included in a selected core team that went to New Jersey to the company's on-sight project. It was indeed a wonderful experience for him. Born in a small town near Chennai, he was now in a sea that consisted of widely different types of people—of various age, nationality, gender, look and cultural orientation—all were there in the melting pot named the United States of America. Not only did Sankaran learn how to work with so many different types of people and understand each other, but he also learned how to look after himself. He became an expert in household activities—cooking, washing, cleaning, shopping and all—which were marked typically as 'women's job' and were never ventured into by men in his circle. He missed his family and particularly his mother, but he was Indeed vastly enjoying the offshore experience as well.

The story of Sankaran was by no way unusual for a boy of his age. In the global village we are in today, this is happening quite often all around us. The geographical borders are porous and people's mobility is certainly much more than yesteryears'. What is interesting to note is the necessity to work with people from different backgrounds.

After reading the chapter, you would know more on this. More specifically, you will learn the following:

LEARNING OBJECTIVES

- What is diversity?
- How does management of diversity lend competitive advantage to an organization?
- What might happen if the work force diversity is not encouraged and properly managed?
- Some special issues in diversity—age, gender, multiculturalism.

There is an increasing amount of diversity in the workplace today which stands in stark difference with yesteryears. If we compare today's workforce with what it was roughly 15 years back, we would find that the number of women professionals has increased significantly. The level of formal education in the present workforce has also increased considerably and there is more mobility among the people. In any metropolitan city, there would always be people from across the country and often from outside. The number of older people who come to work today is much greater, often after completing a career and re-joining the work after retiring from their jobs, as they still keep quite fit and healthy. Now, people belonging to the backward and underprivileged category are found to be present in the working population in a fair proportion, because of the rights of reservation in the country that encourage them to join the mainstream. The family structures have also changed significantly over the years. From the traditional joint family set-ups to nuclear families, comprising only the husband, wife and the children are the most common today along with a sizable number of divorced individuals and single parents. In addition, there are a good number of people with a single or more disabilities who can work, and have to be given employment if they seek by the employment law of the country.

As a result, today's work force is a rich mix of people from various backgrounds. If the business is to survive and flourish, the people at the helm of the organizations must recognize the increasingly diversified workgroups today and discover ways to harness their talents in the diversity. It will not only lend a strong competitive edge to the company, but will also create a sense of pride and belongingness to the minds of the employees, which are immensely crucial for long-term sustainability.

Over the decades, when faced with steep competition from players across the globe, companies have at last recognized that their employees are their biggest assets. Nobody can dare to compromise on the quality of their products or services, as everybody else would maintain a high level of quality to hold their customers. It is that 'extra' that companies are now relying on and are keen to offer, as that only may create the favourable impression so crucial for keeping the customer base intact. And it is the people, the 'human face of the enterprise', that becomes critical in that context. A stable and skilled army of workforce who are dedicated to their organization can only offer that extra advantage—be it in the form of warm courtesy or the willingness to serve them better. And this would certainly make the world of difference so critical for surviving in the market war. Thus, in order to survive and grow in this era of harsh and cut-throat competition, companies must get the best and brightest of employees who are not only superbly skilled and have the ability to handle latest technologies, but also have the willingness to contribute and a sense of commitment towards their organization.

DEFINITION OF DIVERSITY

The term 'diversity' broadly implies that every individual is unique though each one shares a commonality with respect to biological and environmental characteristics. Thus, all of us are similar to the other one, in spite of huge differences that separate us.

The issue of diversity is indeed pertinent for a country like India. Widely different cultures coexist quite happily and peacefully in the nation, as one of the great poets has rightly pointed out 'the similarity in spite of the differences'. However, as noted earlier, diversity does not mean only 'cultural diversity'. There are various sources of diversity that differentiate one individual from the other ones. These may be described as follows:

- **Socio-economic status:** This refers to the differences due to the economic status and social backgrounds of individuals. Today, there is a greater amount of social mobility where anyone irrespective of his background can get good education and be able to climb up the levels of social hierarchy.
- **Age:** Nowadays, a number of retired people join the workforce for a second run of their career. Due to advancements in medical sciences, better provision for food and nutrition and a greater awareness for health and hygiene, people in general are found to remain fit for longer.
- **Gender:** More women are found to come to work because of better educational openings.
- **Caste:** Ours is a nation where there are so many castes. In addition to the four main castes that were there from the ancient times, there are numerous other divisions and subdivisions in the caste systems. Some castes are now protected by the law for employment and are provided with various other facilities. While recruiting, companies must fulfil the 'quota' as specified, the violation of which would take the organization to court of law.
- **Religion:** India being a secular country, people of different religious faiths coexist, with some religions enjoying the 'minority' status that would grant them substantial privileges.
- **Disabilities:** The number of people having one or more disabilities who now come to work has increased significantly. They cannot be discriminated against by law.
- **Marital status:** The number of divorces is on the rise. Single parenthood is also quite common.
- **Affectional orientation:** Some percentage of the workforce may be found to be gay or lesbian.

In this context, the term diversity has three major thrusts leading to three working definitions:

1. Providing 'equal employment opportunities' and 'affirmative actions' for all.
2. The recruitment and selection of minority castes and women.
3. The management of individuals from different cultures.

The first definition represents a rather narrow view of diversity and is found in organizations that follow the rules just to avoid complications, but who do not truly encourage diversity. The second definition helps to ensure that the diversity is protected by law, but organizations that subscribe to the third definition are the ones who are the true champions of diversity.

Primary vs Secondary Dimensions of Diversity

According to Loden and Rosener (1991), there are two dimensions of diversity—primary and secondary. *Primary dimensions* are those characteristics that one is born with and influences us significantly. These include age, gender, race, caste and physical qualities. *Secondary dimensions* are those that are picked up or modified as one progresses in life. These are education, income, geographic locations, marital status, military experience, work experience and parental status. All these are found to have strong impacts on our lives. In fact, these effects are the interactions that are created between the primary and secondary dimensions of diversity rather than the effect of a single factor.

Concept Check

1. What are the primary and secondary dimensions of diversity?
2. How do these two interplay?

Prejudices and Stereotypes

Stereotyping may be described as the process of 'assigning traits to people based on their membership in a social category', and not exactly on the basis of individual experiences. Stereotyping is based on the primary dimensions of diversity, such as age, gender or national origins. These are developed out of our strong need to understand and predict others' behaviour and this becomes easier once we can safely put them under one category or the other, such as young/old, male/female and so on. The problems with stereotyping are that these are rigid and often distorted generalizations as these are devoid of any direct interactional experience. These beliefs are usually handed over from significant others in our life, such as parents, other elders in the family, or teachers and friends at an early age, and become fixed ideas. These could be as innocuous a statement like 'girls should always be modest' to a more damaging one as 'people from a particular state are shrewd'. Stereotyping thrives on the basis of selective perception, when only those facts are accepted that are in line with stereotyped ideas, while others are ignored. Stereotyping does not acknowledge people's individuality and limits their potential, and people are often found to act as they are expected to. If you dismiss somebody as worthless and do not hope anything great from him, he will certainly prove himself truly worthless, thus confirming the expectations.

Self-fulfilling prophecy: *when people tend to act as it is expected from them.*

Negative stereotyping gives rise to prejudice. In prejudice, we tend to feel superior to those who are different from us in some way or the other. There is often the tendency to look down upon people from some nationality or caste or a particular gender. These are indeed found in the organizational set up as well which inhibit people from putting in their best in the workplace. So any organization which values diversity and wants to leverage the differences towards the achievement of organizational goals must identify these and work hard to eradicate them.

Stereotyping: *Attributing typical assumed characteristics to people belonging to a particular class to have.*

In spite of the laws protecting the minority, including women and other backward and underprivileged community, in actual work situation these people still face discrimination.

- *Glass Ceiling*: Though a large number of women and other minority groups are found in the working population today, very few of them are found to make it to the top of large organizations (Stoner, et al. 1995). They can well see the opportunities above but cannot reach there. That is why this is called 'glass ceiling'.

Glass ceiling: *Even when women and people from minority categories are hired in organizations, they face difficulties in getting promoted to senior levels, as if there is an invisible barrier. They can see the opportunities above, but cannot reach them.*

Revolving door syndrome: *Short tenure of work for people from minorities or reserved categories who cannot stay, as they feel uncomfortable in the organization's environment.*

Earning gap: *Discrepancy between earning the power of workers of similar skill level and educational background but belonging to different races.*

- *Revolving Door Syndrome*: Even when women and people belonging to the minority groups get a chance to be employed, they often feel frustrated with the lack of opportunities for career progression. In addition, there is always an undercurrent of thinly disguised contempt and even hostility towards them, which often compel them to leave the job. This is termed as 'revolving door syndrome' when people are found to join but not staying in the organization for long (Stoner, et al., 1995).
- *Earning Gap*: It is a fact that discrepancies may sometimes exist between the earning power between employees of similar background but being women or belonging to the backward or minority category or from lower castes. The racial discrimination is also found to exist and result in disparity in earning. This is referred to as 'earning gap'.

Assimilation vs Valuing Diversity

The best practice adopted by organizations towards managing diversity used to be assimilating the diverse group in the mainstream, thus forcing them to conform to the characteristics of the dominant groups. In the US the prevalent tendency is to measure everyone against the 'white male standard', and bulldozing all the typicality of the diverse population into a homogeneous standard. Assimilation can never be the ideal approach as there is always a perceived feeling of superiority of the dominant group. The pressure of conformity on the diverse group tends to diminish and undermine their cultural backgrounds. We often find this happening to the NRI population, who adapt so completely to the countries they live in, thus suffering from a strong disconnect from their roots and cultural origins. When diversity is not valued, there is always a tendency to undermine their successes and emphasize their mistakes instead. Women and people from minority background are often found to languish in the middle management level with fewer possibilities for career growth. The glass ceiling for women and the revolving door syndrome for employees appointed on the basis of reservations are glaring examples of this.

Assimilation may create enormous pressure on the diverse group and may often result in their eventually quitting the job. This does not help the dominant group either. This reinforces their mistaken idea of superiority and generates the stereotyping and prejudices in the workplace, which is certainly not desirable by any chance.

Valuing diversity and acknowledging the fundamental differences and uniqueness is the first step towards positive management of diversity in any workplace. Allowing equal opportunities to all diverse groups is only complying with the laws of the land and protecting the diverse groups from discriminations. But valuing diversity goes beyond this, and if well managed it would reap rich contributions from the diverse groups.

MANAGING DIVERSITY

Well-managed diversity would not only lead to considerable benefits for the companies, but not doing so may actually incur a considerable cost for them in terms of high employee turnover and subsequently escalated costs of recruitment, selection and training. Possible benefits for well-managed diversity may be as follows:

- **Competitive advantages:** If the diverse groups are given due respect and allowed to grow within the organization, the company would have a greater chance of attaining sustainable competitive advantages over others. Employee satisfaction and commitment are found to be reflected in lesser rates of absenteeism and turnover.

- **Procuring the best talent:** Managing diversity adequately would attract the best talents from such diverse groups as women, and people from minority and/or reserve categories.
- **Employee retention:** Initiating diversity training and valuing the diverse groups would enhance the company's image and goodwill significantly.
- **Reaching diverse customer base:** Having a diverse workforce will indeed help in reaching a diverse customer base, as the chance to pre-empt the customers' demands would be better.
- **Encouraging innovations:** The broader and richer experiences provided by diverse workforce would certainly improve problem solving and decision-making.

DIVERSITY PROGRAMMES

Initial efforts of diversity programmes were aimed primarily towards compliance with the legal requirements only. But subsequently, as companies realized the real benefits of diversity, in terms of cost saving, better company branding and goodwill, and being more effective in handling a widely different array of customers, more effort is now been directed towards diversity management that often goes beyond legal compliance. As asserted by PepsiCo, a global giant in soft drinks and food, 'We take great care to weave diversity and inclusion (D & I) into the very fabric of our culture to improve as a global, multicultural and multigenerational company capable of serving the world's communities effectively'. They have created Diversity and Inclusion Councils in all four continents of their operation, focusing on locally relevant diversity and inclusion strategies and plans, with a particular focus on women. PepsiCo's Employee Resource Groups (ERGs) in the US include African Americans, Latinos/Hispanics, Asians, Native Americans, Women, Colour Women, Caucasian Males, Lesbian/Gay/Bisexual/Transgender individuals, and EnAble, for individuals with disabilities.

Indian Railways, the second largest railway network in the world and one of the biggest employers in the country, has special drives for recruiting people with disabilities, in addition to recruiting people from reserved categories and women.

However, the perception and acknowledgements of the needs for managing diversity is hardly uniform across the organizational cross section. While HR managers are usually enthusiastic about proper diversity management as they are convinced about the benefits of diversity in the organizations, line managers are often found to be rather sceptic. Interestingly, even the top managers tend to look at diversity more as an HR issue and not a key to the company's long-term success.

Diversity Awareness Training

The biggest challenge to diversity management is to change the mindset of the people in an organization so that they can understand the 'different' groups better and accept them. Thus, it is essential to try to change the organizational culture starting from the very top down to the lowest levels. Education in managing diversity as a resource is an ongoing process in any organization.

The basic aim of awareness training is to motivate employees to recognize the worth and dignity of each individual in the workplace and to treat them with respect. The two most commonly used tools for awareness training, role playing and preparing a list of commonly held stereotypes, help the employees see themselves through their co-workers' eyes. In addition, discussing relevant case studies also helps the employees to get a right perspective into the issue of diversity in an organization. Language sensitivity and guidelines for using appropriate language are also required in this context. Keep in mind, however, that the effort to change an attitude and mind-set is never easy and can never be expected to take place overnight by official order.

GLOSSARY

- **Primary dimensions:** Those characteristics that one is born with and influences us significantly. These include age, gender, race, caste and physical qualities.
- **Secondary dimensions:** Those characteristics that are picked up or modified as one progresses in life.
- **Self-fulfilling Prophecy:** People tend to act as it is expected from them.
- **Stereotyping:** The process of assigning traits to people based on their membership in a social category, and not on the basis of individual experiences.
- **Prejudices:** Prejudices are negative stereotypes where one group tends to feel superior to those who are different from them in some way or the other.
- **Glass ceiling:** Even when women and people from minority categories are hired in organizations, they face difficulties in getting promoted to senior levels, as if there is an invisible barrier. They can see the opportunities above but cannot reach them.
- **Revolving door syndrome:** Short tenure of work for people from minorities or reserved categories who cannot stay, as they feel uncomfortable in the organization's environment.
- **Earning gap:** Discrepancy between the earning power of workers of similar skill level and educational background but belonging to different races.

QUESTIONS

1. How can the stereotypes of senior workers be changed? What are the essentials of awareness training?
2. What is the significance of diversity in the present age of globalization?
3. What are the keys to developing a successful diversity programme?
4. How can an employer best recruit and retain a diverse workforce?

REFERENCES

1. M. Loden and J. B. Rosener, *Workforce America! Managing Employee Diversity as a Vital Resource* (Homewood, IL: Business One Irwin, 1991).
2. M. R. Carrel, N. F. Elbert and R. D. Hatfield, *Human Resource Management: Strategies for Managing a Diverse and Global Workforce* (The Dryden Press, 2000).
3. J. A. F. Stoner, R. E. Freeman and D. R. Gilbert, Jr. Management. 6th Edition. (Prentice Hall of India, 1995).

Case Study: Reaching to the Top Through Leveraging Diversity

She is considered to be the 'most powerful business women in US' (with the highest annual earning for her company) and also ranks among the 50 women around the globe to watch for the leadership prowess. The compelling philosophy of Indra Nooyi, CEO of the food and beverage giant PepsiCo, has been a 'performance with a purpose'. This has transformed the company as a 'model organization' and has helped to show the world how to conduct business. The inspiration to think beyond one's personal and selfish well-being compelled Indra to feel passionately to lead a company that is a force for good in the world.

Armed with management degrees from the best management institutes of India and abroad, Indra's personal life and the highly enviable career graph is indeed a glowing example of a lady who shattered the glass ceilings in the corporate world so completely. Indra worked in India before moving to the US and worked in big companies such as Boston Consulting Group (BCG), Motorola and Asea Brown Boveri (ABB) at strategic positions before she joined PepsiCo in 1994. By 2001, she became the CFO and later the President of PepsiCo before becoming the fifth (and the first woman as well as coloured) CEO of the company's 42 years of existence. She made significant contributions to PepsiCo in several aspects. She was the primary architect of PepsiCo's restructuring, including the divestiture of its restaurants into YUM! Brands and company-owned bottling operations into Pepsi Bottling Group. She played a key role in acquiring Tropicana and was responsible for the merger with Quaker Oats that brought the vital Quaker and Gatorade businesses to PepsiCo.

But while establishing herself in the corporate jungle in the US, she could most certainly feel the extra load on her coming from a disadvantageous life position, namely, being a woman and that too from a developing nation like India. Those are possibly the reasons behind her urge to manage diversity at Pepsi, be it in terms of the economically disadvantaged groups of farmers or taking extra care about the female employees of the company. Her achievement so far is to establish the company, which is in the first place a good and ethical company that continuously strives to repay the society and the planet for what it took from the world to establish itself.

But what did it take to make a career as illustrative as Indra's? Let us now try to take a closer look at her personal life. As we have seen earlier, she got the best possible education in the world being in the alumni list of Indian Institute of Management, Calcutta, as well as Yale School of Management. She had also worked in world-class companies before she joined PepsiCo in 1994. But this is as it appears from the outside. What is her inner psyche that holds the clue to her meteoric career?

The real strength of Nooyi is in her authenticity. She is very open and straight in her dealings and always tends to trust people completely. Till date she is often seen attending PepsiCo meetings wearing a sari. She is very religious in her beliefs. Her Indian root has always been very strong, be it in wearing a sari in board meetings or publicly acknowledging the Indian culture where family orientation is considered a priority. She introduced the concept of 'group mothering' and advises aspiring women professionals on how to share some of the motherhood responsibilities among them. She cited examples of group mothering in her life when her receptionist used to take charge of her youngest child by advising her over the phone on whether she could play Nintendo while Nooyi was busy in some important policy meetings at PepsiCo. This is not only a very important piece of advice for the survival of a lady in the corporate world, but it also most certainly speaks about the philosophy of acceptance, inclusion, respect and a sense of caring for others. PepsiCo is a company that attributes its competitive advantage and significant share in the market openly to the people factor. As put by the company, the major sustainable advantages that give PepsiCo a competitive edge in the global markets are big muscular brands, proven ability to create innovative and differentiated products, and powerful go-to-market systems. But all these work so well because of the pool of 'extraordinary talented and dedicated people' in the company. And it is to note that this talented and dedicated pool of people just does not happen at PepsiCo and it takes very carefully synchronized efforts to invest in the human capital to nurture the pool to work for the firm's competitive advantage.

Diversity and Inclusion

For PepsiCo, managing and encouraging diversity is not just the right thing to do. It is *the* right thing to do for the business, and employees at PepsiCo are committed to making diversity and inclusion a way of life. For PepsiCo, managing and encouraging diversity is not just something in the company policy to help polish the company's image. PepsiCo being a multi-location company with its presence all over the globe puts a major emphasis on understanding different cultures, which comes clearly as a major advantage and a key to success from a business point of view with such an extraordinarily diverse array of customers and retailers. To truly understand the needs of the customers and consumers—and succeed in the marketplace—PepsiCo must reflect that diversity in their employees, their suppliers and in everything they do. Thus, offering a workplace where diversity is valued helps the company build a top-quality workforce so critical to their success—by enabling them to attract and retain great people from a wide spectrum of backgrounds.

PepsiCo is a company that actively encourages and supports women employees. Not only does it offer employment to women and support them in their upward movement in the company (Apart from the CEO, the company is comprised of many female employees), but it also tracks the presence of women in the company and keeps a close watch on the ratio of men and women employees in the organization. If it drops at any point of time, it tries to track this and find out why this is happening and subsequently takes steps to correct this anomaly.

The encouragement for having women employees at PepsiCo is not restricted only to those fortunate women who are well-educated and come from a decent family background. The marginalized and the poor and hapless also get a fair share of attention and encouragement from the company. Thus, poor and uneducated womenfolk from the backward locality where the plant is often situated in India are offered employment at PepsiCo as part of a community development effort. This not only helps to improve of quality of life of people around the company and integrate them with the larger societal backdrop, but also helps the company establish itself well in a foreign soil. This helps to win the host country nationals rather completely.

In the same line, PepsiCo also employs those with various types of physical disabilities in different types of jobs that are suitable for them. And of course they never use the term 'disability' and call them instead people with 'special abilities'. For example, in their plant at Sonarpur in West Bengal, they have employees with speech and hearing impairment in the bottling department who have proved to be not only very good at their job but also very conscientious and motivated workers.

Thus, it is apparent that three pivots of PepsiCo are sustainability, diversity and inclusion, which are lending it a great long-term competitive advantage and help to establish itself across the globe. All these became possible because of a strong and almost obsessive passion of its CEO to lead a company that is committed to do good to the people and world around it. India is understandably quite proud of its daughter and showed the affection and recognition by awarding Nooyi the Padma Bhushan Award for her achievement.

Question

Analyse the diversity and inclusion policy of PepsiCo in attaining the long-term sustainability of the company.

Chapter 10

Organizational Change

In the present chapter, we would explore the need for change and factors that force the organization to change. We would also try to understand different models of change.

LEARNING OBJECTIVES

- Organizational change in the present context
- Different models of change
- Understanding and building need for change
- Causes and contexts of change
- Emergent of informal organization and resistance to change
- Change agents and their effectiveness
- Learning and change
- Measuring change

NEED FOR CHANGE

Change is perhaps the only constant in today's world. An organization needs to change and redefine themselves continuously if they desire to stay in the business. Sometimes, organizations may have to go through changes because of some environmental forces. Organizations, even at their prime, need to change to retain their positions. Staying in the business and in good shape is similar to trying to climb uphill through a slippery path—the more you climb up, you possibly slip down more. Thus, to stay ahead one has to be continuously alert and put in efforts for the organization. From the viewpoint of organizational development, organizations must always strive to change the way they function in order to be more effective in the context of the changing environmental demands. So we must try to understand the nature and the forces responsible for the change carefully before chalking out the way for implementing change.

But before we proceed, we must try to define change. Simply put, any change is *a relatively enduring alteration of the present state*. Organizational changes refer to *transformations in the organization's design and structure, technology and/or people, which may be either a planned effort or an unplanned one.* Changes may occur as a natural process in an organization, or it may be initiated deliberately within the organization.

Though the term 'change' includes both planned and unplanned changes, we would consider only 'planned change' here and would thus define organizational change as a planned alteration of organizational components to improve effectiveness of the organization. By 'components of organization' we would consider the entire subsystems within the organization, including the mission and vision of the organization, its strategy, structure, people and processes, as well as uses of technology.

> ***Change*** *is planned or unplanned alteration of the state which is relatively permanent in nature.*
> ***Organizational change*** *is a planned alteration of organizational components to improve effectiveness of the organization.*

Concept Check

1. What is organizational change?
2. Why is change important for the organization?

NATURE OF ORGANIZATIONAL CHANGE

Whether the organization is deliberately introducing a change or is compelled to change as a result of external or internal forces, it is worth noting that any effort to change will have a pervasive influence over the entire organization. In other words, it hardly happens that the change would remain where it has been initially introduced as it will always have its presence felt at almost every corner of the organization. This would happen both in the case of planned as well as unplanned change. It is also to be noted in this context that change may occur either at the behest of the managers or it may slowly evolve within the organization. Apart from this, change of course could take place because of the external pressures operating over the organization.

FORCES RESPONSIBLE FOR CHANGE

There are various factors that may be responsible for driving change in any organization. These may arise from many sources. Some of these are external, arising from outside the company, whereas others are internal, arising from sources within the organization. We will now have a look at each of these separately.

External Forces Responsible for Change

The external environment where the organization is situated is often found to be the biggest driver of change. If we look around we will find that often the extreme turbulence and fluidity in the external environment make it almost impossible to predict what is going to happen next. Globalization saw, among other things, the emergence of multinational network of organizations whose operations span across the world and thus might be most strongly hit by the growing economic fluctuations and terror threats. Nevertheless, the problems, such as the ones faced by the countries within the euro zone may affect even the smaller organizations in our country. Off-shoring of jobs, new technological advancements, changing societal norms and cultural shifts, the new government regulations and laws, and general economic and political policies of the country, to name only a few, are all forcing organizations to alter its strategies and mode of functioning. To face all these and still staying in the business, organizations today have to remain lithe and extremely flexible. But, that is easier said than done. Some of the major external forces for change are globalization resulting in fierce competitions, workforce diversity, technological change, government regulations, changing economic conditions and world politics that compel organizations to change.

- **Globalization:** In today's open market economy, the power players are multinationals or transnationals having their presence felt in every country across the globe. This has undeniably increased the level of competition for every concerned party. Now to survive and remain afloat, an organization will have to compete not only with others in its own country but also with the best in the world. In order to keep pace with the changing demands across the world, organizations have to change themselves.
- **Workforce diversity:** This is one of the powerful forces behind organizational changes in recent times. It is quite apparent that the composition of today's workforce has changed significantly over the past few years. Today the number of female workforce has increased significantly as the quality of education has improved. The average working age is also found to vary a great deal with more and more people joining the workforce after retirement as well as with a sizable portion coming from the student population, joining for either summer jobs or part time ones. Accommodating all these different types of people under the same roof requires a lot of understanding, patience and tolerance, and embracing of various changed policies and practices.
- **Technological change:** Using advance technology can compel organizations to change. The introduction of computers has revolutionized the way an organization may work these days. Internet and intranet have made the day-to-day functioning of organizations very smooth and easy. New advancements in the manufacturing process have also forced organizations to change, which not only are restricted with the application of technology but also involves the people handling these.
- **Government regulations:** Organizations have to cope up and update according to the rules and regulations set out by the operational country's government.
- **Changing economic conditions:** The constantly changing economy, not only in the country of operation of an organization, but all over the world, is posing considerable challenges for organizations. The global recession in the recent time caused lots of change—from freezing recruitment and severe cost cutting to laying-off workers and restructuring—in almost every organization. Organizations have to struggle real hard to adjust to these changing times and had to undergo changes themselves.
- **World politics:** Whatever is happening even at the remotest corners of the world inevitably starts creating ripples within the organization. Events like 9/11, the Afghan war, the US war against Kuwait, the changes in the Indo-Pak relationships as in a sinusoidal curve, the recent upsurge of terrorist movements across the world, the Maoist rebellion, all these are having critical impacts in various forms and influence the way businesses can be conducted.
- **Managing ethical behaviour:** Scandals like Satyam, 3G scam, coal blocks allotments and numerous others have brought the issues of ethical behaviour, or lack of it, in organizations as well as India to the forefront of public consciousness. All these have forced organizations to maintain a minimum amount of transparency and change their style of functioning.

Internal Forces for Change

Pressures for change that originate inside the organization are generally recognizable in the form of signals indicating that something needs to be altered. The following may be considered as some of pointers for change to take place within the organizations.

- **Declining effectiveness** often creates a pressure to change. A company that experiences its third quarterly loss within a fiscal year is undoubtedly motivated to do something about it. Some companies react by instituting lay-offs and massive cost-cutting programmes, whereas others look at the bigger picture, view the loss as symptomatic of an underlying problem, and seek to unearth the cause of the problem.
- **A crisis** may also stimulate a change in an organization. Strikes or an alarmingly high rate of employee attrition may lead management to change the wage structure. The resignation of a key decision-maker is one crisis that causes the company to rethink the composition of its management team and its role in the organization. Sometimes a much-publicized crisis in the organization might lead to a change within the organization as happened in Union Carbide in India after the Bhopal gas leak tragedy.
- **Changes in employee expectations** can also trigger change in organizations. A company that hires a group of young fresh graduates may be met with a set of expectations very different from those expressed by older workers. The work force is more educated than ever before. Although this has its advantages, workers with more education demand more from employers. The new generation work force today is not just career minded, rather they are more concerned with career and family balance issues, thus often favouring flexitime or opportunities to work at their own pace. Thus the various sources of workforce diversity hold potential for a host of differing expectations among employees.
- **Changes in the work climate** at an organization can also stimulate change. A workforce that seems lethargic, unmotivated and dissatisfied is a symptom that must be addressed. This symptom, for example, is commonly found in organizations that have experienced lay-offs in recent times. Workers who have escaped a lay-off may grieve for those who have lost their jobs and may find it hard to continue to be productive. They may fear that they will be laid off as well, and may feel insecure in their jobs.

TYPES OF CHANGE

Change, thus, may be of two types: *planned* and *unplanned*. Planned change is change resulting from a *deliberate decision to alter the organization*. Companies that wish to move from a traditional hierarchical structure with its age-old approach to one that encourages more customer orientations must use a proactive, carefully orchestrated approach. But, certainly not all changes are planned. Unplanned change is imposed on the organization and is often unforeseen. Changes in government regulations and changes in the economy, for example, may come as surprise for the organization and their reactions often tend to be unplanned. Responsiveness to unplanned change requires tremendous flexibility and adaptability on the part of the organizations. Managers must be prepared to handle both planned and unplanned forms of change in organizations.

In order to further understand the nature of change, we may distinguish between the first-order and second-order changes as follows:

- **First-order change**. This refers to the change that is continuous in nature and involves no major shifts in the way an organization operates. We can notice this type of change taking place in the functioning of, say a major steel mill, where the management continuously try to improve the efficiency of its production process.

> ***First-order change*** *refers to the change that is continuous in nature and involves no major shifts in the way an organization operates.*

***Second-order change** refers to more radical change involving major shifts at different levels and different aspects of the organization.*

- **Second-order change.** This refers to more radical change involving major shifts at different levels and different aspects of the organization. When organizations face the second-order change, the basic purpose of the organizations' existence seems to be questionable. An organization going through a second-order change has to revisit its mission, vision and strategy and must make an effort to redefine these in order to position itself better in the market. This is a process of self-renewal when the organization tries to develop an insight into its functioning.

***Fundamental changes** refer to those changes that question the very basic existence of the organization and starts exploring better ways of functioning.*
***Incremental changes** are small changes in the line of the organization's business.*

Change can also be either *fundamental* or *incremental* in nature. *Fundamental changes* refer to those changes that question the very basic existence of the organization and starts exploring better ways of functioning, whereas *incremental changes* are small changes in the line of the organization's business. Understandably, incremental changes are less disturbing for the organizational members, but in the case of fundamental changes, organizational members may even feel devastated under the impact of change.

***Proactive changes** occur when adjustments and related strategies are decided in apprehension of possible changes.*
***Reactive changes** takes place when the organization accommodates itself when facing changes already imposed on them.*

Similarly, when adjustments and related strategies are decided in apprehension of possible changes, these are called *proactive* changes. But when the organization accommodates itself when facing changes already imposed on them, these are called *reactive* changes. In fact, reactive change as a change strategy is actually no strategy, as the organization has to adjust at a considerable cost and waste of useful resources, whereas the proactive changes are wise and effective change strategy that an organization could adopt. Nevertheless, it is not always feasible to adopt proactive change strategy, as it requires wise people at the top who can successfully scan the environment and discern the possible nature of change well in advance to formulate the change strategy.

Change can also be either *fundamental* or *incremental* in nature. *Fundamental changes* refer to those changes that question the very existence of the organization and starts exploring better ways of functioning, whereas *incremental changes* are small changes in the line of the organization's business. Understandably, incremental changes are less disturbing for the organizational members, but in the case of fundamental changes, organizational members may even feel devastated under the impact of change.

Another way of looking at change is to distinguish between *individual* vs. *collective* changes. It depends on the focus of change. If an individual employee becomes the target (How to improve the performance level of employee X?) of the organizational change effort, its activities will certainly be different from when it aims to initiate change at a collective level (How to improve the daily attendance of a particular department?).

THEORIES OF PLANNED CHANGE

Warren Bennis, one of the pioneers in the field of organization development (OD), claimed OD to be a particular type of change process designed to bring about a particular desirable end result. This 'change' as referred to in the context of organization development, no doubt means planned change. These are changes that are deliberately induced in the organization, with or without the help of OD practitioner, with an intention of taking the organization to a greater height. Models for planned change, which are given later in this chapter, provide us with the idea of planning and implementing the change processes in the organization.

Lewin's Force Field Analysis

Borrowing the concepts from physical science, Kurt Lewin tried to understand any state as a state of balance or equilibrium of two sets of forces, which he called driving and restraining forces. As long as the balance is maintained, the status quo will remain the same. If an organization wants to achieve a higher level of existence, the first step it has to undertake is to identify these forces that are acting upon the organization at a point of time. The next step would be to actively disrupt the equilibrium.

The force field analysis is a brilliantly simple and logical approach to understanding the organization's current status and planning strategies for further improvement. The steps are also pretty clear and down to earth which are as follows:

- **Identification of driving and restraining forces:** These may be external and/or internal to the organization. The process of identifying the forces is done in a collaborative way, involving the employees of the organization. This not only encourages the flow of thoughts and new insights, but also helps a greater bonding among the organizational members. After identifying the forces, their perceived relative strengths are also ascertained by the members.
- **Deciding on strategies:** In principle, the action plan is rather simple and straight —to increase the driving forces, to decrease the restraining forces and for maximizing the effect, doing both simultaneously. Relative importance to be given to each of these forces is also decided.

Just planning a strategy is never enough for initiating a change anywhere. To make the change effective, it must be accepted by the organizational members through whom the change will have to be implemented. But if the members think they are quite fine the way they and their organization are functioning, they will surely not trouble themselves for undergoing any change. We will note in the next section why people reject and resist changes and the ways to overcome this problem. But Lewin's three step model of change gives us valuable insights into the process of change and to implement change.

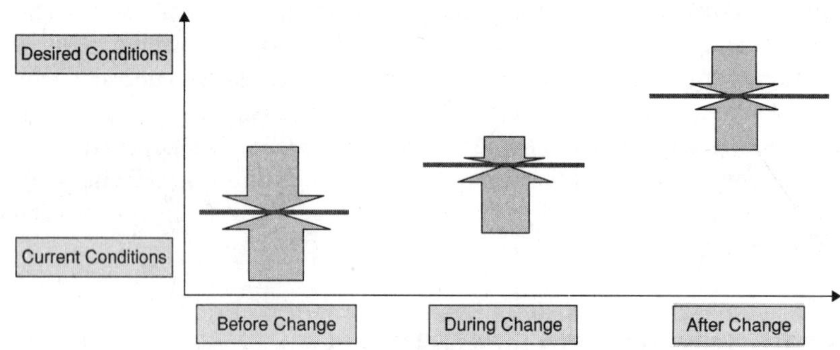

Figure 10.1 Lewin's Force Field Analysis

Source: McShane, Glinow, and Sharma, (2005).

DIFFERENT MODELS FOR UNDERSTANDING CHANGE

Lewin's Three Step Model of Change

Kurt Lewin, one of the pioneers in the field of organization development, proposed his now famous three step model of change. According to him, to make any effective change, one must be led through the following three typical stages, which are:

1. **Unfreezing:** This involves encouraging individuals to discard their present behaviours by deliberately disrupting the equilibrium state that maintains the status quo and 'shaking' them up from their complacency and comfort zones. This becomes particularly difficult when things are seemingly going on well.
2. **Moving:** After the unfreezing state, when people are aroused from their 'slumber' and start realizing the need for change, they feel almost devastated and rather vulnerable. They have understood that what they were doing in the past were not the right thing. But what are those 'right things'? This is the stage when new attitudes, values and behaviours are to be provided as the substitutes for old ones.
3. **Refreezing:** Just enabling change is not enough. The success of any effort depends on how well these are maintained afterwards. This is the stage that involves the establishment of new attitudes, values and behaviours as the new status quo.

McKinsey 7-S Model

The 7-S model of McKinsey was developed by Peter and Waterman (1981) to explain how the organizational effectiveness depends on the right alignment of different components of an organization. The 7-S or the elements of the organization are structures, systems, strategies, skills, staff (or people), style (i.e. managerial style) and shared values (or organizational culture). The model emphasizes the interdependence of all the components. Thus, changes in one component will induce changes in all other components. It also points out that the organizational effectiveness is essentially a function of the degree of fit achieved among the various components and the environment. An effective organization is, thus, the one which can realign the interdependence of these elements or components of an organization to achieve the right fit with the environmental requirements. It is, therefore, necessary to first analyse the external environment and align the key organizational components accordingly. Figure 10.3 depicts McKinsey's 7-S strategy.

Burke–Litwin Causal Model

Burke–Litwin model tries to capture the complexities in understanding the totality and involvement of so many components of an organization. The upper half of Figure 10.4 depicts the transformational factors that include environment, strategy, leadership and organizational culture while the factors in the lower half are categorized under transactional or day-to-day activities. Any changes here would

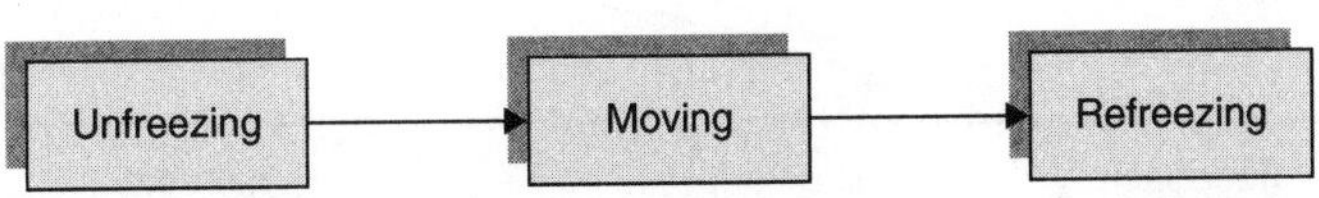

Figure 10.2 Lewin's Three Step Model of Change

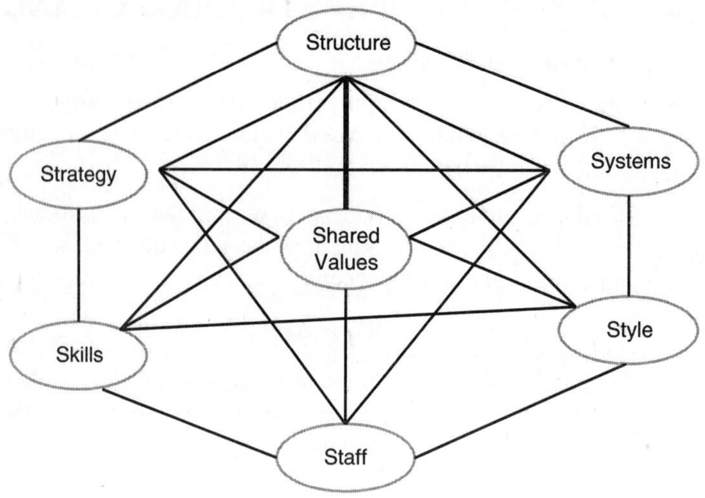

Figure 10.3 McKinsey 7-S Model

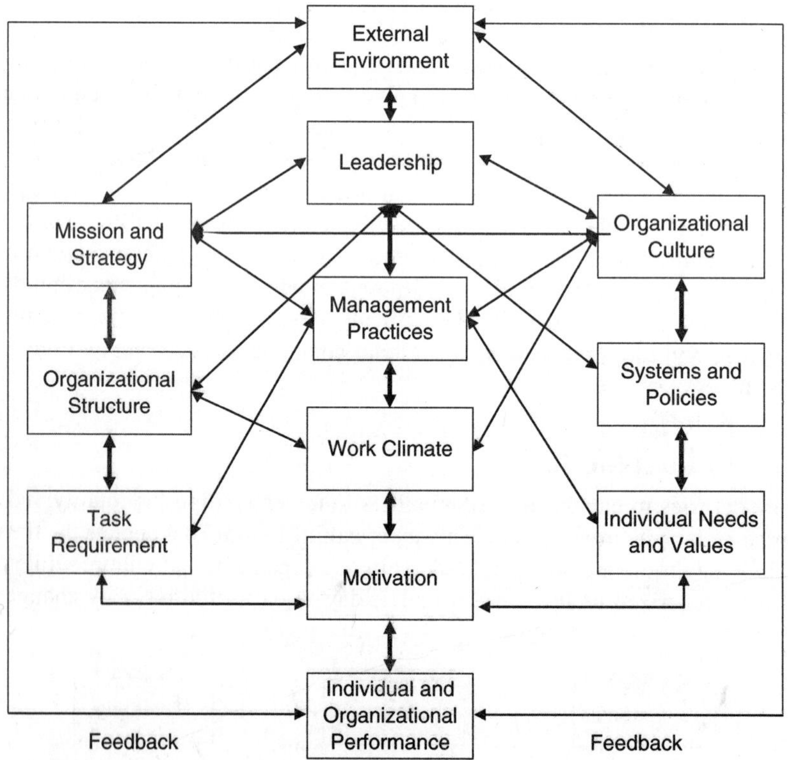

Figure 10.4 Burke–Litwin Model

not necessarily trigger the transformational changes though this may also happen at times. Some transactional changes may initiate the transformational change as well. For example, the effort to improve customer satisfaction in a firm may trigger questions about the existing organizational culture and/or the strategy.

Nadler and Tashman Organizational Congruence Model

Nadler and Tashman model aims to highlight how different parts of the organization fit within the organization as well as with the factors outside in order to determine the organizational effectiveness. This is a systems approach and Figure 10.5 depicts the interrelatedness of different factors. The inputs of the organization include factors such as the environment where the organization is situated, its history and resources. All of these would determine the strategy of the organization. Organizational strategy in turn would determine the nature of task, formal organizational structure and system along with the informal organization and the specific organizational culture and the typicality of the people who will be taken in. All these components are of course intricately interrelated, as shown in Figure 10.5, which would eventually result in the organizational output.

Nadler and Tashman highlighted three critical factors in the context of change framework:

1. **The system is dynamic.** Thus, any organizational diagnosis will change over time with changing concerns and priorities. Any future planning must take this into account.
2. **The fit or congruence.** The fit or congruence between various components is important in diagnosing the organization's performance. Thus, it is essential to understand each component as well as how well they fit to each other to understand why an organization behaves in a particular way and not otherwise.
3. **Good fit.** It is essential to have a good fit among the components. Even when some or more components are extraordinary, the resultant effect may be poor as a good fit is extremely important. Thus, an organization which has amazing employees but may end up performing rather poorly if they do not fit with the general culture of the organization.

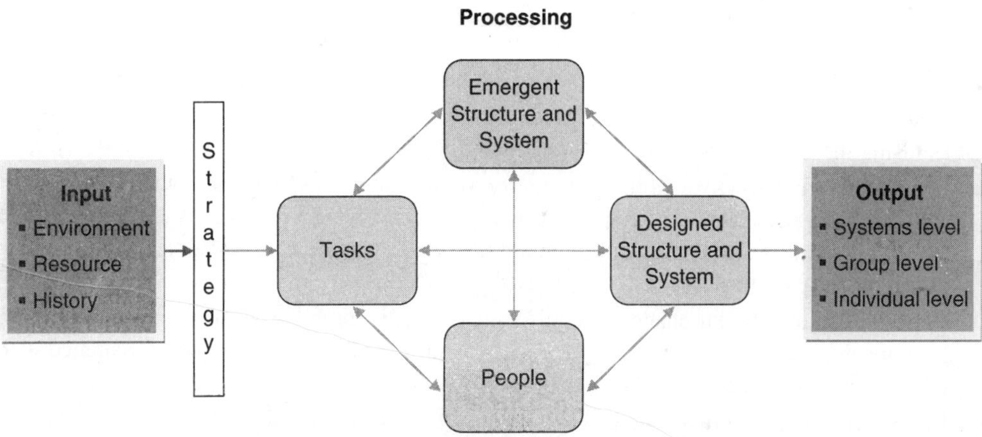

Figure 10.5 Nadler and Tashman Organizational Congruence Model

RESISTANCE TO CHANGE

People often resist change even when they are not satisfied with the way the organization is functioning. They tend to be apprehensive about any proposed change for various reasons. Many of these occur as people usually develop a negative reaction whenever they have to face something different and feel that their personal freedom is at threat.

To understand the nature of resistance to change we can divide this broadly into two categories: resistance at the *individual level* and at the *organizational level*.

Individual Resistance

The major reasons for resisting change by the individuals concerned are due to the basic nature of human beings that can be summarized as follows.

- **Fear of the unknown** Change often brings with it substantial uncertainty. Employees facing a technological change, such as the introduction of a new computer system, may resist the change simply because it introduces ambiguity into what was once a comfortable zone for them. This is especially a problem when there has been a lack of communication about the change.
- **Fear of loss:** When a change is impending, some employees may fear losing their jobs, particularly when a digital technology like computer controls is introduced. Employees also may fear losing their status because of a change. The professional chartered accountants, for example, may feel threatened when they feel their expertise is eroded by the installation of a new software.
- **Fear of failure:** Some employees fear changes because they doubt their own ability. Introducing computers into the workplace often arouses individuals' self-doubts about their ability to master the required computer skills. Often resistance can arise from a fear that the change itself may not be as effective as it is being projected.
- **Force of habit:** Jobs that are well understood and that become part of habit are easy to perform. The prospect of change might imply developing new job skills that might be threatening to the employees.
- **Economic factors:** Any change in job most often than not have the potential to threaten one's livelihood either in the form of loss of job or reduced pay. Thus, resistance to such changes is but natural.
- **Disruption of interpersonal relationships:** Employees may resist change that threatens to limit meaningful interpersonal relationships on the job. The prospect of too much automation can be seen as losing the opportunity to interact with their colleagues.
- **Personality conflicts:** When the personality of the person in-charge of change (the change agent) engenders negative reactions, employees may resist the change. A change agent who appears insensitive to employees concerns and feelings may meet considerable resistance, because employees perceive that their needs are not being taken into account.
- **Politics:** Organizational change may also shift the existing balance of power in the organization. Individuals or groups who hold power under the current arrangement may be threatened with losing these political advantages in the advent of change.
- **Failure to recognize need for change:** Unless employees are fully convinced about the need for change they will not support the change.

- **Breach of psychological contract:** People usually develop a psychological involvement with the organization they come to work. Apart from the clear, tangible and legal contracts between the employer–employee, this gives rise to what is called the *psychological contract*. Any threat of change, particularly the harsh ones, might disrupt this. For example, in the time of ruthless downsizing, people become sad with the prospect of losing their jobs even when it was clearly mentioned in their appointment letter that the nature of job is purely contractual. They tend to feel betrayed as they feel that the organization has not kept their promise and lacked the reciprocity of feelings.
- **Cultural assumptions and values:** Sometimes cultural assumptions and values can be impediments to change, particularly if the assumptions underlying the change are alien to employees. This form of resistance can be very difficult to overcome, because some cultural assumptions are deep rooted.

Organizational Resistance

Like individuals, organizations also resist changes in various ways. These can be summarized as follows:

- **Structural inertia:** Organizations are created to ensure stability, and jobs in an organization are designed in a standardized way. Thus, it often becomes difficult to change all these because of the inherent inertia.
- **Work group inertia:** Inertia to continue performing jobs in a specified way comes not only from the jobs themselves but also from the social work group within the organization.
- **Limited focus of change:** Organizations are made up of a number of interdependent subsystems. Change at one subsystem can only be effective when the other subsystem also changes accordingly. But often this is difficult to attain.
- **Threat to expertise:** Changes in organizational patterns and functioning may threat the expertise of specialized groups and that is why it may be strongly resisted by the concerned members.
- **Threat to existing power equation:** Any redistribution of decision-making authority can threaten long-established power relationships within the organization and so resisted by those enjoying the power.
- **Threat to established resource allocation:** The groups in the organization who have access to more resources often see change as a threat.
- **Commitments or contracts already made**: Sometimes organizations resist any prospect of change because of commitments already made. For instance, when the organization had signed the contract of supplying certain amount of product, it is not possible for them to reduce the workforce immediately.
- **Previously unsuccessful change efforts:** Any organization that has faced a disaster in the past will naturally be resistant to initiate any new change.

Managing Resistance to Change

Resistance to change makes it difficult for the organizations to implement the proposed changes required for the development of the organization. As discussed earlier, resistance to change is an innate psychological response of human being to anything new, and it is wiser to acknowledge it. Instead of all the time trying to overcome it, this can be treated as valuable feedback from the people subject to the change and can be used to effectively manage the change process in the organization.

There are various approaches for managing resistance to change that can be summarized as follows:

- **Identify and convince the key individuals:** For changes to be effective and accepted, it is often essential to win the support of the most powerful individuals in the organization. This surely facilitates the change process.
- **Identify and neutralize those who resist change:** During the times of impending change, some people become too nervous and tend to verbalize their apprehension openly. And the whole thing might be quite infectious and more and more people start feeling panicky. People in authority should be prompt enough in responding in such situations and clarify the doubts of the concerned people as candidly as possible.
- **Education and communication:** Resistance to change can be reduced significantly if employees can be helped to appreciate the need for change. This can be achieved through clear and extensive communication. Open communication, participation and emotional support can go a long way towards managing resistance to change. Managers must realize that some resistance is inevitable, however, and should plan ways to deal with resistance early in the change process.
- **Involve employees in the decisions for change:** In order to win the support of the employees, it is always wise to involve them in the decision-making process. Then they will feel that the decision is their own and will feel committed to it.
- **Facilitation and support:** During the times of change, offering support in the form of counselling or arranging training programmes for mastering new skills required in the changed situation, helps in reducing resistance considerably.
- **Reward constructive behaviour:** A time-tested tactics for accepting change is to reward those who have learned to adopt the changes successfully.

Behavioural Reactions to Change

In spite of attempts to minimize the resistance to change in an organization, some reactions to change are inevitable. People may show four types of basic identifiable reactions to change: disengagement, disidentification, disenchantment and disorientation.

- *Disengagement* is psychological withdrawal from change. The employee may appear to lose initiative and interest in the job. They lack drive and commitment, and they simply comply without real psychological investment in their work. The basic managerial strategy for dealing with disengaged individuals is to confront them with their reaction and draw them out so that they can identify the concerns that need to be addressed.
- Another reaction to change is *disidentification*. Individuals reacting in this way feel that their identity has been threatened by the change, and they feel very vulnerable. Many times they cling to a past procedure because they had a sense of mastery over it. When employees are allowed to participate, they are more committed to the change. Another strategy for managing resistance is providing empathy and support to employees who have trouble dealing with the change.
- *Disenchantment* is also a common reaction to change. It is usually expressed as negativity or anger. Disenchanted employees realize that the past is gone, and they are mad about it. They may try to enlist the support of other employees by forming coalitions. Destructive behaviours like sabotage and backstabbing may result. It is often difficult to reason with disenchanted employees. Thus, the

first step in managing this reaction is to bring these employees from their highly negative, emotionally charged state to a more neutral state. They can then be dealt in such a way to acknowledge that their anger is normal. This can reduce the negativity in their feeling.

- A final reaction to change is *disorientation*. Disoriented employees are lost and confused, and often they are unsure of their feelings. They waste energy trying to figure out what to do instead of how to do things. Disoriented individuals ask a lot of questions and become very detail oriented. They may appear to need a good deal of guidance and may leave their work undone until all of their questions have been answered.

A final note of caution on organizational change. The success of any change in fact depends on the person handling the change. His capability of handling any change sensitively and winning the trust and confidence of those facing the change will determine the effectiveness of any change programme.

Manager's Essence: Initiating Changes in Tata Motors

Tata Motors is one of the largest Indian automobile companies with a revenue of $14 billion. It was established in 1945 and was initially focused primarily in the commercial vehicle sector. But during the economic slowdown around the late 1900s, the market for commercial vehicles shrank almost 40 per cent. It was this time that saw the entry of Tata Motors into the small passenger car sector, with the introduction of Tata Indica and Indigo. However, this was not a very happy phase for the Tata. The commercial vehicle sector was already struggling to cope with a heavy loss. On the top of it all, was the acute financial pressure because of the heavy investment made in the production of small passenger cars, along with cost of compliance with the new emission standards and increasing threats from the global competitors. All these resulted in an unprecedented loss of nearly ₹5 billion in the year 2001. Driven by the urgent need for cost cutting, Tata Motors could eventually make the biggest turnaround in the history of automobile industry. Over the next two years, there was severe cost cutting ventures at Tata Motors which enabled the company to save ₹8 billion to be pumped in to restore the corporate health. There was also a refocusing of its investments in light commercial vehicles, buses and spare parts along with the production of the passenger cars.

Today Tata Motors is the world's fifth largest manufacturer of medium and heavy trucks—it has 61 per cent domestic market share in this segment—and has taken the number two position for sales of passenger vehicles in the Indian market. It has also built a significant global presence. But the turnaround was uneasy. People were always Tata's assets. They typically had a large, dedicated and loyal workforce. But they were also the most frozen layer in the company, defying any attempt to change. Instead of forcing the change and shooting orders, Tata Motors took a different approach. They rightly understood that the best way was to involve people into the change process rather than ordering. Thus, they conditioned their workforce to listen to their customers about the problems they are facing; they exposed their workforce to the products of their competitors by tearing their products apart and analysing the good and bad and compared with their own products, thereby making people see why customers prefer buying someone else's products than theirs.

Change Agents and Their Effectiveness

Just recognizing the need for change is never enough. Change agents, who are the managers of an organization, usually at the higher side of the organizational hierarchy, need to check whether the organization is ready for the change or not. They must be able to create a sense of urgency for the change before any change effort could take place. This often requires revisiting the mission and vision statements of the organization down to the day-to-day functioning and interrelations among all the components of the organization.

Characteristics of an Effective Change Agent

The following are some of the qualities that will be necessary to become an effective change agent.

- Pleasant personality and good man management skill helps the change agent to be successful in his endeavour
- A strong determination even in the face of odds and persistence to the attainment of the objectives
- Willingness to bring in change and dissatisfaction with the status quo
- A high level of intelligence for scanning the environment, analysis and determining the possible impacts of the change efforts
- Communication and interpersonal skills
- High level of emotional intelligence

Concept Check

1. How would you identify effective change agents from ineffective ones?
2. List down the important characteristics of an effective change agent.

Measuring Change

It is essential to measure the impact of any change effort as this will help in correcting the direction, content and outcomes of the change initiatives. The following are a brief index of what are to be measured:

- **Identifying critical factors:** Factors that have significant impact on the organizational operations and functioning. If the measurement reveals the difference, this will be helpful in initiating and sustaining change.
- **Fair measures:** The measures should be perceived by the people as fair and appropriate. The success of an entire change effort depends on the fairness of the measure as it will increase people's acceptance.
- **Clear message:** A confusing or ambiguous message may offset the change effort. If some behaviour elicits both positive and negative responses in the organization, people will be confused.
- **Role models:** Change leaders must act as the role models and show what is ideal and expected.
- **Simplicity of the measure:** The measures should be simple for effective implementation.
- **Measures should be appropriate in the environmental context:** Measures should be appropriate in the environmental context.

It should be noted that organizations should always do a reality check before plunging into any change programme. Whenever there is a change of baton, for example, the new CEO as a rule tends to reject whatever has happened so far in the earlier regime and urges for change. This is often done for the sake of change. This should be avoided as far as practicable.

QUESTIONS

1. In the context of organizational change, what are the things that are typically changed? List down the forces that lead to change.
2. How can you, in your role of the change agent, make people willing to change in the organization? Explain your strategy with the help of appropriate examples.

3. Refer to the organization with which you are associated. Describe the change/s that has/have occurred during the recent past. Analyse that in terms of the concepts that you have picked up from this chapter.
4. You have just taken over as the top executive of an organization and found things are not in shape. You have planned a major restructuring of the organization. Explain why people might resist the change effort.

REFERENCES

1. A.R. Rosoff, *Insight*, 9 (2), 2012.
2. T. Cawsay, and G. Deszca, *Toolkit for Organizational Change* (Sage, 2007).
3. Waterman, R., Jr. Peters, T., and Philips, J. R. (1980). Structure is not organization. *Business Horizons*, 23(3).
4. W.W. Burke, *Organizational Change: Theory and practice* (Thousand Oaks, CA: Sage, 2002).
5. D.A. Nadler, and M.L. Tushman, 'A diagnostic model for organizational behaviour' in J.R. Hackman, E.E. Lawler, and L.W. Porter (Eds.), *Perspectives in behaviour in organizations* (New York: McGraw-Hill, 1977).
6. McShane, S. L., Glinow, M. A. V. and Sharma, R. R. (2005). (McGraw-Hill).

Case Study: Change Effort in a Nationalized Bank

They were deliriously happy with their success, all four of them. They just graduated from one of the premier management institutes in the country and already had lucrative jobs in their pocket even before the last semester examination. They started their professional life after their final result was published. The interesting thing was that all of them are posted in the head office in the same city where they had studied, with two of them being residents of the city itself. The job was not only well paid but prestigious as well. They were employed in the HR department as scale one officers and were excited at the huge learning opportunity lying in front of them.

The office was actually fun. They were not yet been given their work stations. They were instead given a big room where four of them sit together with just one desktop to share among them, and that too without the Internet connection. But they did not really mind. It was almost an extension of their college days and they used to work, discuss, talk, chat and discuss and chat again, and of course, work—just like what they were used to do at their College. They were two boys Shuvendu and Mahindra and two girls Sumedha and Rini, all between 23 and 25 years of age. Both the boys had a worse experience and they were slightly older than the girls. Shuvendu, the city boy, was of serious type who naturally assumes the leadership role within their small group, as he had always assumed earlier in the college. Mahindra was from Punjab, a strikingly handsome and infinitely naughty boy. Both Rini and Sumedha were good students and would often poke fun at the boys in a friendly way. They were not only happy, but also looked very happy. And that was a sore point for the other employees in the bank. Most of the employees in the HO were middle aged with a sizable number of them being practically on the verge of retirement. What is there to be so happy about? They could never understand why all of them were posted together in the same branch, and that too in the HO? And what they talk about all the time? What is there to talk about in the first place? The other employees could not understand a thing about this 'gang of four'. They were almost hated for their happiness, youthfulness, excitement about life in general and also for their die-hard enthusiasm.

However, after around a month in their job, they were called by Mr Sanyal, the chief manager in his room. He looked straight into their eyes and said, 'I want you to work on a pretty serious project. This is about employee competency mapping which had long been planned by the authority but couldn't be implemented so far for lack of trained people in the bank. Now that you people are there, I hope you know the basics about the competency mapping. Prepare a detailed plan, check with me and after my approval start working straight from here. You got me? Are you OK with this?' This got them really exited. They were looking forward to putting their hands on anything, and competency mapping is surely a challenging assignment. They said so. Mr Sanyal looked at them a shade too long this time and then said slowly, 'Never discuss it with anybody else here, and don't rush. You wouldn't take a step without informing me. It is serious.' They were puzzled. They could not fully understand the worry of the chief manager. Nevertheless, they started working on the project with their usual enthusiasm. Shuvendu took the lead role and they all would sit together for hours chalking out the general outline of the project and got busy in preparing questionnaires.

For the next two weeks, the four worked hard on the project. The questionnaire they initially prepared went through detailed scrutiny and was eventually approved by their boss after several revisions. Then they started interviewing the employees armed with the questionnaire without expecting the reactions that were in store for them. The very first interview with a mid-level manager in the HO taken by the girls was a real shocker. The gentleman was amazed to see the 'audacity' of these new joinees and said he was 'being gentle' with them only because they were girls, otherwise he would have thrown them out. Though they hardly found him to be 'gentle', they did not argue and politely told him that they are doing just as instructed. The person was still terribly agitated and pointed out that being fresh from the college, they hardly had any idea of the real world. He was working in this bank before they were born and now they are asking him what he is good at. The girls hurriedly tried to explain that they were no doubt inexperienced and they really had no clue about such a complex business as banking. And that was precisely the reason. They wanted to learn. This pacified him to some extent. The boys had a worse experience. They met a senior staff, actively involved with union activities. He was in his late 50s, a bald headed thin springy kind of a person who is thoroughly bitter with life and believes that he knows everything under the sun. He seemed to take extra pleasure to be rude with them, these 'professionally' educated fools in front of him. He told them on their face that he knew all their tricks and was well aware how they landed up in this coveted post and started their career right from the HO. He gave a careless attitude to them.

The experience was more or less the same across the branch. The main refrain was how could these youngsters dare to ask them what they do in their job and how good they are at that. What did they know? Having a high sounding degree from a prestigious business school never gives them the license to do whatever they wish to. But whoever at high levels might have supported them, he didn't care.

Questions

1. Why do you think people reacted in this way?
2. What is happening here?

PART 2

Organizational Development

Chapter 11

Organization Development

Opening Case: Strategic Rethinking at TCS

Tata Consultancy Services (TCS) was founded in 1968 by Ratan Tata. Headquartered in Mumbai, it was initially created to give technical support to the Tata group of companies. But soon TCS started to serve clients outside the Tata group, and by the 70's it started outsourcing its services. During late 1990s, the infamous virus Y2K was a problem for both computer-based and non-digital documentation and data storage all over the world. TCS developed software tools to enable automated conversion process so that third-party developers and clients use it. With this, TCS earned a lot of revenues for Tata group, the parent company. But, as it was recounted by Ramodorai in his *The TCS Story and Beyond*, TCS was still dominated by industry giants such as IBM, Accenture and EDS (now part of HP). Apart from these giants, a host of younger competitors had also emerged, thus making it impossible for TCS to ignore the mounting competition any more. Ramodorai felt it was 'time to pause and take stock' to reinforce the achievements and focus on the challenges ahead. So he created a corporate 'think tank' consisting of six or seven people who would meet every week at his residence for a 'strategic rethink'. This eventually crystallized into new mission statements and paved the way for the company to go public in 2004. The corporate think tank decided that if TCS is to be transformed from a relatively small IT service business into a global giant, they have to expand the services offered along with capturing more market share. From just 'IT Solutions and Services', they added Global Consulting, Engineering and Industrial Services, Asset-based Offerings, Infrastructure Services and IT-enabled Services (or BPO).

This soul searching and strategic rethinking paid indeed. Over the next few years, TCS emerged as the largest provider of information technology in Asia and second largest provider of business process outsourcing services in India. TCS has offices in over 47 countries with more than 142 branches across the globe and accounts for 20 per cent of India's total IT exports. It has registered the revenue earning of $8.355 billion while the profit margin was $2.024 billion in 2011.

As we trace the history of TCS, one of the most powerful IT companies in Asia, we see the amount of strategic thinking that went in making the company such a grand success. It evolved from where it started. This is the history of its development.

In the present chapter we would explore the concept of organization development and its various techniques.

LEARNING OBJECTIVES

- What is organization development (OD)?
- Brief history and background of OD
- Phases of OD cycle

INTRODUCTION

As illustrated earlier, even the best of the organizations need to ponder, take stock of their position and change to retain their present position of excellence. Change is all around us, and to cope with the ever changing environment, both inside and outside an organization, it is essential to develop some well thought out strategies, be it to retain the present position or to alter the current status to enhance growth and excellence.

Organization development (OD) is essentially an effort towards initiating planned changes within an organization in order to improve its effectiveness and current status. The term OD was introduced by eminent behavioural scientists such as Herbert Shepard, Robert Blake and Jane Mouton, Douglas McGregor and Richard Beckhard in the 1950s and early 1960s (Porter 1974), when they started applying theories and principles of behavioural science in understanding and improving the functioning of various organizations. The field of OD is largely the offshoot of the human relations movement or the behavioural school of management thought. It started with the now famous Hawthorn studies, which was the first to point out that the best way to understand an organization is to view it as a socio-technical system, and acknowledge and appreciate the social and psychological context of work organizations. As it was revealed by the Hawthorn studies, the social relationships among the employees on the job are very important for them, often even more important than economic benefits. This was the beginning to seriously consider issues like employees' social needs, sense of belongingness and acceptance, and a personal identity while focusing on organizational effectiveness.

WHY ORGANIZATION DEVELOPMENT?

What compels an organization to go for organization development? After scanning the occurrences of OD in various organizations, the most cited reasons are usually short and simple—the level of competition, survival and improved performance. The level of competition faced by the organization in question is the driving force behind initiation of OD, as the threat of competition may jeopardize the very survival of the organization. In order to stay in the business and survive the threats, the organization has to redefine itself and renew its capacity. And all the time, it is not possible to bring in the desired change through improvement in structure, function or technologies. Until the people and culture of the organization change, no sustainable change can be achieved.

Why Organization Development?
- *The level of competition*
- *Survival*
- *Improved performance*

DEFINITION OF ORGANIZATION DEVELOPMENT

Organization development has been defined in various ways by different scholars in this area. According to Beckhard (1969), OD is an effort that is planned organization-wide, and managed from the top to increase organizational effectiveness and health through planned interventions in the organization's

Organization development is a planned process of change in an organization's culture through the utilization of behavioural science technologies, research and theory.

processes, using behavioural science knowledge. Bennis (1969) described OD as a response to change, and believed it to be a complex educational strategy intended to change the beliefs, attitudes, values and structure of organization, so that they can better adapt to new technologies, markets and challenges, and the 'dizzying' rate of change itself. French and Bell (2001) define OD as a long-term effort led and supported by top management to improve an organization's visioning, empowerment, learning and problem solving processes through an ongoing, collaborative management of organizational culture—with special emphasis on the culture of intact work teams and other team configuration—using the consultant-facilitator role and the theory and technology of behavioural science, including action research. Burke (1994) simplified OD as a planned process of change in an organization's culture through the utilization of behavioural science technologies, research and theory. Beer (1980) defines OD in a more comprehensible way as a system-wide process of data collection, diagnosis, action planning, intervention and evaluation aimed at:

- Enhancing congruence between organizational structure, process, strategy, people and culture.
- Developing new and creative organizational solutions.
- Developing the organization's self-renewing capacity.

It occurs through collaboration of organizational members working with a change agent using behavioural science theory, research and technology.

CHARACTERISTICS OF OD

There are a host of other definitions of OD as well. But there is a common thread and the same underlying emphasis in all these definitions, which may be summarized as follows:

- Organization development relies specifically on the principles and applications of behavioural sciences in the context of organizations with the aim of improving the individual and organizational effectiveness.
- OD is essentially an interdisciplinary field of study that has been developed over the years on the contributions from an array of social sciences, starting from psychology, sociology and anthropology to economics and political science.
- OD subscribes heavily to the system's concept and views organizations as an open system with a number of interdependent subsystems under it. It recognizes the influence of one or more subsystems of an organization upon the overall functioning of the entire organization.
- OD puts its primary focus on the people in the organization and views organizational culture as one of the major areas to drive changes in an organization.
- OD does not believe in a prescriptive approach on the part of the OD practitioners while trying to improve the organizational effectiveness. The emphasis is always on the participatory approach with a collaborative client–consultant relationship, where they both actively engage in the process of diagnosing and problem solving. Here the consultant acts as a facilitator and helps the client to help himself by developing capability. Thus, the consultant is not like a doctor who prescribes a medicine after hearing the nature of the malady from the client. He is more like a personal trainer in your gym or yoga class, where he actively helps you to 'do' and experience the movements and its effect, but does not do it for you.

- OD is a continuous process. It starts with diagnosing the real problem which is not necessarily the one reported by the client and searching for a solution jointly. But then after implementing the solution it may lead to newer problems. The problem itself also changes with time and so the entire process would have to be repeated in order to ensure the development is sustainable.

Who Does OD?

OD practitioners are those who are specialists and have the expertise to apply OD principles and practices in day-to-day work. They may be either external to the organization as OD specialists or consultants or they may be someone from within the organization in the capacity of managers and leaders.

Concept Check

1. What is OD?
2. Who does OD in an organization?

HISTORY OF OD AS A DISCIPLINE

As mentioned earlier, the OD movement started at around the 1960s. Approaches towards OD, however, changed over time, and we can identify three distinct phases in the development of OD as a discipline. These are as follows:

1. **The first generation of OD** (French and Bell, 2001; Ramnarayan and Gupta, 2011) attempted to improve the organization by focusing primarily on individuals and small groups within the existing framework.
2. **The second generation of OD** paid more attention to the macro environment of the organization and aimed at improving the organization by equipping it to adjust effectively to the external

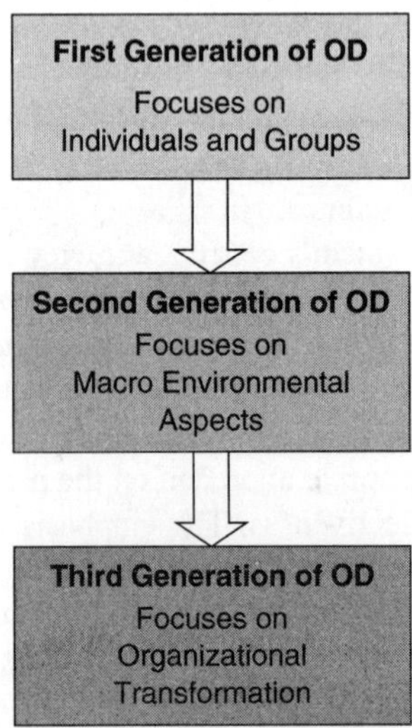

Figure 11.1 Phases of Development of OD as a Discipline

challenges in the form of market conditions, technological advancements, competition, stakeholders' demands and so on. The issues such as leadership and its role on initiating and managing change were in the forefront.

3. **The third generation of OD** was marked by the efforts of extensive transformational changes in the organization, keeping in mind the past history and values existing in the organization.

First Generation of OD

There are four different categories of the initial phase of OD. These are termed as 'pillars' of OD (French, Bell and Vohra, 2006) and are as follows:

1. **Action research approach:** The behavioural scientists, who were primarily responsible for the OD movements, insisted upon an objective and strictly scientific approach to be employed in the effort to improve the organizational effectiveness. They believed that an effective action can only be taken on the basis of adequate research. Kurt Lewin (1946) was remarkable in terms of his contribution to the action research approach, which is based upon a collaborative effort between the client and the OD consultant, instead of the unilateral approach. Thus, the action research is essentially an objective approach following a cyclical process such as gathering data, feeding the data back to client group, discussing and analysing the data jointly with the client group to arrive at an action plan and continuing to evaluate the impacts of implementing the action plan and reviewing the entire process. Action research thus follows an iterative cycle for improving the organization's effectiveness on a continuous basis.
2. **Survey feedback approach:** Rensis Likert founded the Survey Research Center at the University of Michigan in 1946 and was responsible for bringing in the survey feedback approach to the field of OD research. It is based on gathering data from across the organization and its various groups and subgroups with the help of conferences and structured questionnaires. After analysing the data, the results and the implications of these are then fed back to the client group who are now engaged in conferences and discussions with the consultant. The organizational members then work together with the consultant to decide upon an action plan. The consultant shares his critical insights into the functioning of the organization, typically in terms of the processes involved, and makes them aware of the research methodology.
3. **Sensitivity training or T-group training:** This is also known as laboratory training, which is essentially an unstructured small group without any explicit agenda. Individuals develop better insight from the interaction with others and learn the meaning and consequences of their own behaviour, how they are being affected by others' behaviours and the dynamics of group behaviour. These insights, along with the development of skills in diagnosing help them become more effective in interpersonal and group actions. The Research Center for Group Dynamics (RCGD), founded by Kurt Lewin, and the National Training Laboratory (NTL) in group development, developed by behaviourists like Benne, Bradford and Lippit around the later part of the 1940s, conducted a number of training sessions with participants from different walks of life. The participants used to meet with a facilitator and observers for three to five day sessions. The stated goals of these sessions were enhanced self-insight, understanding conditions facilitating or inhibiting group functioning, and developing the skills to diagnose individual, group and organizational behaviour.
4. **Socio-technical approach:** OD research gained impetus in England in the 1950s. Wilfred Bion and John Rickman, along with a few others, started experimenting with Lewin's theories of group

dynamics and related areas at Tavistock Clinic in the UK and developed the socio-technical systems approach to understand people's behaviour in organizations. Eric Trist's work in the coal mines revealed the effect of work redesign on the changing social relationship and autonomy that in turn affects the productivity of the workgroups.

Second Generation of OD

The focus of the second phase of OD research was predominantly organizational transformation and dealt with large-scale organizational changes, taking the entire organization as the unit of analysis. The major areas under this phase are described below:

- **Organizational transformation:** Organizational transformation (Levy and Merry, 1986) is considered a second-order change as it is multidimensional and multifaceted in nature and involves different levels across the organization. The change that the organization goes through in the process of transformation is discontinuous and radical rather than continuous or incremental. It often involves questioning the fundamental set of values and organizational culture and urges to review the basic organizational strategy. In order to succeed, greater commitment on the part of both the top management and employees alike are necessary. It indeed requires more time, more experimenting and simultaneous management of a host of other variables such as stakeholders' demand, organizational structure and policies, to name a few (French, Bell and Vohra, 2006; Ramnarayan and Gupta, 2011).
- **Emphasis on total quality management (TQM):** There is in fact a striking similarity between successful application of TQM and the basic principles and philosophy of OD. As noted by Ciampa (1992), successful TQM efforts 'encourage true employee involvement, demand teamwork, seek to push decision-making power to lower levels in the company, and reduce barriers between people'. These values are at the core of OD as well. Burke (1994) also believed that OD could lead to TQM efforts in an organization.
- **Focus on team building:** There is a renewed interest in developing successful high performance and self-managed teams in the organization in the context of increased pressure on organizations in the face of steep competitions. Organizations are now compelled to improve quality, reduce layers of management and enhance flexibility and employee morale. A number of OD interventions thus focus on team building, as there is increased reliance on teams in the work field.
- **Visioning and future research:** This involves typically a two-to-three day future search conference (Weisbord 1989), where the participants are asked to build a database and to look at it together to interpret the findings and decide future actions. As Senge (1990) points out, the most important thing that results from this effort is actually the development of the 'shared vision', which truly binds the people in the organization and indeed enhances their commitment towards the organization.
- **Getting the 'whole system into the room':** In this type of OD effort as formulated by Weisbord, all the organizational members from top management to the lower level employees meet in a one-day conference and jointly decide the future action plan for the organization and allocation of responsibility to different groups or individuals to accomplish the task.

Third Generation of OD

The third or the latest phase of OD focuses on employee participation across the organization. It takes into consideration the past of the organization and builds the intervention techniques around that. There are two important OD activities belonging to the third phase or third generation of OD.

1. **Learning organization:** In today's cut-throat competition and constantly changing environmental conditions, the only hope for an organization is to stay ahead of others by learning new things fast and quick and mastering new skills. According to Senge (1990), a learning organization is one that is 'continuously expanding its capacity to learn'. With the development of new technologies at a great pace, skill obsolescence is a major threat for organizations and their members alike. Learning organizations put strong emphasis on enhancing the capability of its members to learn on a continuous basis and facilitate the process of learning by ensuring their accessibility to knowledge and information (in the forms of Internet connectivity, library, etc.).
2. **Appreciative inquiry:** It believes in focusing on the positive strengths of the organization and leveraging the same for future growth and development (Watkins and Mohr, 2001). It helps in:
   - Identifying the positive as focus of enquiry.
   - Inquiring into stories that highlight the life giving forces.
   - Locating common themes appearing in the stories and select topics for future enquiry.
   - Creating shared image of a desired future.
   - Finding innovative ways to create the future (Ramnarayan and Gupta, 2011).

OD IN INDIA

In India, OD movements started around 1960 when a group of Indian professionals, Udai Pareek being one of them, went to NTL at Bethel, Maine, USA, to be trained as OD specialists. Around the mid-60s, some of the OD intervention techniques, namely, the grid programmes, became quite popular at places like Small Industries Extension Training (SIET) Institutes in Hyderabad, State Bank of India and IIMs. However, these programmes were rather restricted and could not make the OD movement widely accepted in the country. In the mid-70s, OD was formally initiated at Larsen & Toubro by the ministry of HRD. But, overall it must be admitted that the OD movements in India were restricted mostly to the confines of academic institutions. However, a number of professional bodies committed to OD philosophies and practices emerged over the next decade or two, including ISABS (Indian Society for Applied Behavioural Sciences), Indian Society for Individual and Social Development (ISISD) and HRD Network.

Interactive Exercise

1. Refer to the case at the beginning of the chapter. Do you think that was an OD effort?
2. What is the nature of the OD activities that are involved here?

SEVEN STAGES OF OD CYCLE

As mentioned earlier, organizational development can never be a one-time effort on the part of the organization. Rather, it is a continuous process and can best be viewed as coming in cycle, with seven distinct phases (Burke 1994). These are given in Figure 11.2.

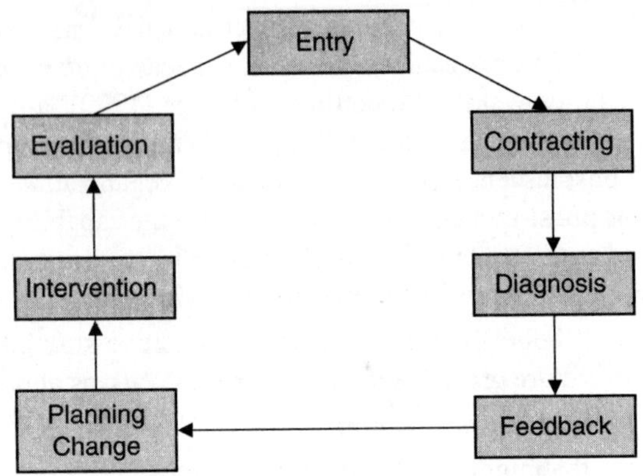

Figure 11.2 Phases of OD

Source: Ramnarayan and Gupta

1. **Entry:** This refers to the point of entry of the consultant. This is the initial phase of the OD cycle when the client meets the consultant for the first time with some perceived problem in his organization. The client usually checks the background and credential of the consultant before contacting him. The entry state is indeed a critical phase when the client and the consultant agree to analyse the issues jointly and explore ways to rectify the same. If, however, the parties do not agree, any one of them can backtrack.
2. **Contracting:** The second phase in the OD cycle is contracting when both parties enter the contractual agreement that clarifies the expectations (from each other), time limits and roles and responsibilities in clear and tangible terms. The contract also mentions the provision of termination if either party views the project as futile or inappropriate.
3. **Diagnosis:** The consultant hardly accepts the issues reported by the client as 'the real' problem. Just like a doctor never treats his patient on the basis of the reported symptoms only, but starts looking for the real causes behind the malady through diagnostic testing, the OD consultant also strives to unearth the root causes behind the malady. However, there in lies an important difference—unlike the doctor prescribing some medicine or course of action, the OD consultant adopts a collaborative approach when he searches jointly with the client the possible causes behind the malady. In order to understand the problem in its entirety, the consultant tries to identify the problem only after analysing the present state of the organization in terms of its structure, systems, policies, culture and processes. This fact-finding state explores both explicit and implicit aspects of the problem through two distinct stages: data collection and analysis. The purpose of diagnosis is not merely identifying the root causes or real issues, but also ensuring a joint understanding of the problem. The primary emphasis is given on generation of valid data and maintaining confidentiality.
4. **Feedback:** Feedback is a highly powerful tool to enhance personal awareness and attain a right perspective. In this phase, the consultant gets engaged in the process of sharing the data and analysis with the client, and develops a joint understanding and insight into the problem. This phase involves members of the organization from across the entire cross-section and is very critical as this ensures that the organizational members own the problem. A primary condition for attaining this must ensure that the consultant must carefully plan and ensure that the feedback session

remains a non-defensive and non-reactive environment. Only in a non-threatening atmosphere will organizational members be willing to receive, examine and assimilate information in a constructive manner.

5. **Planning change:** In this stage the task is to generate solution alternatives to the problem that has been identified at the previous stage and to analyse the possible consequences of each of these on the organization. Like all OD efforts, this too is based on a collaborative approach between the client and the consultant to decide upon the action plan. In the process, organizational members are encouraged to analyse the difficulties, if any, of the proposed action plan and to suggest ways to overcome these. The present phase is restricted to planning only and not implementing these plans, which would come next.
6. **Intervention:** This refers to the implementation stage when the agreed upon and modified plan of action is put into action. This involves well-defined sets of structured activities related to organizational improvement. It is indeed one of the most critical phases of the entire OD cycle as only after implementation can one assess whether the specific plan would actually take the organization to an improved stage or otherwise.
7. **Evaluation:** After the specific action plan is implemented in the organization, it's impact is evaluated. It becomes imperative to assess the gaps between the desired and the actual changes. If the changes do not meet expectations, required rectifications are to be made now. This phase also helps in identifying any unplanned events which might crop up either in the unit where the change has been initiated or it may have repercussions in a remote part of the organization.

QUESTIONS

1. What is OD?
2. What is the impetus for OD growth?
3. What are the seven stages of OD cycle?

REFERENCES

1. R. Beckhard, *Organization Development: Strategies and Models* (Reading, MA: Addison-Wesley, 1969).
2. M. Beer, *Organization Change and Development* (Santa Monica, CA: Good Year Publishing, 1980).
3. W.A. Bennis, *Organization Development: Its Nature, Origins and Prospects* (Reading, MA: Addison-Wesley, 1969).
4. Blake, R. R. and Mouton, J. S. (1964). The Managerial Grid. Houston: Gulf Publishing.
5. W.W. Burke, *Organization Development: A Process of Learning and Changing* (Reading, MA: Addison-Wesley, 1994).
6. D. Ciampa, *Total Quality* (Reading, MA: Addison-Wesley, 1992).
7. French, W. L. and Bell Jr., C. H, and Vohra, V. (2006). *Organization Development: Behavioral Science Interventions for Organization Improvement*. Dorling Kindersley (India) Pvt. Ltd.
8. French, W. L. and Bell Jr., C. H. (2001).'*Organization Development: Behavioral Science Interventions for Organization Improvement*', 6th ed, Englewood Cliffs, Prentice-Hall.

9. A. Levy and U. Merry, *Organizational Transformation* (New York: Praeger Publishers, 1986).
10. Lewin, K. (1946). '*Action Research and Minority Problems*', Journal of Social Issues, 2, 34-46.
11. L. Porter, 'OD: Some Questions Some Answer—An Interview with Beckhard and Shepard', *OD Practitioner*, 1974, Autumn, 6:1.
12. S. Ramnarayan and Neha Gupta (2011) contributed a chapter (Chapter 1) in '*Organization Development: Accelerating Learning and Transformation*', 2nd ed, edited by Ramnarayan, S. and Rao, T. V. Sage.
13. Ramnarayan, S. and Rao, T. V. (2011). '*Organization Development: Accelerating Learning and Transformation*'. Sage.
14. S. Ramodorai (2011). *The TCS Story and Beyond.* Portfolio (Penguin Group).
15. P. Senge, *The Fifth Discipline: The Art and Practice of the Learning Organization* (New York: Doubleday Currency, 1990).
16. J.M. Watkins and B.J. Mohr, *Appreciative Inquiry: Change at the Speed of Imagination* (San Francisco: Josse-Bass, 2001).
17. R.M. Weisbord, 'Future Search: Toward Strategic Integration', in W. Sikes, A. Drexler and J. Gant (Eds), *The Emerging Practice of Organization Development* (Alexandria, VA: NTL Institute for Applied Behavioural Science; San Diego, CA: University Associates, 1989).

Case Study: JPT—Where Things Do Not Change

Jagannath Precision Tools (JPT) Limited was founded in the early sixties as a small scale manufacturing unit in the industrial area in Hyde Road, near Calcutta Port by Shree Jadunath Mukhopadhyaya in his father's name. Mukhopadhyayas were an established family of repute in Howrah, the twin city of Kolkata. Though Jadunath was a student of literature with a poetic bend of mind he was a passionate person always itching to try his hands in something that is different. His love for literature and poetry did not rob him of a keen sense of practicality and pragmatism. At the suggestion of an engineering friend he started a business in manufacturing precision tools for holding automotive parts. There were hardly any such manufacturing facility in India at that time and one had to depend solely on importing these parts from abroad. Jadunath decided to venture in this completely new territory, partly accepting the challenge from his engineer friend and partly because of the lucrative offers and benefits from the Government to enhance local production to minimize reliance on import. Not only just that. Jadunath was a man with a vision. Even though he did not have any engineering background, instead of that being a hindrance, it actually helped him to appreciate things in the proper perspective as he had an open mind with genuine curiosity. Soon Jadunath targeted his market abroad from where India used to import these holding tools for automotive parts and started exporting his products to countries such as USA, Canada, UK, Germany, Switzerland, Australia, New Zealand and South Africa. The dream of manufacturing world's 'most accurate tools', over a relatively short period of time Jadunath was able to craft a small yet immensely profitable niche market and a worldwide reputation of being one of the largest exporters of precision tools. Because of its reputation in the precision tools manufacturing sector across the globe, JPT soon started selling its products through world renowned distributors such as Ford Motors, Tapmatics, Scully Jones, Hoffman and Weston Engineering, to name a few.

Over the years, JPT became a hugely profitable organization and did not have to rely on the home market at all as it had the strong demand from the foreign market across the world. This all was possible because of a simple 'mantra' that was followed by Jadunath throughout his life – *the continuous pursuit to excel in tool making technology and manufacture the most accurate tools.*

JPT is a relatively small organization with only hundred odd employees, including staff and workers. It however had created a very positive and warm organizational culture and a high degree of employee satisfaction. It is one of those rare organizations which have employees who have been associated with the company for more than 40 years and still maintain a satisfied grin on their faces whenever asked about their views on working for this company. The organization has a very congenial atmosphere where employees enjoy a very cordial relationship with their superiors along the hierarchy. There is complete transparency within the organization and, trust and reliability along with quality and dedication are the four pillars of its success.

The dedicated work force at JPT is fortunate to work with the latest and world's finest tool making machines. From the blocks of metal they craft the most precise pieces of equipment with their love and sweats following structured and standardized procedures to ensure the products strictly match the international standards. Continuous investments by JPT towards maintenance and improvement of the existing machines over the years to conform to international standards have ensured company's success for years to come.

Some of the products manufactured by the company are listed below:

- JPT Mandrel System
- JPT Special Expanding Collets
- JPT Double Angle Collets
- JPT BT and ISO V shanks
- JPT Quick Change Tap Chucks and Adaptors
- JPT Floating Holders
- JPT Utility Collets Chucks

Though JPT is a thriving and profitable organization, it does not mean it did not have its usual share of occasional lows. One such time was during the late nineties when world recession hit it very hard. There was the loyal and dedicated workforce who overnight became a burden as there was hardly any order coming. Paying employees' salary became a huge challenge. The auditors and financial advisors all suggested a workforce rationalization in order to make the organization tide over the hard time. The company was then run by Jadunath's only son Jayanto who had taken over after his fatther's demise. Jayanto was a Managing Director with a brilliant academic record and a management education from one of the premiere management institutes in the country, but more importantly he also possessed a compassionate heart. After having repeated meetings with his auditors and financial advisors who insisted that there is no way out than to go for workforce rationalization to tide over the present financial crisis faced by the company. At least, they suggested, Jayanto may start with people who were past the retirement age, but were never shown the door because of their skills and expertise and contribution to the company. When time was good, it was all very fine, the advisors pointed out, but not now. Jayanto should start with Nripen Samanta, one of the finest machinists, who was with company from Jadunath's time. He has lost his wife to cancer a couple of years back and his only daughter stays with her husband in Kanpur. The company was actually his home.

Jayanta had to agree as he could not argue with the advisors with their perfect reasoning. They said start with Nripen who was already sixty five. This will not only save the monthly salary and related costs, but also would give message to others, and it would eventually be possible to trim the flab in this way. Jayanto was feeling wretched and visibly restless. Watching him for a couple of days like that, his wife was forced to say, 'Come on, try smiling for a change. You are not the only company hit by recession.' Jayanto did not say a thing. Today he would have to go to factory and ask Nripen to leave. He was feeling awful. To try to get over the brooding, he went to take a cold shower. While standing under the shower, the cold water running all over his body, Jayanto suddenly heard his father's voice. Of course it was a trick of his own overburdened mind, he argued later. But for that moment it was a reality. He heard him as if Jadunath was standing next to him and addressing him in his typical manner, half jovial, indulgent but earnest at the same time. 'Are you a fool, my son? Who owns the company? You or those advisors of yours? Who knows each of your employees like your own relatives? You or they? Take the decisions of your own heart, son.'

Jayanto felt that the scales from his eyes were removed. He got dressed and started for the factory. Reaching the factory, he sent for Nripen babu. Nripen babu came with a sad smile on his face and asked 'Are you looking for me?' Jayanto said yes. Nripen Samanta nodded and said 'I know', because the bad news has already travelled. Jayanto asked, 'What do you know Nripen babu?' 'I know you would ask me to go. Truly, the time is tough. There is no order. I come every day and stand beside the machine, with practically no work to do, as there is no order coming these days. I know it's time for me to go…' 'You know nothing, Nripen babu', barked Jayanto. ' I called you to say, you ARE NOT going anywhere! The company will not be saved by saving your salary. That is too small an amount and that will not help the company to overcome the recession. If we are to die, we will die together. If good time ever comes, we will enjoy that together. You are staying with us, because you are one of the most loyal employees that JPT ever had!' when he finished, both of them had tears in their eyes.

The tough time eventually got over and the company was flooded with orders at least three times more than it ever had in the past. The work demand was easily met with the group of loyal and dedicated workforce cultivated over the years. Nripen Samanta is still with JPT and continues to be a pillar of strength. It is not only his workmanship and expertise that make him a distinguished employee, but his love and unstinted loyalty set a glorious example for the next generation to follow and idolize. The legendary success of JPT lies not only in the captured overseas market but also in the love and devotion of the workforce at a time where people vie largely for materialistic prosperity. In other words, it lies chiefly in tapping the human resources of the firm.

Questions

1. Comment on the focus of organizational change in the present context.

Chapter 12

Agents for Organization Development

Opening Case: Change of Guards at Tata Sons

Ratan Naval Tata was the chairman of Tata Sons for 21 years, during which he has led the group become stronger and more efficient, not only within the country but also across the world. He is widely credited for 'changing the architecture' of the group after taking charge from JRD Tata in 1991. Under his leadership, the revenues of the Tata Group soared 20 times with around 32 listed entities at over ₹4.5 trillion. During this time, Tata Group aggressively took over a number of well-established companies around the globe, starting from Corus and Tetley Tea to the later takeover of the prestigious carmaker Jaguar Land Rover, which was turned around successfully. The journey, however, could hardly be claimed to be smooth and was bereft with turbulence and a lot of ups and downs.

Ratan Tata, an architect graduated from Cornell University joined Tata Steel (then known as Tata Iron and Steel Company or TISCO) as an apprentice on the shop floor in the Jamshedpur plant in 1962, as he had to come back to India for personal reasons. JRD Tata was the Chairman at that time. He used to be surrounded by a group of highly successful executives such as Russi Mody at Tata Steel, Darbari Seth at Tata Tea and Chemicals, Ajit Kerkar at Taj Group of Hotels and Nani Palkiwalla, a director on the boards of several Tata companies and chairman of the erstwhile Associated Cement Companies (ACC Ltd), in which the Tata Group was one of the original promoters. These celebrated executives used to enjoy a lot of autonomy and seemed to be more closely associated with their companies than perhaps the Group Chairman JRD himself. It was rumored that most of them cherished the desire to succeed JRD. So when JRD chose Ratan Tata as his successor in 1991, it was not taken too kindly by this group of chairman aspirants, who used to wield a lot of power within the group. They let their feeling known as well, with almost an open hostility towards Ratan Tata, who was percieved as a dark horse. It is true that he had a number of success stories of turning around several group companies by that time, but with almost an equal number of failures to his credit. So it was indeed a surprise choice! In his initial years at Bombay, Ratan Tata was considered an outsider at the head office.

The major challenge for Ratan Tata as the group chairman was not to lead the company to right direction so much, but as to rein in these strongly influential and fiercely ambitious group of chairman aspirants, who had become extremely bitter after Ratan Tata's appointment as the group chairman. And Ratan Tata did rein in these satraps successfully and with considerable tact and eventually established his stronghold over the Tata Empire. Mody was sacked over an issue of the appointment of senior executives, Palkiwalla quit and Seth and Kerkar retired in close succession after Ratan Tata brought in a new policy setting the retirement age of directors at 70 and senior executives at 65. Business analysts in the country had credited Tata in bringing about a 'group vision from individual fiefdoms' and establishing the Tata Sons over the group companies. He was the one who gave importance to Tata brand over everything.

Ratan Tata turned 75 on 28 December 2012 and stepped down as the Chairman of Tata Sons, though he will remain the Chairman Emeritus of the group. Cyrus Mistry, whom he had been grooming for the last one year as his successor, has taken over from him.

As we see in the opening case, the most critical issue in running an organization is not devising brilliant strategies but implementing the change and acceptance of people in the organization. In this case, for Ratan Tata, it was realigning the power equation within the organization so as to establish his unquestioning supremacy as the chairman.

After reading this chapter, you would know how to implement changes successfully in an organization and who will be the right person for that. More specifically, you will be learning the following:

LEARNING OBJECTIVES

- Who can act as agents for change?
- External vs. internal agents for change
- Skills for effective change agents: organization development practitioner
- Competencies for effective OD practitioner
- Values and ethics of OD consultants

CHANGE AGENTS: WHO WILL TAKE THE CUDGEL?

Organizations need to strive for development on a continuous basis in order to ensure survival in the business. The change agents are those who can implement organizational strategies into realities and are located in the human resource department of the organization. In fact, the most important role for senior HR professionals is the role of a change agent who can create a renewed organization.

Change agents are those who can implement organizational strategies into realities.

ROLE OF CHANGE AGENTS IN AN ORGANIZATION

The most important mandates of change agents may be summarized as follows:

- To ensure the present functioning of the organization as well as enhancing future performance.
- To enable the organizational members to work effectively as they plan, implement and experience change.
- To enhance the organizational members' preparedness to manage future change.

WHO PRACTICES OD?

Who practices OD in an organization? Does it involve people employed within the organization or are they brought in from outside? In fact, there could be two types of OD practitioners who could drive in the required changes in an organization.

OD Specialists and Practitioners

The first category consists of the specialists and experts who have been trained as OD practitioners. These are the ones who practice OD principles and advocate and assist others to implement the same. External consultants can be summoned into the organization for tackling a specific malady. When faced with a problem, people in charge of running an organization look for an expert outside the organization who could set things right. They are located on the basis of their reputation and credentials in the market, and certainly from references. They are professionally trained as OD specialists and have a track record of helping organizations take the right course of action. People tend to open up to them relatively easily, as they are believed to have an open mindset without any preconceived notions. There are, however, certain problems with the external OD consultants. The first, of course, is the hefty fee they charge for their service. To locate a suitable consultant is also not always easy.

OD specialists and practitioners are people who practice OD principles and advocate and assist others to implement OD.

Internal Change Agents

The second category of OD practitioners would include the managers and leaders in the organization who can spearhead the changes from within and help in implementing specific OD intervention techniques. Being insiders, they have a better clue to the nature of the people in the organization as well as the overall functioning of the organization with the possible bottlenecks. On the other hand, people feel apprehensive and do not easily trust them.

Concept Check

1. Who are OD practitioners?
2. What do they do?

As noted by Ramanarayan (2011), the internal change agents may assume four typical leadership roles in the capacity to drive in changes within the organization. These are:

1. **Leader as cognitive tuner:** Who can have a feel of the peoples' mindset and can prepare them for changes both within and outside the organization.
2. **Leader as people catalyser:** Who can get people at his side and change them to a desired direction by virtue of his communication and clear vision.
3. **Leader as systems architect:** Can imply designing, building and sustaining a 'social architecture' by replacing old routines with new ones.
4. **Leader as efficacy builder:** When he enhances people's self-efficacy by enabling them to muster new skills and attitudes necessary to face the changed scenario.

SKILLS AND COMPETENCIES REQUIRED FOR EFFECTIVE CHANGE AGENTS

The following skills and competencies have been identified as essential qualities of change agents:

- **Diagnosing the problem:** The change agents must have an adequate understanding of both the business and the organization in order to identify the key performance issues and the possible impacts of these on both the long-term and short-term functioning of the organization.
- **Developing trusting relationship:** One of the most critical tasks of the change agent is to create an ambience of faith and mutual respect and to develop a trusting relationship with the client and the organizational members. It is evident that without this, there will be absolutely no progress.
- **Articulating organizational vision:** It is the task of the change agent not only to articulate and interpret the vision of the organization to the people but also to align their aspirations and motivate them.
- **Create teams and define leadership roles:** The change agents must be able to define the ongoing processes in the organization including communication, role modelling, reinforcement of desired behaviour in the context of the past history of the organization and the group dynamics in order to create and sustain effective teams and leaders.
- **Problem solving:** One essential skill of the change agent is to decipher the emotional and political overtones of the problems that arise in organizations. The task of a successful change agent is to enhance the sensitivity of the organizational members and involve them in collaborative problem solving as opposed to the prescriptive one.
- **Managing resistance to change and conflict:** As when the change agents would initiate changes in the organization in a deliberate and planned manner, people would instinctively try to resist those changes. These would also disrupt the old status quo and result in increased conflicts among people. The change agents must have the ability to tackle these change-induced problems effectively.
- **Risk taking:** The change agent must be able to take risks and tolerate ambiguity, as in changed situations things will have to chalk out anew and often without any cut and dried solutions.
- **Ability to change himself:** It would never work to urge others to change and maintain one's own status intact. The change agent must have the flexibility to change himself if that is required.

- **Planning and project management skills:** The change agent must be an impeccable planner with a thorough knowledge of project management skill as the entire effort of change has to be time bound and cost efficient.
- **Implementing the change:** The task of the change agent is not only to identify the right strategy but also to implement it through appropriate change in organizational culture as well as supportive people policies, systems and processes.

Concept Check

What are the skills and competencies of an OD practitioner?

VALUES AND ETHICS OF OD CONSULTANTS

The pioneering authors and researchers in the field of OD, such as Warren Bennis, Richard Beckhard, Robert Tannenbaum and Sheldon Devis listed down a number of OD values that are essential for OD practitioners.

These may be summed up as follows:

- Implicit assumptions about the nature of people to be basically good.
- Accepting people to be in process and evolving slowly over time.
- Viewing and accepting individuals as a whole person rather than just a job holder.
- Allowing people to be in touch with their emotions and expressing them rather than suppressing.
- Allowing and encouraging authentic behaviour instead of 'maskmanship' and 'game playing'.
- Trusting people.
- Not to avoid facing people and encouraging appropriate confrontation.
- Being sensitive and appreciating the processes involved as essential to effective task accomplishment.
- Encouraging collaboration and not competition.

QUESTIONS

1. Who are change agents?
2. What are the roles of change agents?
3. What are essential skills of change agents?
4. What are the important values of change agents in order to be effective and successful in their task?

Case Study: Bringing in a Gradual Change

Amit Vasani looked beyond the young lady sitting in front of him at the picture of Vasani Sr. and smiled. He was having a silent dialogue with his dad as he often did. 'What a mess you had landed me in! It was certainly not fair, dad. I was only 24 and you pushed me mercilessly!'

He took off his spec and started polishing it slowly while looking at the lady who had come from a well-known English daily to take his interview. He was a well-known figure in Indian industry today and people like to read about him and the Vasani group of industry. Yes, he knew that. But he did not know how to portray his plight during those initial days when he was suddenly thrown into the deep water of managing the entire Vasani Empire at the age of 24.

The last question the lady had asked him took him on a nostalgic trip down memory lane. '*What were your mandates Mr. Vasani when you took over the charge of Vasani group of companies from your father at a very young age*?' He wore the spec and smiled at the lady. How can he explain that he never took charge of anything from anybody? His father simply disappeared from the scene and permanently migrated to the United States to help develop the group's international business, thrusting everything to his son who had just graduated from one of the premiere engineering colleges in the country. Vasani Jr. was entrusted with the total responsibility of running the business of Vasani Group of Industry in India. It was still a mystery to Amit as to why his father had taken such a decision. In retrospect, he believed his father actually took a calculated gamble, which he figured could be taken because should the ship start sinking, nothing would prevent him from flying back. In fact, he promised his son that he would fly down whenever any crisis arose, but it was only to be used as a 'fire-brigade'. In the first two years after he left, he came back four times every year; in the third year, he came back twice and in the fourth year only once. From the fifth year onwards, he stopped coming altogether. Although Amit felt quite unprepared for this daunting task, it was apparent that his father had full confidence in his abilities.

It would surely be unfair to say that Vasani Sr. did not groom his son for finally taking charge of his empire. In fact, he started preparing his son from a very early age. Amit had a different kind of childhood. Like many others from the similar social strata, he had studied in the best residential school in the country. But while others used to go home or other tourist spots on vacations, Amit used to spend his holidays on locations where the Vasani group was either erecting a new plant or renovating an existing one, within or outside the country. Vasani Sr. would camp in these places with his entire family, which consisted of his wife and son. Mrs. Vasani was completely devoted to her husband and his passion and never minded those 'camp lives'. And for Amit, these were simply wonderful. He had the sweetest and fondest memories of those 'camp lives' at various locations where he used to accompany his father to the plants. He was no doubt thoroughly pampered by all the people around who used to call him *chhota sab*. However, on looking back he understands how much he learned from those trips. He learned about people and learned to love the smell and sights of the plant. He was initiated to engineering drawings during these 'camp lives', long before he enrolled into formal engineering classes. Actually he learned to love his father's passion.

The Vasani Group began its journey in the early 1950s under the entrepreneur-owner Vasani Sr. in Kolkata in eastern India. Since then, the Vasani Group has grown to 10 companies and more than 500 employees with manufacturing plants and offices throughout India. Vasani Group has been India's dominant manufacturer of foundry equipment, combustion equipment and industrial furnaces. Twenty per cent of the group's sales come from foundry equipment, 30 per cent from combustion equipment and the remaining 50 per cent from industrial furnaces. It has corporate and head offices at Kolkata, with regional offices at six major industrial centres—New Delhi, Ahmedabad, Mumbai, Pune, Bangalore and Chennai, covering entire India.

But all these did not happen overnight. There was a strong effort behind every successful step that the company took. However, Vasani Jr. believes that whatever success he achieved was because of the fact that he had a loyal and committed group of people behind him. In fact, the company had many senior people in the organization as it had a principle of not throwing anybody out of the company as a policy. It certainly helped to build a loyal and committed workforce. But, at the same time, just having a group of old loyalists may not always help. He could sense that the old timers who had been in the company from his father's time had become complacent, basking in the glory of past success. Amit was painfully aware of this but was hardly in a position to change anything during his initial days. He understood that these people were his main asset. They were an integral part of Vasani Group and were fiercely loyal and emotionally attached to Vasani Sr. and the company they worked for. Taking any harsh or drastic decision would undoubtedly ruin the morale of the entire group.

As Amit experienced, these people were mostly old timers who were loyal to his father, Vasani Sr. Amit, of course, was cherished as *chhota sab* as they had seen him grow. But, at the same time, they did not take him too seriously. It was indeed delicate for Amit to occupy the highest position in the organization at a time when he was not mentally prepared.

But, at the same time, Amit was sure that this state of affairs would not go on forever. If they had to survive and retain the number one position in the market that they used to enjoy in his father' regime, the company and its people would need to turn around and take things seriously. Amit knew that to remain in the business, the company would need to keep growing and have to be the first choice of the customers even if the company's products became an expensive choice. And in order to achieve this, Amit put an extra effort to identify strong and well-known international partners and thus become one of the most respected companies with the latest available know-how and technology. Vasani now formed joint ventures with two German sister companies. In 2000, Vasani entered into a technology licensing agreement with Furnace Construction Company Plc. of the United Kingdom to manufacture oil- and gas-fired cremators. With the liberalization of Indian economy, Vasani Group also set up an exclusive export company and targeted the rapidly growing industrial markets in Asia-Pacific, Middle East and Africa. In addition, it became the marketing agent in India of several leading international foundry equipment manufacturers.

But a lot of changes were needed within the organization as well. Amit understood that being hasty would certainly backfire. Instead, he decided to bring about incremental rather than harsh and abrupt changes in the organization. He respected people's seniority and involvement, and learned a good deal in the realm of managerial and operating issues from their experience. He nevertheless initiated the change process in a gradual way, which was never intimidating to the people involved. These were thus transformative in nature and became embedded in the very fabric of the organizational life of the Vasani Group. He did not touch the policy of life membership in the group, but at the same time introduced the concept of accountability by maintaining a basic performance standard in the organization. As there were hardly any threats involved in the process of change, people slowly started accepting these and eventually Amit was able to change the outlook of the people and face the challenges of modern times. But more importantly, from Amit's perspective, it was a bloodless battle that he won, in which mutual love and respect had been reinforced and enhanced in the organization, making it a truly joyful place to be.

Questions

1. How did the organization change from one generation to the next?
2. How did Vasani Jr. bring in the change in the organization?
3. Comment on Vasani Jr.'s change handling style.

Chapter **13**

Organization Development and Its Steps

Opening Case: An OD Intervention Effort

Debmohan Chatterjee is already sixty-five and is now seriously worried about the fate of the family business, a paper mills machinery manufacturing company 'Tara Sundari Paper Mills'. It was founded by his late father Debdas Chatterjee. The company had grown rapidly and once it employed a workforce of over 500 in addition to the engineers, managers, accountants and other white-collar employees. The good time for Tara Sundari was, however, slowly coming to an end. The eastern part of India began to be troubled by militant trade union movements, which eventually forced many big companies to wind up and shift their production base to other parts of the country. The demand for machinery and parts was dwindling down at Tara Sundari; the large workforce became a concern because of the union politics and the negligible support from the ruling government in the state. After completing his education, Debmohan took over from his father. Debdas however foresaw that the troubles faced by the company would increase and perhaps it would be more judicious to slowly wind up the company. But Debmohan did not listen to his father's advice. Debdas died a few years later. With the tireless effort along with the support of a group of trusting and loyal employees from his father's time, Debmohan sailed the company through.

Now, Debmohan was feeling lost again. Over the past few years, the profit margin kept on showing an obstinate downturn and the company also had to face labour unrest. The company certainly needs to be pulled up. Employees were losing the passion to work for the company. They seemed to take everything for granted and never bothered about how to survive. Debmohan was feeling strongly perturbed. Finally, he decided to take the help from his alma mater. He requested two professors—from a premier management institute from the city where he graduated from—to work as management development consultants for 'Tara Sundari Paper Mills'. The professors, one senior and the other relatively younger, came to the organization and met the senior managers to find out the challenges met by the company and to discuss strategies to overcome these. The consultants organized a workshop to plan appropriate steps that can be taken and to prepare the employees to embrace the change. However, hardly anything came out from the 3-day workshop. Most of the managers acted as mere spectators. Instead of committing themselves and being truly participative, they relied on the top echelon comprising the president to take steps, if any.

As the case illustrates, attempting to develop the organization through a series of well-thought out, planned changes never guarantees that changes would actually take place. The greatest hurdle for any change effort is getting people's acceptance of those changes before there is any hope for implementing them.

The pivot of any OD effort is the action research model, where specific actions are decided only on the basis of organization diagnosis, which is firmly rooted in research. We will discuss more about the action research model when we learn various OD intervention techniques later.

After going through this chapter, you will be able to understand how to implement changes in the organization to achieve organization development. More specifically, you would know the following:

LEARNING OBJECTIVES

- Diagnosing the organization
- Diagnosing the groups within the organization
- Gathering diagnostic data
- Feeding back the diagnostic data
- Deciding on organizational interventions
- Monitoring and stabilizing Organization Development (OD) intervention

DIAGNOSING THE ORGANIZATION

The first step of any effort towards organization development is to identify the typical characteristics of the organization in question. It is similar to the process of deciding on a particular course of action by a physician while treating a patient. In the first place, he is to know the exact state of the patient before choosing a particular line of treatment, as what can work for one patient may not work for another. Similarly, the person in charge of organization development must first meticulously diagnose the state of the organization before taking any action.

The organization diagnosis process typically starts with the collection of data from various levels of employees. Apart from accurately identifying the antecedent causes within the organization, the very participative approach ensures people's involvement and subsequently a higher possibility of their accepting the changes.

Organizational diagnosis is the collection of data about the total system, its subunits, its processes and its culture.

As has already been noted in the earlier chapters, organization development is essentially a scientific endeavour, where every step is taken objectively on the basis of existing data. The diagnosis of the organization is in fact an ongoing process that depends on 'collection of data about the total system, its subunits, its processes, and its culture' (French, Bell, and Vohra, 2006). Like the clinical diagnosis, organizational diagnosis is also multilayered, involving employees across different levels in the organization to identify factors leading to the status quo, unearth the real underlying causes leading to the problems faced by the organization, the strengths and weaknesses of the organization along with possible opportunities that await the organization.

The effort to diagnose an organization can start at different levels, which may be described as follows:

Total Organization: Diagnosing the organization starts with the total organization including its complex subsystems such as employees in various groups starting from top management teams, customers, suppliers, various regulatory bodies and the like, as in the case of a large business firm or a university.

The stated objectives or missions of the organization, for example, would provide some clue to the basic functioning of the organization. Similarly, the exploration includes organizational culture, climate, processes and performance, to name a few. To understand the state of a particular organization, one has to probe into all these areas.

Large Subsystems: The next focus would be the complex and heterogeneous subsystems within the large organization, such as its different divisions, departments, subsidiaries and subunits in multiple locations, with typical orientations and shares of their own issues. It also tries to identify the attitudes and feelings that are held by these subgroups towards others, namely, different divisions, departments and subsidiaries within the larger set up, in addition to the total organization.

Small Subgroups: Small subgroups with relatively homogeneous structure, such as top management, task force or cross-functional teams, faculty members and non-teaching staff in a teaching institute, important subordinate groups and the like, would be the next level of analysis for the organization development consultants or practitioners. The focus could be further fine-tuned when directed to dyads (pairs such as superior-subordinate, interdependent colleagues) or triads consisting of multiple group members, down to individuals when the attention is focused at the micro level. Understanding and specifying individual roles and expectations also falls under this level.

Between-organization Systems: It probes into the relationship and interaction patterns that might exist between two separate but interacting organizations, such as the functioning of a particular organization within the jurisdiction of state law agencies.

As already pointed out, organizational diagnosis is a systematic and ongoing process. It can however be thoroughly pre-planned and specifically structured or it could even evolve over time while analysing the emergent data carefully. Information for organization diagnosis can be obtained by employing several methods such as personal interview, observations and administering structured questionnaires, and from secondary data source such as organizational records. The way the information is collected is also very important from the perspective of organization development. It is to note that the main thrust in any OD effort is the collaborative approach to develop between the OD practitioner and the organizational members, in almost everything—from identifying the target group, the method of diagnosis, organizational processes to focus on or how to use the data for action planning. So much so that the information generated in any OD effort is treated as the property belonging to those who generated these. Thus, it is imperative to give them the feedback and in fact the process of giving an honest feedback to the different groups and subgroups from whom the data was generated is a vital part of OD process.

Concept Check

1. What is diagnosing the organization?
2. Why is it important for the OD consultant?

Weisbord's Six-box Model

Marvin Weisbord (1976) developed his six-box model as an excellent framework to diagnose the organization. This model identifies six critical areas to look into in order to understand the state of an organization and is critically important for organizational success.

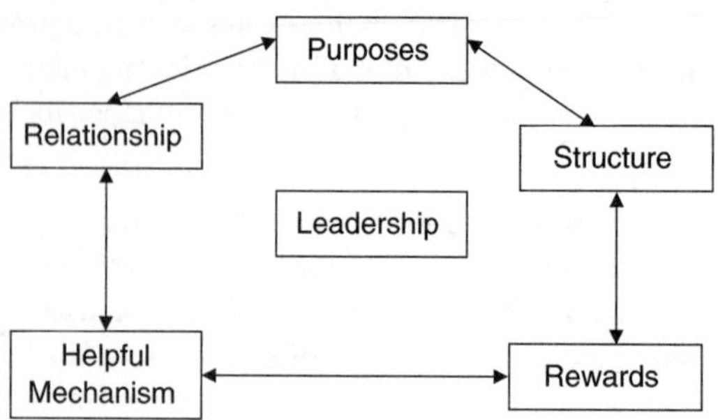

Figure 13.1 Weisbord's Six-box Framework

Source: Weisbord, (1976).

The six critical areas are as follows:

1. **Purpose:** This refers to the objectives and the basic purpose for the existence of the organization.
2. **Structure:** This denotes the specific structure of the organization along with the existing reporting relationships.
3. **Rewards:** This tries to find out whether the needed tasks and behaviours are properly rewarded with adequate incentives.
4. **Helpful mechanisms:** This attempts to check whether there exists adequate amount of coordination among various subunits within the organization.
5. **Relationships:** This keeps a check on whether the relationships among the people within the organization are positive and without major conflicts or otherwise. This also attempts to find out, even when conflicts ensue, what the usual ways of dealing with these in the organization are.
6. **Leadership:** Organizational leadership is actually the balancing mechanism among all these different aspects within the organization.

It is to note that all the six boxes are within the broader environmental context that encompasses everything around us and in turn may influence the functions of the boxes as well.

As pointed out by Weisbord, the OD consultant must check both the *formal* and *informal* aspects of each box, as often what is formally announced is not what is practised. The consultant must check

Manager's Essence: Slow but Steady

When Mehta Junior took the mantle from his father at a young age of 24, he found that many things needed to be addressed in the relatively old and by then almost rusty organization. But the problem was that nothing could be done in haste as most of the employees were from his father's time and were fiercely loyal to the company. Hence, he decided to devote more time to bring in the desired changes. He was very patient and did not thrust the changes on the people. He engaged a reputed OD consultant who started to work from the very top management level down to the lowest echelon. Many were interviewed and they were also asked about opinions, views and suggestions regarding the betterment of the company. After several feedback, and brainstorming sessions, the outline of changes was formulated in joint collaboration of the employees and the consultant. The changes were brought into the system and the technology was updated, along with increased training support. There was also an effort of 'cutting the flab' but that too was rather incremental than drastic. More reliance was on natural attrition or voluntary retirements.

In less than 5 years, the group became India's dominant manufacturer of foundry equipment, combustion equipment and industrial furnaces. Now, 20 per cent of the group's sales come from foundry equipment, 30 per cent from combustion equipment and the remaining 50 per cent from industrial furnaces. It has corporate head office at Kolkata, with regional offices at five six major cities in India.

Mehta now formed joint ventures with a French company. In 2000, Mehta entered into a technology licensing agreement with a British Company to borrow the latest technology. With the liberalization of Indian economy, Mehta group also set up a separate export-dedicated company and targeted the rapidly growing industrial markets in South East Asia, the Middle East and Africa. In addition, it became the marketing agent in India of several leading international foundry equipment manufacturers.

in the first place whether the formal system is correct for a particular box and secondly, whether the evolving informal system is acceptable for the overall functioning of the organization. According to Weisbord, the formal/informal distinction provides a powerful insight in understanding and diagnosing an organization.

THE DIFFERENT PHASES OF OD PROGRAMME

According to Burke, whenever any organization decides to go for organization development, it has to go through several logical phases, which are as follows:

- **Entry:** This denotes the first contact between the client and the OD consultant or practitioner. It happens when the client feels there are some problems faced by the organization that need to be addressed. The client or the person in charge of the organization searches for a competent person who can lend his expertise in this area. Usually this is done on the basis of references.
- **Contracting:** In this stage, the client and the consultant meet and clarify the mutual expectations. This includes specifying expected time frame, cost and other resources on the one hand as well as what can be delivered by the consultant.
- **Diagnosis:** This is exploring the problem as stated by the client in all its complexities and perspectives. It is essentially the fact-finding stage through various methods—interviewing people, administering questionnaires, observing and scrutinizing important and relevant organizational records—to get to the bottom of the problem.
- **Feedback:** After collecting the relevant information from various sources and methods, now it is time to give the analysed information to the client system across various levels. This helps checking the accuracy of the consultant's understanding of the organization in its totality as well as having a better clue to the specific problem.
- **Planning change:** In this stage, specific action plans are made by the consultant along with the organizational members. Exploring various alternatives and their possible consequences are discussed in detail before agreeing on a particular course of action.

- **Intervention:** This refers to the stage of implementation of the action plan as agreed upon by the consultant and key organizational members.
- **Evaluation:** This refers to the process of assessing the effects of implementation of the programme—whether it is providing the desired result or otherwise. If it is found to be not in the desired direction, required corrective steps are to be taken.

QUESTIONS

1. What is organizational diagnosis?
2. Why is organizational diagnosis necessary before any OD effort can take place?
3. What are the levels in the organization that the OD consultant needs to address?
4. Explain Weisbord's six-box model of organizational diagnosis.
5. Identify different phases of OD programme in an organization.

REFERENCE

1. French, W. L., Bell, Jr., C. H. and Vohra, V. (2006). *Organization Development: Behavioral Science Interventions for Organization Improvement* (Dorling Kindersley (India) Pvt. Ltd).
2. Weisbord, M. R. (1976). "*Organizational Diagnosis: Six Places to Look for Trouble With or Without a Theory*," Group and Organization Studies, 1(4): 430–77.

Case Study: Shift in Business at United Engineers

The attraction was mutual and from the very first moment. When Shantanu Roy, a middle age practising foundry-man trouble shooting in and around Kolkata and Howrah, was looking for someone to prepare a very precisely finished machine component, he stumbled into a cubbyhole workshop in the interior of Howrah, fondly referred to as the 'Manchester' of India for its population of indigenous craftsmen who could create miracle in small workshops. The proprietor, a young man of around 30 years of age, quoted a price of ₹60 only for that piece of machinery, which was far too low for Shantanu's expectation. He was delighted, as that would leave a pretty good margin for him before he would supply it to the end user at the rate of ₹250. When the material was at last delivered after a longish wait, the proprietor fumbled that it had actually cost him ₹160 and not ₹60, as quoted by him initially. Without a question, Shantanu put the amount on the table. The young proprietor however took only ₹60, leaving the hundred-rupee note. Shantanu was genuinely pleased to see the honesty of the young fellow. He was seeing a near-extinct species of human race—a *gentleman*! Anil, the young proprietor of United Engineers, also found Shantanu quite a fascinating, if not slightly quirky, individual. He was around 20 years older than Anil, had long practical experience in this field, a tough nut to crack. He was a proper *sahib* in his English accent, terribly sharp and rather intuitive, as far as the business was concerned, and at the same time indulgent and affectionate in his own ways. In spite of his elite background, Shantanu could easily relate to the working class people and always showed a genuine respect to them.

That was the beginning! Within a year or so, Shantanu joined Anil, and lent him his expertise in developing his modest workshop into a prospering business. Anil hailed from an educated upper middle class Bengali family, and according to Shantanu, 'without an iota of business sense'. Shantanu, however, visualized the tremendous growth opportunity for Anil's modest workshop, with a yearly turnover of only ₹8 lakh. In spite of the bleak business scenario and consistently low profit margin, which made even the salary payments to the employees often a daunting task, there were a few good things that could certainly save the firm. The fact that this modest workshop was a registered vendor of Diesel Locomotive Works (DLW), Varanasi, a part of Indian Railways, was indeed the 'silver cloud' as the entire products they could yield were taken by Indian Railways. In addition to the Indian Railways, it was also enrolled with the Gun & Shell Factories in Cossipore and later in Ishapore as registered vendors. Though the rates were not exactly lucrative as the usual practice with the large Public Sector Organizations the orders were steady and the payments assured, even if delayed.

When Shantanu joined Anil, he correctly identified the chief causes of the malady, that is, the sluggish business with a low profit margin. The most troubling one was evidently the cash crunch. Secondly, the huge quantity of rejection was posing dual problems—wastage as well as storage cost. The third culprit was the lack of an intelligent product line with fewer competitors, which was responsible to a large extent for the low profit. As most people in the business were creating similar kinds of products, it was imperative to keep the price low, thus severely eating away the margin of profit. Shantanu worked very hard to allay these. In the first place, he approached the bank for funding. However, this was never hassle free, with the bankers' primary emphasis on conforming to the rules without much concern to the small manufacturing unit's various predicaments and enormous backlogs in payments from the Government concerns, which were the major clients with United Engineers.

While trying to tackle the second problem, that is, the huge rejection rate, he found a solution to the third problem, that is, creating a new product line less fraught with competitors. Shantanu had more than four decades of experience in the foundry line and as an active member of the Institute of Indian Foundrymen he was aware of the shift in general demand for non-ferrous foundry products. He steered the company to the production of non-ferrous foundry products (copper- and aluminium-based alloys), which, apart from responding to the market demands, could also successfully address the issue of huge rejection. The rejected parts of the iron and steel products had to be simply sold off at an abysmally low price as these could not be recycled and would incur unnecessarily high storage cost. However, these non-ferrous rejected materials could be either recycled or would fetch a considerable higher price when sold as scrap.

Around this time, the DLW was changing the model of their diesel engines and adopting the General Motors' models of locomotive engines (GM Loco), with higher HP and better hauling capacity, and was in the process of slowly replacing the existing diesel engines in the Indian Railways with GM Loco. In the GM Loco, the machine parts required were all non-ferrous, especially with copper- and aluminium-based alloys, the areas where Shantanu had a wide exposure and specialization. The shift from ferrous to non-ferrous foundry was truly a Midas touch for United Engineers, and it did not require any major change in technology or know-how and the existing in-house skills and expertise could produce the products with ease. Thus, after a long time in business, United Engineers started to taste real success for the first time.

The shift in the product line from ferrous to non-ferrous (aluminium- and copper-based alloys) foundry solved two gnawing problems at United Engineers—reducing the rejection cost and entering into an area with relatively lesser number of competitors with adequate expertise.

By this time, the reputation of United Engineers had gone up well in the market with more contracts pouring in. Eventually, United Engineers started venturing into the foreign market. They already had the import-export license and after entering into collaboration with a local organization having export-oriented business, United Engineers took the export seriously for two main reasons. Firstly, the scope for increasing the profit in Indian soil was largely limited because of the fierce competition and conservative pricing of the PSUs, the main customers for United Engineers. The business pattern here was thus largely growth deterrent, as it required blockage of huge investment with poorest Return on Investment (ROI). Secondly, in the export-oriented business model, the possibility of remaining competitive by offering the lowest price and still enjoying a good ROI in terms of INR was feasible owning to the drooping INR value.

Thus, United Engineers is at present doing brisk businesses with countries like Vietnam, Canada and Brazil, with possibility of further business scopes in other countries. The saga of United Engineers highlights how a changed outlook can turn around a modest small-scale workshop to a flourishing business.

Questions

1. What do you believe is the real reason for success at United Engineers?
2. Would you agree to call Shantanu an OD practitioner rather than just an expert engineer? Why?

Chapter **14**

Different OD Intervention Strategies

Opening Case: Wesman Group of Industries

Wesman group of industries is a leading company in industrial furnaces and kilns, combustion and foundry equipment, and thermal plants. It started its journey in 1951 as Wesman Engineering Company Pvt Ltd under the leadrership of Arjan Vaswani, the founder member, and since then has travelled a long path. In 1973, it became Wesman Thermal Engineering Processes and in 1993 it ventured into export. The year 1996 onwards, Wesman started importing latest technologies in its related fields of operation and went for technical collaboration with various European giants. Wesman's proven track record, spanning a period of more than six decades, has established itself as a trusted and reputed group of companies in the Indian market as well as abroad.

The journey, however, was never easy. It was more of a family-oriented business with a group of loyal and faithful employees, a number of whom were associated with the company from the time of its inception. They adored Vaswani, the senior, were devoted to him and were very proud of their company. That however did not exactly help the company to explore newer possibilities and charting out new business ventures. It was evident that the people, particularly the old timers and fiercely loyal ones, were getting rather complacent, basking in their past glory and a stagnant stage in business seemed to set in. In the meantime, Vaswani junior had taken the rein of the business from his father and felt that quick steps had to be taken if he was to save the company and put it in the right track.

He eventually brought in a team of qualified OD practitioners to look into the problem in the company, which were many—from dwindling profit margin to shrinkage of market share and overall stagnation. These people were not only smart, intelligent and knowledgeable, but were also quite sensitive and could well understand the people issue and various behavioural dynamics in the organization. They started talking to various groups in the organization right from the top and down the line to even the shop floor employees in the Kolkata office and plant of the company. They thoroughly examined the work processes and involved the organizational members in the search process to find out ways for improvement. They collected a lot of data from across the organization and extensively discussed the feedback with the involved groups. At the end of nearly more than 2 years they came out with their recommendations and suggested changes in a number of areas. The consultant team remained with the company a little longer until the process of implementation was successful and was accepted by the majority of the employees, including of course the management groups. The beauty of the present OD effort was that they never rushed the people, which helped remove any psychological fear they might have during the transition phase.

After the consultants left Wesman, there were indeed a number of changes in the organization. Employees were embracing changes and were not shying away from trying newer ways of doing something, be it technology or otherwise. The market share and profit margin also improved and the company was seriously considering the business beyond the national boundary, which they eventually did successfully, along with venturing into newer business.

What you see in the above case illustration is an OD intervention. You may take a note of the sequence of steps taken and the outcome of the effort. The present chapter describes different OD intervention strategies that are used by the OD consultants. We would make an effort to classify different strategies and their expected impacts on the organization. More specifically, the following interventions will be discussed:

LEARNING OBJECTIVES

- Human process intervention: individual, interpersonal and group process approaches
- Team building interventions
- Process consultation interventions
- Inter-group team building interventions
- Third-party peace-making interventions
- Organization mirror interventions
- Comprehensive OD interventions
- Search conferences

ACTION RESEARCH AND ORGANIZATIONAL DEVELOPMENT INTERVENTION STRATEGIES

OD is strictly a scientific endeavour and is based on a systematic research. Before deciding on any specific intervention strategy, OD practitioners have to conduct their research to identify the root of the problem and find out ways that would solve these and improve the conditions prevailing in the organization. According to Lewin, one of the most renowned and applied social scientists of his time, a thorough research on possible action programmes must be conducted to ascertain any social change programme. These would address several important issues: greater understanding of the root of the problem; its possible negative effects and the dynamics of 'social ills'; the need for collaboration between the practitioner and the organizational members to find out workable solutions that can be implemented to allay the maladies; and the need for generating a database to arrive at generalized principles to explain 'complex social phenomena'.

Action research: *The process of systematically collecting research data about an ongoing system relative to some objective, goal or need of that system; feeding these data back into the system; taking action by altering selected variables within the system based both on the data and on hypotheses; and evaluating the results of actions by collecting more data.*

French, Bell and Vohra (2006) define action research as 'the process of systematically collecting research data

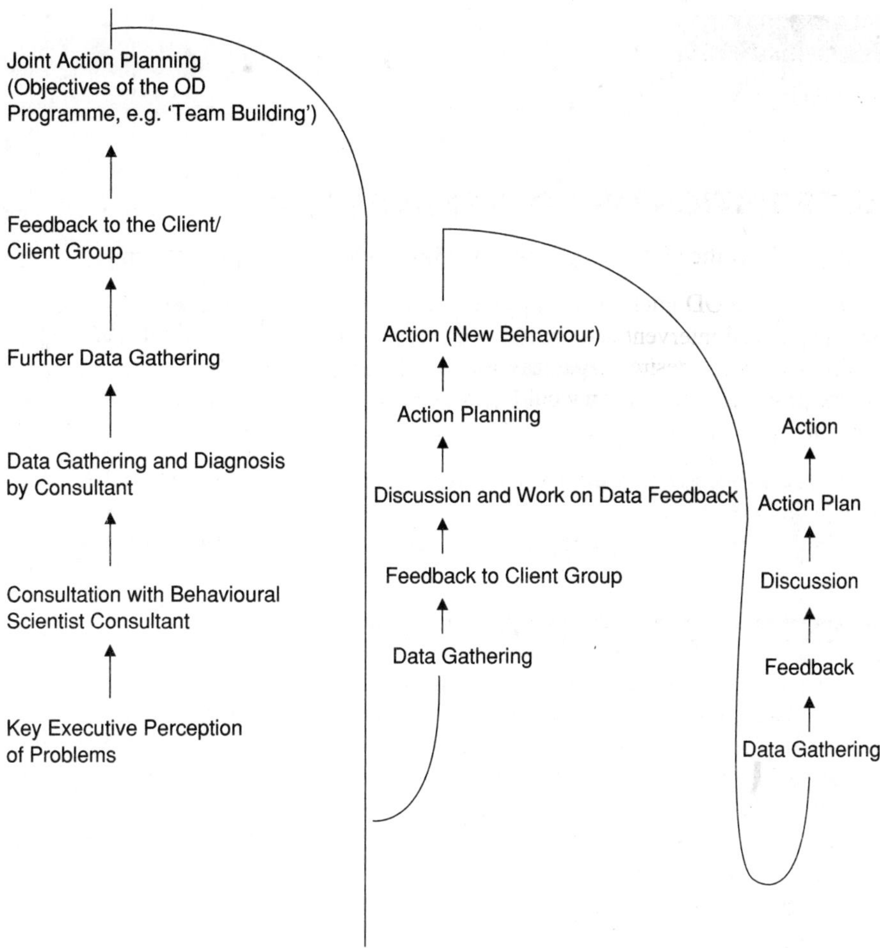

Figure 14.1 Action Research Model

about an ongoing system relative to some objective, goal, or need of that system; feeding these data back into the system; taking action by altering selected variables within the system based both on the data and on hypotheses; and evaluating the results of actions by collecting more data'. The key aspects of the model are diagnosis, data gathering, feedback to the client group, data discussion and work by the client group, action planning, and action.

WHAT IS AN OD INTERVENTION?

OD interventions are a set of activities in which selected organizational units, that is, individuals or target groups, are engaged (French, Bell and Vohra 2006). These are a sequence of tasks with specific goals of organization development. Cummings and Worley (2001) define OD intervention as 'a set of sequenced and planned actions or events intended to help the organization increase its effectiveness.' According to them, interventions are purposely designed to disrupt the status quo and thus help initiating change.

Concept Check

1. What is OD intervention?

CHARACTERISTICS OF OD INTERVENTIONS

Before selecting any specific OD intervention, it is imperative to check the following:

- Whether the specific OD intervention matches the needs of the organization.
- Whether the planned interventions are firmly based on an established causal relationship between the intervention and the desired organizational outcomes.
- Whether the proposed intervention would help to transfer the required competence in order to manage change to organizational members.

In addition, it is also necessary to ascertain whether these would be feasible to implement in the organization and whether people involved would accept these. It is also needed to determine the possible consequences, both positive as well as negative, of the planned interventions beforehand.

IMPLEMENTING OD INTERVENTIONS

The success of any OD intervention strategy clearly depends on its effective implementation. There has to be some plan to tackle the inherent uncertainty arising out of changes in the prevalent conditions and some unanticipated consequences that may eventually crop up. The entire process of implementation is rather a tentative one, often requiring constant monitoring and refinement. Before implementing any change, it is necessary to foresee its consequences in terms of the organizational members' willingness and/or ability to change. Also, a lot depends on the capability of the change agent or the consultant to drive in the desired change.

More specifically, implementation of any OD intervention requires the following:

- Clearly defined long-term and short-term objectives of the OD effort.
- Key organizational members must be involved in the process, which should be collaborative in nature, in order to ensure smooth implementation.
- The goals to attain should be arranged in order of difficulty and to start with the ones that are easier to achieve. Feedback of success would be powerful motivators for the people and would ensure commitment.
- In order to effectively involve the organizational members, emotional appeals, and not only rational approach, are necessary.
- The intervention activities should be carefully sequenced to provide a feeling of psychological safety to the people.

EVALUATING OD INTERVENTIONS

The impacts of any OD intervention should be evaluated on a continuous basis so that the required corrective measures, if any, can be taken before it is too late. Criteria for evaluation must include both hard and soft approaches. Thus, in addition to the hard criteria of productivity, quality assurance, reduced absenteeism, employee attitudes and feelings should also be considered. These criteria should ideally be pre-determined before any OD intervention takes place.

CATEGORIES OF OD INTERVENTION STRATEGIES

The major classification of OD intervention strategies can be made in terms of two dimensions: static, dynamic or a combination of both on one hand and structured, unstructured or a combination of both on the other. Table 14.1 comprises some of the usually practised organizational strategies.

Table 14.1 Categories of OD Intervention Strategies

	Static	**Dynamic**	**Both**
Structured	MBO, RAT	■ Role negotiation ■ Organization mirroring	Survey feedback
Unstructured	■ Team building ■ Internal facilitator	■ T-group ■ Conflict resolution	Process consultation
Both	Job enrichment	Managerial Grid	Confrontation

BRIEF OVERVIEW OF DIFFERENT OD INTERVENTIONS

Another way of looking into OD interventions is in terms of the specific groups for whom the intervention processes are aimed. French, Bell and Vohra (2006) identified a number of OD intervention strategies specifically designed for five-category target groups in the organization. These are described as follows:

1. **Individual level:** Life and career-planning activities, providing coaching and personal counselling, creating scope for skill enhancement (including both technical and behavioural skills) by organizing training and education of the individual employees, sensitivity training or T-Group, work redesign and behaviour modelling are some of the OD intervention techniques that are aimed at individual employees.
2. **Dyads/triads:** Process consultation, third-party peace-making, role analysis and role negotiation techniques are used at this level.
3. **Teams and groups:** A large variety of OD intervention techniques are aimed for teams and groups within an organization. These include team building exercises (aimed at both task and process), force field analysis, self-managed teams, interdependency exercise, appreciative enquiry, responsibility charting, process consultation, role analysis and role negotiation techniques, visioning, quality of work life (QWL) programme, quality circle (QC), etc.
4. **Intergroup relations:** Organizational mirroring, intergroup activities (both process and task related), process consultation, partnering, survey feedback, and third-party peace-making at group level are some of the important intervention techniques for this level.
5. **Total organization:** Some of the intervention techniques involving the entire organization are socio-technical system, MBO, confrontation meetings, visioning, interdependency exercise, survey feedback, appreciative inquiry, search conferences, QWL programmes, total quality management, etc.

Some of the intervention techniques have been described below:

Life and Career Planning

Life and career planning includes career anchors and life's goals exercises. According to Schein, career anchor for an individual is his 'self-perceived talent, motives, and values that serve to guide, constrain, stabilize, and integrate his/her career and tend to remain stable throughout one's career.' Schein developed a questionnaire named 'self-analysis form' which would provide information to the individual in order to determine his career anchor. The life goal exercise helps individuals to understand and focus on his personal goals through various interesting activities such as making a symbolic representation of their life to write one's own obituary.

Mentoring, Coaching and Counselling

While coaching is more focused on employees' job performance, mentoring is broader in its scope and focus on general career growth and personal development of the protégé. It is provided either in the form of one-to-one training or as part of a group. Group training has the possibility of evolving in learning teams and may inculcate coaching skills in the team members. Counselling could be either *directive* or *non-directive*. In directive counselling the counsellor plays a more active role in discovering the strengths as well as inadequacies of the individual. In non-directive counselling the counsellor helps the individual client to discover his own potentials and weaknesses and develop the required action plans. In the non-directive counselling, the counsellor plays the role of a sounding board instead of providing direct advice.

Education and Training

This focus of education and training of the organizational members as part of OD intervention effort includes both technical skill training and social and behavioural skill improvement. The social skill enhancement programme covers a wide array of human process-related areas such as interpersonal effectiveness, team building, developing emotional maturity and the like. In some cases, an OD consultant may recommend the organization to sponsor its members to outside courses, if that is deemed required for the betterment of the organization.

T-Group

T-group or training group is also known as laboratory training or sensitivity training, which evolved in National Training Laboratories in USA under the supervision of Kurt Lewin. It is essentially an unstructured and agendaless small group consisting of 10–12 individuals who meet in the presence of a trainer (who is called facilitator). The group typically meets for a span of at least three days to two weeks. In between, a database comprising actions, reactions, interactions and concomitant feelings generated in the group is formed. With the help of the facilitator, the group members learn the art of being aware about each other and their respective surroundings. The main objective is to learn experiential learning, though additional conceptual learning materials are also provided. The aim of the group is to gain knowledge about increased sensitivity to emotional reactions and understanding one's own behaviour through each other's feedback. It is believed that the participants will gain from these experiences and would become more sensitive individuals. Use of T-groups in OD intervention is primarily aimed at addressing interpersonal process issues and enhancing interpersonal skills. This technique has been widely used in many Indian organizations as an OD intervention technique.

Team Building

People in organizations function more as a team rather than as individuals. The purpose of team building is primarily to (1) set goals and/or priorities, (2) analyse the way work is allocated and performed, (3) examine the way a group is performing and analyse the processes, such as goal setting, communication, norms, etc., and (4) examine relationships among each other within the group (Beckhard 1972). It is a common experience that whenever a team is engaged in any activity, in addition to the task accomplishment, the team members develop a feeling of belongingness, bonding and commitment. Team building is one of the most widely used OD intervention technique.

Process Consultation

Process consultation (PC) as an OD intervention was introduced by Schein (1969). A process consultant helps the organization to 'solve its own problems' by increasing awareness about organizational processes, the consequences of these processes and the mechanisms by which these can be changed. In particular, the process consultant, the third party, helps the client perceive, understand and act upon the process events. These refer to what is going around him, within him and between him and others in the environment in order to improve the situation as defined by the client. PC is essentially an approach where the consultant helps the organization and its members to be more sensitive towards the human and social processes that take place in the organization and makes them learn to solve problems stemming from social processes. The basic underlying assumptions of the PC are that the client needs help not only to diagnose the problem faced by him, but also the nature of the improvement that is needed, and he has the intent to find these out. Schein believes that organizations would be far more effective if they can learn and diagnose their own problems and this is what the process consultant strives to pass on to the clients. In addition, the consultation provided would be strictly non-directive where the consultant can generate alternative courses of action from which the client must choose what would be more appropriate for his organization. PC has been found to be an effective OD intervention technique especially in resolving conflicts in the organization.

Intergroup Team Building

The intergroup team-building intervention attempts to improve the intergroup relationships by increasing communication and reducing dysfunctional conflicts between them. The suggested steps of intergroup team building are as follows:

- The leaders (or all the members) of the two groups who have a history of conflicts meet in the presence of the consultant and are asked whether they want to improve their relationship. If both agree, the process would start.
- The groups meet in separate rooms and produce two lists: one where they put down their thoughts, attitudes and perceptions about the other group and the second describing what the other group thinks about them.
- The groups then meet and exchange the lists they have produced.
- The groups return to their respective rooms and deliberate on the two lists handed over to them—one what the other group thinks about them and what the other group thinks they feel and think about them. No doubt a heated discussion will ensue. But eventually each group would discover a lot about themselves and the other group. They would also find that most of the disagreements and frictions are largely due to lack of communication and in fact the differences are not as great as they thought.

- Each group now makes 'priority issues', which need to be addressed. This list is invariably much shorter than what they started with.
- The groups come back to the common meeting room and again share the lists.
- They jointly now set the priorities that must be addressed. They generate action plans together.
- There must be follow-ups and more meetings of the two groups or their leaders where they monitor the progress.

The intergroup team-building efforts help remove misunderstanding between the groups and often prove to be an effective intervention strategy.

Organization Mirror Intervention

Unlike intergroup team building where only two groups are involved, organization mirror intervention is used when the host group seeks and receives feedback from more than one group. The objective of this exercise is to improve relationships between the host group and other groups and also to increase the work effectiveness of the groups. The host group (or the unit) in the organization that faces problems with other groups in the organization invites key people of other groups/units in the meeting and requests them to provide feedback regarding their view of the host unit. The consultant however meets the concerned people and interviews them before the meeting in order to feel the magnitude of the problems; answer any questions they might have; and prepare the participants beforehand to avoid any major unpleasantness and smooth conducting of the meeting. The consultant starts the meeting by giving feedback from the interview session to the participants. In the first phase, the outsiders, that is, the members from other groups, sit in a circular fashion, surrounded by the host group members. This arrangement is known as 'fish bowl' where the members of the inner circle discuss issues related to the host group, while members of the host group sit in the chairs surrounding the outsiders, listen to their discussion without making any comment. In the next phase, the members of the host group sit in the inner circle of the fishbowl while the outsiders sit in the outer circle. The members of the host group discuss what they heard from the outsiders, and ask for clarification if required. At this point, a general discussion involving all the participants might start taking place to make the host group members clearly understand the problem. Next, the participants are divided into smaller groups with members from both the host group and the outsiders to identify the most important changes that need to be made in order to improve the host group's effectiveness. After the smaller groups identify the problems, all the groups now meet to prepare a comprehensive list of all that needs to be done and develop specific action plans accordingly. The subgroups then prepare summary lists as to the action plans and these are then confirmed in the total group. Adequate monitoring as to the true compliance of the host group members to the suggested action plan and the follow-up should take place.

Force Field Analysis

Lewin (1947) suggested the force-field analysis as a useful and easy to implement OD intervention technique. Lewin applied the principles of vector analysis in physical science in the field of social science to understand social problems, the factors that create the social equilibrium, and ways to bring in changes in an organization. A state of social equilibrium, just like the physical equilibrium, results when the opposing forces operating at a given point of time balance each other. Lewin believed that the state of social equilibrium or status quo could be disrupted and moved to a desired state by carefully identifying the driving forces and the restraining forces operating in the environment. The organization can be pushed to attain a higher level of equilibrium by increasing the driving forces, reducing the restraining forces, and ideally both at the same time. The force-field analysis is typically conducted in a group. The steps of force-field analysis are as follows:

- Deciding on a problem situation that needs to be improved. It is important to describe the current situation as completely as possible along with identifying the needs for change.
- To describe the desired condition in specific details including *what* are desired and *why*.
- To identify the forces operating at a given point of time, namely, the driving forces that help the organization to go up and the restraining forces that inhibit further improvement. The process of identification of the restraining and driving forces should be as exhaustive as possible to get a clear idea for the members.
- The next task is to examine the nature of the forces in detail—which forces are strong and which ones are weak, which ones are amenable to change and which are not.
- Decide on the strategies for moving the equilibrium to the desired state, and how to achieve that—increase the driving forces, reduce the restraining forces or doing both simultaneously. This stage will help to develop the action plan for reaching the desired state.
- To implement the action plan that is generated, and check whether the movement is indeed in the desired direction.
- To stabilize the equilibrium.

Survey Feedback

Survey feedback is the process of systematically collecting the data about the functioning of the organizational system by the OD consultant which he feeds back to individuals and groups across the organizational level so that they can analyse and interpret the data to design specific action steps. The steps of survey feedback are as follows:

- The OD consultant involves organizational members at the top level for preliminary planning for the organization development.
- Data are collected from members from all levels across the organization to understand the functioning and the underlying processes in the organization, such as the attitudes, organizational climate and expectations of the organizational members. This could be achieved by administering appropriate questionnaires and recording the responses.
- Data are fed back to the top level of management and down the hierarchy.
- At each level, the supervisor holds a meeting with his subordinates where they discuss the data. The subordinates, in the presence of the supervisor, try to make sense of the data given to them and attempt to interpret them, make plans for change or improvement, and decide how to introduce the data to the next lower level.
- The feedback meetings are conducted in the presence of the OD consultant who facilitates the meeting and acts as the resource person.

The survey feedback is clearly having two distinct components—*survey* to create and collect objective data about the functioning of the organization and *feedback*, that is, feeding back these data to individuals and groups from the top most level downward so that they can try to improve the functioning of the organization.

Third-party Intervention

Resolving or controlling conflict is one of the major aspects of organization development. The third-party intervention aims at resolving conflicts in an organization. The basic condition for the third-party peace-keeping intervention to be effective is that the conflicting individuals or groups must be willing to resolve the conflict by acknowledging that conflict actually exists (confronting) and that it is having negative consequences for both of them. The third-party (the OD consultant) must know how, when and where to bring in the issues into the open so that the parties face the conflict and try to find out ways to resolve this in the presence of the facilitator or the third party. The third-party intervention technique has been found to be quite effective in various forms of either individual or inter-group conflict resolution.

Managerial Grid

The managerial grid as an intervention strategy was introduced by Blake and Mouton (1969) which is based on the concept of their managerial grid model. Managerial grid is essentially a two-dimensional model with the dimensions of 'concern for people' and 'concern for production', and helps to identify the most effective manager as the one who is high on both the dimensions. The managerial grid as an OD intervention uses a number of instruments for enabling the participants to assess their innate tendencies, strengths and weaknesses. The six phases of managerial grid are as follows:

Pre-phase 1

When an organization decides to implement the managerial grid, selected key individuals from management levels are sent to attend the week-long grid seminar to gain experiential learning of the grid concepts, and learn to assess their own leadership style from the questionnaire. These people would eventually act as the instructors in their organization, who sometimes are also sent to attend advanced grid seminars.

Phase 1: The Managerial Grid

These managers would conduct grid seminars in the organization for all the managers. The focus of this seminar would be to identify their leadership styles, communication skills and enhance the problem-solving skills. The managers now learn how to reach the high-high style of management.

Phase 2: Development of Teamwork

The focus here is on enabling the participants to create perfect teams through the analysis of team and organizational culture, and enhancing the skills related to planning, goal setting and problem solving.

Phase 3: Intergroup Development

The focus here is on improving the effectiveness of intergroup relationships. The emphasis is given on learning and adopting the win-win or collaborative approach instead of the traditional win-lose one. The dynamics of intergroup cooperation and competition are analysed and action steps are designed to reach the ideal state of relationship between the groups. Usually people who have close working relations with each other are brought in for this session.

Phase 4: Development of an Ideal Strategic Model

At this stage, attention is given on developing an ideal strategic model by learning concepts and skills required for achieving corporate excellence. Here, the task of the corporate managers become to design an ideal strategic corporate model, which are open to evaluation and scrutiny by other members, who might offer help in fact-finding and other technical inputs. The comparison of the ideal versus real corporate strategy may provide valuable insights as to what areas need serious changes in order to achieve excellence. This phase may continue up to even a year.

Phase 5: Implementing the Ideal Strategic Model

The organization now strives to implement the ideal strategy in stages. It may require serious reorganization in order to implement the ideal strategy in the organization. Competent planning teams are developed for each area of corporate strategies, namely, product lines, profit centres, geographical locations, etc., along with appointing a coordinator for this phase who would act as the resource person. The effort of these teams and the coordinator would chiefly be the 'conversion study' as to how the real organization can be transformed in to the ideal one. With the completion of the planning, followed by assessing the processes, the implementation of ideal corporate strategy is achieved.

Phase 6: Systematic Critique

Here, the results from Pre-phase 1 to Phase 5 are measured and evaluated. Barriers to the implementation of ideal organization, if any, are also identified and steps to overcome these are designed.

Grid management as an OD intervention is indeed a systematic and methodical approach, though a bit complex. However, the success of this strategy has been recorded, particularly in large organizations.

Appreciative Inquiry

The concept of appreciative inquiry (AI) was first introduced by David Cooperrider in 1985 in his doctoral thesis where he noted how the level of positive collaboration in the organization facilitates in bringing in changes. AI is based on the principles of positive psychology (Seligman 1996), which focuses on what *works* with a person or individual rather than what *does not*. The AI approach in an organization is based on the interview of the organizational members followed by discussions in small groups around the core questions such as the following:

- What have been the most exciting and greatest moments in the life of the organization? When did people feel most happy, energized and committed?
- What are the things that the organizational members value most about themselves, their job activities and the organization as a whole?
- What are the areas where the excellence has been established (structure, system, leadership, values, etc.)?
- What are the organizational potentials for becoming a better organization?

The AI approach is based on the conversational approach to change and believes that change happens when people meet and talk together and not necessarily after the process is over. The new relationships that emerge during the process, and the different conversations that they have in these sessions, bring in important changes in the life of the organizational members and their understanding of the organization. The 'stories' or the experiences they share with each other which they have not told anybody before, the *dreams* they have created for the future in the organization and their ideas regarding how things need to be done, all changed their experience of the world, and thus *effectively changed* the world. According to Lewis, Passmore and Cantore (2011), the energy generated in the AI session is supported by the action plans and is *not* a product of the effort.

Search Conference

The search conference and future search conferences are rather similar, the only difference being the former originated in Europe and Australia, while the latter was in the USA. The rationale of the search conference is simple and has three essential phases:

- **Phase 1: Environmental appreciation** that makes an effort to understand the probable changes in the environment and identify what would be the desirable and probable future.

- **Phase 2: System analysis**, which will probe down in the history of the organization, analyse the present system and what would be desirable state for it.
- **Phase 3: Integration of system and environment**, by taking care of the constraints and designing strategies and action plans.

The search conferences typically involve a large number of representative organizational members and might span several days. The members note down the outcomes in flip charts for later analysis. The focus of the search conferences is three-fold, the *past*, the *present* and the *future*.

Confrontation Meeting

The confrontation meeting, as designed by Beckhard, refers to a one-day meeting of the entire management group to take stock of the organizational health. The management tries to find out the major problems faced by the organization and the probable root causes for these, designs specific action plans to remove the maladies and sets a time schedule within which these have to be accomplished. This is indeed a fast and simple technique.

QUESTIONS

1. What do you mean by OD intervention strategies?
2. Why and when does an organization require these?
3. Who decides a specific strategy for an organization?

REFERENCES

1. R. Beckhard (1972). '*Optimizing Team-Building Efforts*', *Journal of Contemporary Business*, 1(3).
2. R. R. Blake and J. S. Mouton, *Building a Dynamic Corporation Through Grid Organization Development* (Reading, MA: Addison-Wesley, 1969).
3. T. G. Cummings and C. G. Worley, *Organization Development and Change*, Eighth Edition (Thomson South Western, 2005).
4. W. L. India, C. H. Bell (Jr.) and V. Vohra, *Organization Development: Behavioral Science Interventions for Organization Improvement* (Dorling Kindersley (India) Pvt Ltd, 2006).
5. S. Lewis, J. Passmore and S. Cantore, *Appreciative Inquiry for Change Management: Using AI to Facilitate Organizational Development* (Kogan Page, 2011).
6. K. Lewin (1947), 'Frontiers in Group Dynamics', *Human Relations* 1(2).
7. E. H. Schein, *Process Consultation: Its Role in Organization Development* (Reading, MA: Addison-Wesley Publishing Company, 1969).
8. M. E. P. Seligman, *The Optimistic Child* (New York: Houghton-Mifflin, 1996).

Case Study: The Battleground

It was a pleasant day at a small quaint university town around 150 km from Kolkata. The place was beautiful in the early days of spring, with a bounty of blossoming flowers all around. It has a small stream flowing around the campus. Initially all the classes used to be held under the sky—from pre-primary school level to the post-graduate level. However, with the advent of time and encroaching modernity, the university has now become a huge complex of fine buildings. Apart from the usual graduate and post-graduate courses that are run by the university, it was especially famous for its Fine Art Faculty—including the Music and Dance Faculty, Faculty of Fine Art and Sculpture, various Language Centres and Faculty of Agriculture. There are also two schools including the Primary and Senior Secondary in the sprawling campus of the university.

The focus of our present discussion was the Senior Secondary School. The school could boast of a group of excellent and talented teachers coming from as far as Gujarat and Chennai. There used to be a constant scuffle between the principal and a few of the teachers as one group with the rest of the teachers. The divide among the teachers became clear and there used to be a war-like situation between these groups, which often took quite an ugly turn. It would often result in loud outbursts, particularly during the teachers' weekly meetings. As the days went by, the skirmishes between these groups kept on increasing. Practically every move taken by the principal was opposed by the other group. The exasperated vice chancellor at last decided to bring in two faculty members from a premier management institute in Kolkata to probe deeper into the problem and search for ways to reduce it.

The two management faculty members, Dr Radhika, the senior professor, and Uma, the assistant professor, came over from Kolkata. They arrived in the evening and were taken to the university guest house where they would stay for a couple of days. The guest house was not luxurious, but quite nice and comfortable. They took a shower and were barely settling down with the evening cup of tea when they had their first visitor, the principal himself. Dr Sanath Halder was politeness incarnated. After enquiring about their comfort and well-being and asking whether they would need anything, Dr Halder came straight to the point. He briefed them about the 'rebel group' of teachers who would not work and would do everything to put the daily running of the school next to impossible. They were 'shirkers', and would not take any responsibility. 'Come in any teachers' meeting and you would see for yourself. They think they belong to a different class and would protest every step, no matter what.' He was so visibly upset that he refused the tea offered by Uma and stormed away.

Barely had Dr Halder crossed the entrance gate of the compound entered a senior lady teacher of the school. She ostensibly came to ensure the comfort and well-being of the professors, as they were the VC's 'guest'. After a little chit chat over a cup of tea on various topics such as the general environment of the place, the current trend of the students and so on, she too came closer to the point. She was refined in her way of talking; nevertheless she pointed out the lack of finesse of the principal, who, according to her, belonged to an altogether different school of thought. It was indeed difficult to work with such a person who totally lacks 'sensitivity'. And according to her, the students were suffering the most, and the authority must do something. Radhika and Uma could rightly sense the tension prevailing in the atmosphere. They remembered the briefing of the

VC who summed it up as 'It is unbelievable how a group of so well educated people could fight so much among themselves!'

The next day Radhika and Uma reached the school at 10.30 am with the VC. It was a Wednesday, the school's weekly off day, like all other departments. In spite of the holiday, all the teachers were asked to come to the school in time. They made a nice seating arrangement on the floor. A few colourful carpets were spread in the hall, with a liberal number of cushions put around. Some flowers from the garden were put in the corner in earthen pots. They all, including the two professors and the VC, sat in a circle facing each other. After the introduction of the professors by the VC and explaining the purpose of the workshop, which was put as 'an effort to improve the functioning of the school', the VC left.

Radhika looked at the faces. Some were tense and worried, the principal among them. Some were perfectly relaxed, talking to each other. Bhatt and Suryamohon were among them, the names Radhika picked up later. But what Radhika and Uma clearly noticed from the very first moment was an inevitable feeling of underlying tension all over the place. They now divided the entire group of teachers, around 18 of them, into smaller groups of four or five members in each. They allowed them to choose their group members. After the smaller groups were formed, they were asked to find out the problems faced by their school, if any, at the present moment, and what could be the possible ways to resolve those. The groups were asked to spread out so that each group had their own privacy and asked to jot down their points on the sheets of papers given to them.

The entire day went into this. First, each group presented their list of problems. They wrote them on the flip chart put over the easel. After each group finished their presentation, there was the lunch break when Radhika and Uma carried the sheets with them to the guest house. They had a quick glance and identified the common themes, omitting the repetitions. These were roughly five:

1. Lack of trust among the teachers
2. Lack of innovative teaching
3. Lack of motivation among the students
4. Indiscipline
5. Lack of conscientious among the teachers regarding any issue

In the after-lunch session, Radhika and Uma presented these back to the entire group. Now they urged them to brain storm and find out solutions to each of these problems. The group got themselves involved and after a two-hour debate unanimously came to the following suggestions:

- To bring in more openness in the running of the school.
- Tolerance to each other to be enhanced.
- More attention to be given to correct the students' attitude rather than simply teaching.
- The academically backward students to be given extra time, either before the school starts or after school hours.

The next day Radhika and Uma spent time to the teachers individually. After the initial stonewall of the teachers, they started to pour out their heart to them. Sushila was a beautiful lady in her late 30s who grew up there. She was very refined in her taste, could sing well and had a natural talent in drawing and painting. She was the English teacher and she took pains to create a sense of appreciation for the language in the students. She broke down while talking to the professors and narrated how she was ridiculed and humiliated by the principal on several occasions. The principal's favourite refrain was that he did not really care for those sophisticated 'accents', nor the 'love for language', but just good marks from the students. And his complaint against Sushila was that she spent too much time on making the students read extra books, which were clearly beyond the syllabus. Amol Bhatt was a senior Physics teacher, who came from Gujarat. He loved the students and the feeling was certainly mutual. He firmly believed that the students should be treated with respect and this was the only way to discipline them. Not by the rule of stick any more at this stage of adolescence. The principal used to dismiss him as too soft a person who knew nothing about discipline. And the list was almost endless.

Radhika and Uma could understand that the root of the malady was deeper than it appeared. There was a deep cultural divide between the two groups. In fact, a majority of the teachers had graduated from the very same schools there (junior and seniors) and later from the same university. Even those who came from other states were actually residential students here from an early age and spent all their life in this university town. The bonding of these teachers with the school and the entire place was very different from a usual workplace relationship. It was more of a family, of siblings growing together and sharing a strong passion—for the school, for every flower in bloom in different seasons, the local tribal people around the place, its abundant greenery, the wide open space, their dear 'Kaluda's' modest tea shop, all the 'Dadas' and 'Didis' (elder brothers and sisters) at every residential households, most of whom were associated with various departments of the university or the two schools there as teachers or otherwise. The teachers in the school loved the children, were innovative in their teaching and used to imbibe a strong passion for nature and beauty in the children, a legacy they got from their own teachers. Things were going peacefully and harmoniously till the new principal joined after dear old Benudi retired. Benudi, as everyone would call her, was also from this place. She had a Ph.D in English and devoted her life to the school. She never got married and the school was everything for her. The teachers used to adore her, as she was very dignified, soft spoken and extremely committed. Nobody had ever heard a harsh word from Benudi, but nobody could escape from their responsibility either, as Benudi was good at getting the job done from her colleagues.

Dr Sanath Halder, the present principal who joined last year, was indeed a very qualified person, with a Ph.D in education from the University of Calcutta. He, however, had to struggle for his education, and for that matter for almost everything in his life. His family, consisting of his parents, six siblings and the old grandmother, migrated from the erstwhile East Pakistan after the partition of the country. Getting the opportunity to be the head master of the Senior Secondary School after a stint of around 15 years in a local school was certainly a welcome break in Sanath's life. He was a down-to-earth, pragmatic and practical type of a person and never suffered from too much emotion. He was not exactly artistic in nature, to say the least. In contrast to most of the teachers for whom it was an extension of life, for Sanath it was just a better career move. The job of the head master gave him a status, a better pay package, some amount of comfort and that is all. The teachers, who had been from this very place, felt a distinct difference in their values and those of Sanath's. Only some of the younger teachers who were mostly from outside the place were to some extent aligned with Sanath.

Questions

1. What OD intervention techniques were applied here?
2. If you were the OD consultant, what else would you have done?